WHAT IS GOOD
FOR GENERAL MOTORS?

What Is Good for General Motors?

Solving America's Industrial Conundrum

Thomas A. Crumm

Algora Publishing
New York

Library of Congress Cataloging-in-Publication Data —

Crumm, Thomas A.
  What is good for General Motors?: solving America's industrial conundrum / Thomas
A. Crumm.
      p. cm.
  Includes bibliographical references and index.
    ISBN 978-0-87586-777-9 (soft cover: alk. paper) — ISBN 978-0-87586-778-6 (hbk.:
alk. paper) — ISBN 978-0-87586-779-3 (ebook) 1. Ford Motor Company—Management. 2.
General Motors Corporation—Management. 3. Automobile industry and trade—United
States—Management. 4. Industrial policy—United States. 5. United States—Economic
policy. I. Title.
    HD9710.U54F5345 2010
    338.7'6292220973 — dc22
                        2010019773

Front cover: 1950s-vintage Dodge and General Motors cars, imported before the
Castro revolution, serve as a fleet of taxicabs in Havana, Cuba.
  Image: © Jeremy Horner/CORBIS
  Date Photographed: August 21, 1996, Location: Havana, Cuba
  Photographer: Jeremy Horner

Printed in the United States

One writes out of one thing only—one's own experience. Everything depends on how relentless one forces from this experience the last drop, sweet or bitter, it can possibly give.

Walter Bagehot (1826–1877), "Shakespeare," *Literary Studies*, 1879

TABLE OF CONTENTS

PREFACE

The often-repeated misquote of General Motors President Charles Wilson, "What is good for General Motors is good for the country," was a sound bite in the fifties that epitomized the arrogance of America's mighty industrial complex. It was said at a time when GM, Ford, and Chrysler were the dominant leaders and soon to become America's Big Three. That arrogance is gone now. A half century of robust ascension has been followed by a half century of devastating decline. Something happened in the locker room at half time and the Big Three began to lose.

America's hunger for goods is not waning. Imported goods are increasingly meeting the demands of this hunger, and the trade deficit hurts the US economy. Bottom line, Kevin Phillips in *American Theocracy* argues convincingly that America, like other prominent nations in the past, is slipping into rentier collapse. When a nation begins to focus on finance, insurance, and real estate (FIRE), and to neglect its industrial sector, industrial prowess slips and rentier collapse ensues. It happened to Spain, Holland, and England, in turn, in the past four centuries, and America's descent has already begun.

It is still possible to climb back from the edge, but only by gaining a deeper understanding of what is happening. The chapters that follow are an attempt to save America's industrial sector by raising awareness: the auto industry is a likely candidate to lead the United States back into balance in the global economy.

CHAPTER 1. SETTING THE STAGE

I had been avoiding travel to Flint, Michigan, since leaving General Motors (GM) in 1998 after gambling my career on the need for fundamental change. Following the protocols of the nineties, I submitted a "white paper" to the Board of Directors. Its step-by-step plan proposed sweeping changes in nearly every segment of the business. Perhaps it was more than any Board could have been expected to contemplate, but I had high hopes. When my proposal was rejected in favor of continuing to build wealth through mergers, acquisitions, and divestitures in foreign lands, I requested and received permission to leave.

In 2003 my eighty-two-year-old father lost his battle with cancer. We laid his ashes to rest in Flint Memorial Park on a sunny morning in July. The respectful, worn faces that emerged from the surrounding ghost town confirmed what I had feared. In voices and in faces, I no longer heard or saw any hints of pride or suggestions of hope for the future. The people whose last names matched those on the oldest tombstones were the saddest. Surely the cemetery reminded them of their own grandparents and the tales they were told as technical knowledge was handed down. Our ancestors came to Flint to build carriages long before anyone dreamt of transforming this community for auto production. The memorial service for my father was filled with eerie reminders as I realized some of the long faces mirrored in the mausoleum's polished stone had their names chiseled in their reflections.

Perhaps guilt heightened my awareness, but there seemed to be undertones in every condolence. Was there something I had not yet seen? At the funeral home the night before, the conversations circled around old commonplace myths. The people of Flint used them to explain what they could not understand about the loss of their livelihood. They were myths that would bring even the most optimistic leaders to their knees: twelve things that I knew were not true but that they believed were the reasons for their plight:

1. Of course the auto industry needs to be located in Michigan.
2. Of course the role of unions should be to fight for all they can get from management.
3. Of course an assembly line is the most efficient way to build cars.
4. Of course American autoworkers are paid too much.
5. Of course it takes years and billions of dollars to design and develop a new vehicle.
6. Of course there are unbeatable advantages to high-scale operations.
7. Of course outside sources can make parts for less than the auto companies.
8. Of course transfer lines (lines of machines connected by automation) and automated body shops are the only avenues to quality.
9. Of course "lights-off" factories (factories run by robots) are the future.
10. Of course cars have to be sold and serviced through dealerships.
11. Of course research has to be done by scientists and protected by patents.
12. Of course imports will always be cheaper than American-made cars.

I left the cemetery in a rental car and drove aimlessly, nostalgically through devastated neighborhoods. I stopped at a familiar overlook along the Flint riverbank and sat there, stunned. Below should have been "Happy Valley"—where William Durant launched his low-priced Chevrolet intent on staking his claim in the midst of Henry Ford's market share—but it was empty! Plants 2A, 2, 4, 5, 6, 7, 8, 9, 10, the Main Office, the Personnel Building, the Service Parts Warehouses, the Power House, and even the Apprentice Shop had all been razed. Only the perimeter fence remained to guard a vast sloping field of dirt and weeds leading down to the silent, winding river. Nature was already beginning to reclaim what it had lost a century earlier. Every brick of every building had been hauled away. So much for future generations holding fundraisers to turn historic industrial ruins into a museum. Annual rainfall would soon return this valley to a hickory forest.

I stared across the barren landscape to the far rim, where I saw abandoned houses with broken windows. The culture that had nurtured apprentices for more than a century had also disappeared. These were the neighborhoods where my grandfathers had lived until the Great Depression drove them back to ancestral farms. It was where my parents' generation had found their first homes, and where I had rented my first apartment. All evidence of the largest auto company in the world was being erased. The culture of the carriage makers who knew how to hand down centuries of accumulated knowledge and experience had vanished. Even the best archaeologists were never going to uncover the contributions of my family.

Nearly overwhelmed with sadness, I leaned back against the rental and began my first one-sided conversation with my father. I told him it was probably best that his father's generation hadn't lived to see this dreadful end. There is no one left to tell the stories, no one left who has a clue as to how to rebuild.

I was born in 1945 while my father was operating a naval radar station overlooking the Leyte Gulf. After the war, my parents set to work building our house, one room at time, at the far end of the family farm. It was located fifteen miles west of Flint and sat back a hundred yards from River Road, which churned up clouds of dust in the summer and developed ruts in the spring. Living a mile and a half from town and half a mile from the nearest boy my age, my social life was limited to Sunday gatherings in the beginning. All the breadwinners in our family were autoworkers. Before I was ten, I could grasp both sides of the blue-collar/white-collar issues, and I was still seventeen in 1963 when I set out to seek my fortune in Happy Valley. I would become the first in our extended family to hold the coveted title of engineer. A slow and steady rise through the ranks took me to every corner of operations over the next twenty-five years. In 1987, I was appointed to join General Motors' inner sanctum, where I would spend a decade serving the leadership. I did my best to carry on the family legacy, but the valley below was confirmation of how badly my attempt had failed. Only memories remain to testify as to how my family gave its full measure of career energy. Three generations of life's work have been wiped clean. This was what the people at the funeral had not wanted to tell me. It was going to take time to come to grips with this new reality.

I hiked along the ridge to the spot where my mother and her father, Frank, had stood and witnessed the violence that birthed America's United Auto Workers (UAW) in 1937. From there I recounted how I had spent a decade offering advice to two of the great wizards (chairmen of the Board of Directors at GM). What had I learned? The challenges of leadership are daunting. Once you reach the top, the winds attack from four directions.

I returned to lean against the car, stricken with the finality of my father's death. He was gone. I remembered family gatherings in the fifties, where I watched my grandfathers lapse into periods of silence, while my uncles were joking and recounting tales from the shop floor. There was something bigger than a generation gap holding my grandfathers back, and now I know what it was. They had premonitions of what was going to happen here and how their life's work was going to be erased. Today's funeral was not like the ones in the fifties and sixties. There's no longer any pride of accomplishment in Flint's residents. There are just too many misconceptions for them to deal with, and the myths are too deeply ingrained. No one has a clue as to the origins of the myths they parrot. They just hand them down like interpretations of folk tales.

My reflections turned to the sixties and how the old craftsmen could reconfigure the buildings in Happy Valley during the "annual rearrange." Each summer this valley had to be prepared to produce for the coming model year. The knowledge of the craftsmen who performed the rearrange has disappeared in my lifetime. There was more that has been lost—the practice of counting on seniors for the long-term lessons that bind a craft culture together. The consequence of no longer handing down skills is evident in valleys like this and the surrounding ridges across the country. Michael Moore's 1989 film *Roger and Me* touched on this subject but failed to capture the reasons behind it. His movie insinuated that it was GM Chairman Roger Smith's fault, at a time when Roger was on the verge of becoming a hero of America's industrial sector. The timing of the movie's release overshadowed the production start for GM's Saturn in Springhill, Tennessee. It was as if the movie were intent on clipping the wings of hope for Saturn just as it left the ground. Perhaps the timing was part of some master plan by a threatened faction of GM's leadership—certainly not the ones pulling my strings, nor the ones leading Saturn.

Moore failed in his attempt to capture the big issues of Flint and the other Happy Valleys. Why is it that America's ability to manufacture consumer electronics, cameras, and so many other things has all ground to a halt in my lifetime? Why did Roger Smith fight so hard during his tenure to change the business model of the auto industry—from confrontation with union leaders to making them partners, from mindless positions along a line to holistic involvement of the workforce, from out-sourcing to in-sourcing, from specialized equipment to universal equipment, etc.? Perhaps Saturn really was on the verge of giving imports a run for their money. Perhaps investors in New York had more to gain if Saturn failed, or perhaps someone in Washington had negotiated it away in some high-level trade-offs. Moore should have dealt with these bigger issues instead of taking out a corporate leader on the verge of changing the direction of the largest auto company in the world. His movie should have focused on how workers did not choose their own leadership in the fifties and sixties. The few who bothered to make the trip to the union hall didn't vote for visionaries. If Saturn's approach to the role of unions had survived, the UAW side of bargaining tables would now be leading the United States toward a very different future. Instead, what has evolved is a cast of elected radicals that counter the aggression of eager "professional managers" pumped up with Peter Drucker's thinking and lacking any semblance of hands-on knowledge in auto making. The old masters who erected factories in valleys like this, including my mother's father Frank, simply walked out in the late thirties. Frank left when it became clear that the shareholders were going to fight to protect their newly amassed wealth and were going to select executives willing to focus on counter threats. Frank walked out in 1939, taking his paint process expertise with him. The UAW's membership began electing leaders charged with energy and ready to counter the emerging wave of feisty executives. Both sides cooked up plans while World War II and the Korean War raged. Michael Moore should have delivered a much more balanced message about this critical time in history and how it evolved. Instead he drew a bead on Roger Smith.

It was hard to come to grips with the reality of the empty valley below. It had been forty years since I first walked down the slope at 5:30 a.m. to take my place in one of the stanchions along the motor assembly line. This is where I was taken under the wing of several of the masters of their craft. I served as an apprentice die maker and then as an apprentice electrician. I spent a year working through the chairs of the white-collar office jobs before ever being allowed to assume the responsibilities of an industrial engineer. I returned to this valley twice, as a foreman and then general foreman. It would take a lot of remembering to piece it all together and figure out what had made this valley so successful in the industrial race.

During the summers of 1966 and 1967, I was assigned a minor role as a plant layout man and got caught up in the excitement of the annual model change. Workers would come from all corners of the valley to join in the rearrange of their capital investments. Over the winter, engineering staffs would bid against other component operations to win allocations of component business. The bids they won were known by March, when they started to plan the annual rearrange. Winning a contract to produce a component meant the rest of the Chevrolet Division's more than hundred thousand employees would be counting on your site's ability to manufacture and deliver on time. When June rolled around, workers rallied, ready to shoulder the risks of tearing the place limb from limb and getting it all back together in time. By the first week of August, the perennial pride of accomplishment would be restored and workers would return to their roles in the other grand scheme of this valley: keeping production running no matter what happened.

During the 1966 rearrange, I watched some of the first outside contractors stumble in their attempts to match the skills of the valley's groomed masters. The old-timers had already realized that fewer apprentices were being hired and had concluded that these outside contractors were going to take over. I didn't believe it at the time, but in hindsight it is easy to see that the long-range strategic decision to walk away from the annual model change had already been made.

That summer one of the outside rigging crews had begun to fall behind in its contract to relocate one of the large stamping presses. Once behind schedule, they began to make mistakes; the haste-makes-waste proverb had proven to be true. A shortcut in rigging led to the collapse of the booms on two of the rental cranes, and the press fell to the ground, causing needles to flutter on Richter scales. It was the day that I got my first glimpse of what the last of Happy Valley's master riggers could do. The shudder beneath our feet had hardly stopped when a silver-haired crew came roaring out of Plant 7 on a rescue wagon. Within minutes they had the hundred tons of cast iron jacked up and sitting on logs they called "rollers." It was winched through the doorway into Plant 2A—steered using sledgehammers to reorient the rollers.

Once inside the building, the press was lifted up on its feet using one of the overhead cranes that were rated at just fifty tons. The Plant 2A crane operator was instructed to step down, and one of the silver-haired masters climbed up into the cab. The crane soon whined as its cables stretched tight enough to play a tune. The building structure strained as the top half of the press rose into the air. As it passed the balance point, the old master shifted the gantry, catching it and letting it settle gently on its feet. The heavy load yanked at the building structure as if to wrestle it to the ground. Within minutes the press was still rocking as it snaked winding its way through the plant, reeled in by straining D-9 Caterpillars chained to the bases of building columns. The press was on its new foundation in a matter of hours instead of days, and I was lucky to have had a ringside seat. It was one of the last great performances of some of the masters who once led this valley's culture. I still think of them whenever I stop to watch a crew moving a house or something equally heavy. I keep hoping to once again catch a glimpse of a crew that confident and competent.

There was something else about Happy Valley. In the early sixties, the machine repairmen were still building the automation. The American machine tool industry was just beginning to settle its grip. Threats of automation displacing UAW members were being stacked on bargaining tables, and the big poker game that would end in a loss of competitiveness had just begun. Twenty years later America's auto plants would be fitted out with capital-intensive Rube Goldbergs that lit up like holiday trees, displaying their coolant in waterfalls and playing monotonous tunes. The sixties was still a time when the masters who rearranged equipment in the summer were also the masters who reworked fixtures and tooling throughout the winter. The culture inside the auto plants was very different back then. So were the choices of equipment and the roles of skilled-trade workers.

As I peered into the valley, memories came back of the unusual roles of the plant layout men. Their collective performance under fire is still something I aspire to emulate. They were the pioneers of modern-day program management careers. They were expected to handle the pressures of completing the summer rearrange on time. Bob Asp was one of them and a particularly feisty fellow. He was charged with rearranging the gas tank lines in Plant 10 each summer. He would conjure the new manufacturing system and define it on a quarter-inch-equals-a-foot scaled blueprint that only hinted at what he was carrying in his head. Today, manufacturing system designs are created in Auto-CAD by dozens of screen jockeys far from the hands-on pressures of implementation.

I was there in 1967 to witness Bob in the midst of his corner of the fray. I caught him drawing things in the air with his hands or on the sides of coffee cups with a few members of one of his dozens of crews—often tinsmiths. At some point his audience would nod and set off to construct what he had been describing. It was impossible to define where Bob's imagination left off and the skills of the masters of the crafts took over, but it was very clear that they were not talking in a language taught in engineering schools.

My rounds that summer as the solo night overseer of plant layout responsibilities allowed me to observe the complete transformation of Plant 10. With just two weeks to go before production start, Plant 10 more than the others was still a tangled jumble of steel and equipment. I couldn't fathom how Bob was going to make it. On Sunday night preceding the Monday production start, I walked the rounds from plant to plant confirming finishing touches, like fresh coats of battleship-gray paint. At 6:30 a.m. I was in Plant 10. The power panels were switched to "on" as the factory whistle blew, and within minutes the year's stream of two million gas tanks began to flow in all sizes and shapes toward waiting boxcars. There were no circles of frantic MBAs wringing their hands or program managers and leaders of contactors standing around. Just Bob Asp and the returning production foremen, making sure all workers knew their new tasks. Bob was just one of many automotive manufacturing craftsmen who were vital to the competitiveness of this valley. The Bobs in valleys like this shouldered the risks each summer in exchange for a lifetime of income. A little recognition by a member of leadership at retirement was all the praise they ever expected. They found their rewards in a job well done. America's rise to economic and technical prominence was erected on shoulders like theirs. Flint's culture once nurtured youth that could do more than trek off to dorm rooms to grow up. Being selected for an apprenticeship was an invitation to a rewarding career that was challenged by constant change in materials and processing and filled with the rewards of a good income. The Bob Asps are gone now, and what has taken their place is expensive and inflexible.

Immersed in memories, I recalled how "the rearrange" began; the crews of journeymen backfilled with line workers. When most production workers were headed for the gates and a little vacation with sub-pay, a few would wander into Plant 7, the hub for maintenance activity and control central for the annual rearrange. These few would enter the building quietly and lean against a wall or pillar to wait for an assignment. They brought nothing with them but their handed-down skills and accumulated experience from previous summers. They came ready to help assure that the new-production deadline would be met. The ones I got to know didn't come for the money, but rather to get caught up in the excitement and maybe pick up a few more stories to help ease them through another long year of boredom in their stanchions along an assembly line.

Frank loved to repeat his tales of being seventeen and driving horse-drawn wagons filled with trimmed, notched, mortised and tenoned stacks of beams from the sawmill to the site of the next barn raising. Once all of his loads were delivered and stacked in just the right places and in the right order, farmers would come from all directions on an appointed morning. Beginning at dawn, by sunset they had turned piles of beams and boards into a barn. "The barns would rise into the air as if by magic," Frank would explain to my cousins and me. "Everyone just knew his job." The annual rearrange in Happy Valley was similar. It brought people together on an appointed day, including the production workers who came to Plant 7 for the excitement and the satisfaction of making something rise into the air. They too "just knew their job."

Bob Asp could be likened to the sawmill operator Frank had worked for. Bob would ensure the pieces were cut to the right length and piled in the right order. He would conjure the systems of manufacture that would match the limits of human capability at each stanchion. Somehow Bob would always manage to get the gas tank line moving in time to reach the waiting assembly plants.

As the sun went down, I made a silent promise to my predecessors: "I will remember the culture that once thrived along this river and never forget the importance of the knowledge and experience you handed down." I drove south toward Detroit Metro and tried to come to grips with my father being gone. Sadness shifted to anger as I realized that so much had been wasted. The knowledge and skills of Happy Valley would no longer be passed down to succeeding generations. I sensed that someday my own eulogy might read, "He was given every opportunity to correct the great ship's course and failed. Perhaps he did not do enough; perhaps he left too early."

The weeks following the funeral brought further reflections. Things I had never been able to grasp began to make sense. In 1987, when I was called out of GM operations to join the Corporate Strategic Planning Group (CSPG), a think tank, a major internal struggle was already underway. Factions were busy with alterations to the plans laid down by Roger Smith in the eighties. Harvard's finest were prepping GM's controlling shares of EDS, Hughes, Military Vehicles, Locomotives, and even Saturn for divestiture. I had been asked to fill a room in the heart of CSPG with charts, graphs, photos, and articles that would defend the direction Saturn had taken. Someone wanted a vision of how to alter the fundamental business model of the company that would incorporate what was learned at Saturn. My next task was to convey the vision. It was the opportunity of a lifetime for a guy from operations. Looking back, I see I might have been the first up-from-the-ranks person to be invited back into the inner den of strategic thinking since 1959 when antitrust legislators came to Detroit to clip wings. Someone must have pulled a lot of strings to enable operations to speak out on the future. My goal had been to convince all reviewers that the Big Three were going to fail without a fundamental change in operations. My audience was the top one percent of the company, 1,100 of them, and for two years they kept coming in groups of two or three without my sending an invitation.

I didn't reach my goal, and when I walked out of GM in April 1998, I was quite sure that America's auto industry could not be saved from itself. It took the death of my father to bring me around to try again. Five years had passed and I had to begin by updating myself. I found that Richard G. "Skip" LeFauve, the president of Saturn Corporation, had stepped down when it was clear that Saturn Corporation was being shut down. His parting words to Saturn's leaders were significant: "The lesson here is that you never want to become holier than the pope." Saturn had become a threat to the status quo, and people in Detroit on both sides of the bargaining tables began working together to overpower Roger Smith's dream. Unknowingly they were cutting off perhaps the only chance for GM's survival. Saturn's engineering prototype culture was good enough that it might have impressed even Henry Ford. Its approach to engineering together with its approach to operations just needed to be set free.

It is now obvious to all that America's Big Three have fallen behind. Market share has declined even faster than the most pessimistic projections in the late 1980s. The Big Three are busy abandoning America and setting up manufacturing overseas. The largest of these foreign plays was cemented in March 1997, with GM in Detroit signing a symbolic joint-venture agreement with China's State Planning Committee and the assistant to the mayor of Shanghai. GM was eager to close the deal. With production moved offshore, the business school graduates in middle management would be released from all responsibility for operations. They could move toward something more comfortable—managing mergers, acquisitions, and divestitures—something more familiar. They could simply fire up production in whatever country had the lowest labor costs and most favorable exchange rate at a given time. The United States no longer realizes that what it needs is a return to handing down industrial skills from generation to generation.

Industrial companies are moving to places like China even though the resulting technology transfer means they will soon become irrelevant there. It is my prediction that when the usefulness of American manufacturers is exhausted, they will be driven out of China like dinosaurs to the tar pits.

BEGIN BY TRACKING THE MYTHS

The conversations during the days of my father's funeral were an introduction to the fatalistic myths now hanging over the Midwest. The reasons why Flint and the other auto towns should just give up had spun out in one tale after another. If I could somehow introduce disbelief into their myths, I thought, I just might get someone to consider recovery. At the same time, recovery would require getting some segment of America's financial district excited about invigorating the industrial sector. It would not be easy. The financial sector is rarely excited by the long-term proposals from the industrial sector. Financiers have become infatuated with entrepreneurial dreams of submitting a patent and living on a tropical beach off a slice of revenue from a single thought.

The things that made America's industrial sector great are still around, but the country has developed some bad habits; too focused on artificial changes in share price and not enough on size of dividend, too enamored with penny stocks, too ready to step aboard the next bus headed back toward Atlantic City, too easily led astray by the values of corporate leaders at WorldCom, Enron, and others, too willing to participate in the promises of Ponzi schemes orchestrated by the likes of Bernie Madoff, too willing to take out high-risk loans and bundle high-risk debt. Proposing that America get back to perfecting its craftsmanship probably sounds like a pitch for a slow-growth fund, that is, unless you are part of the craftsman's culture.

The excavators have scooped out the roots of the US auto industry, erasing all pointers left by past generations. What is left is a set of inaccurate myths. Defaming and rewording those myths would be a place to start. I searched libraries and private collections from Ohio to Illinois and from Michigan to Kentucky, and a few in Florida. At first I read the modern historians, until I discovered that their interpretations did not match my family's accountings. There were just too many family experiences that did not match their assumptions. I shifted gears and launched another search for the old accounts, things written by people on the inside during the industry's formative years. My questioning challenged the best of librarians across the Midwest and even at the Library of Congress. They looked through their archives, bringing out the musty books published before 1930 and no longer on the shelves—books that hadn't been opened for half a century—books that never made it onto a best seller list. I read wearing the lenses ground by my grandfathers, rediscovering their language—something I had not heard spoken for forty years. The jargon and nuances were all familiar. I visited the old photo archives at the *Detroit News* and the *Flint Journal* and thanked their historians repeatedly for what they had saved. The photos of crews in the early plants had backdrops that filled in the blanks for an industrial engineer trained in the same factories. The photos picked up where the written accounts left off, and I became convinced that some really good systems of manufacturing predated the 1913 assembly line. It amazed me that modern historians were not referencing these old accounts. Perhaps they didn't understand the language.

It wasn't long before I could match what I experienced with things I found and began to compile arguments to discount the myths.

— *"Of course the auto industry needs to be located in Michigan."*

In studying the oldest accounts of the Midwest, I came across the names of European carriage builders who came to southern Michigan to be close to the world's finest hickory forest. Oak had been the material of choice for centuries in Europe until the Midwest's hickory proved to have a superior strength-to-weight ratio and just the right amount of flex for carriages. To a carriage connoisseur, the difference was significant. If you wanted to give your favorite horse a slight advantage, you looked for the ultra light and responsive surrey. Catalogs and other advertising in the late 1800s lauded the lightweight achievements rolling out of the hickory forests of the Midwest, and prepaid buyers as far away as Europe began ordering them.

The masters of the carriage industry were skilled in the fine art of lightweight construction and understood the requirements for durability over rough terrain in all weather conditions. This knowledge was exactly what the early automakers needed—to get the most performance out of their tiny gasoline engines. The Midwest was also valued for its nurtured apprentices, much as the Czech Republic is valued for its industrial capability today. It is little wonder that the only auto companies to survive were those that had set up shop in the Midwest. Within two decades, automobiles were no longer made of hickory or any significant amount of the iron ore that traveled the Great Lakes. Still, the Midwest automakers stayed and prospered. It wasn't the hickory that made their cars better. It was the culture of the Midwest that nurtured craftsmen who made them such a success.

My research began to make it even easier to empathize with the seniors who had attended my father's funeral. Some of them were holding onto memories of the culture of their ancestors, just as I was. They remembered Happy Valley and the craft skills of the ancestors who erected it. Many in their families had been forced to retire or leave town and had left them behind. Yes, Flint has been abandoned, but the belief that Flint was still the ideal place to rekindle an auto industry was no longer valid. The hickory is still there, but the culture that handed down its knowledge is gone.

THE MISSION

The other myths passed around in funeral homes would not be so easily defused. Their origins stretched back a century and were part of some complex evolutions. To counter their gloom and doom was going to require more explanation. I decided to go back to 1903 and try to track all the major strategic decisions over time—decisions that would lead to where the auto business is today. My mission became the building of confidence that a comeback is possible. Somehow I would find a path to survival for America's industrial sector. It will mean picking up the struggle again to counter the leadership that had unseated Roger Smith. This time I would be working from the outside in to facilitate change—to return craftsmanship to prominence. My target would need to be the segment of American culture that stands to benefit the most from a reversal of industrial decline. My target audience would be wholesegments of the economy that stand to gain. Change would be needed in legislative and foreign policy. I would have to reach voters who could steer the politicians who draft legislation.

A fictional work titled *The Riddle of the Sands*[1] was first offered in bookstores in England in 1903, the same year the Ford Motor Company was founded. It has been reprinted and is a tale of plans for the invasion of England by the forces of Wilhelm II, German Emperor and King of Prussia, using thousands of small sailboats launched from the shifting sandbars along Germany's northwest coast. One among many publications before World War I, it was intent on raising awareness of mainland Europe's growing military ambitions. Great Britain's citizens needed convincing that their current defenses would not be enough. Perhaps comparable works on the plight of America's industrial sector and why it should be rekindled could shift the United States back into gear in time to save its economy. Writing something of equivalent impact and aiming it at average trade readers might be a good place to start. My version of *The Riddle of the Sands* would have to rekindle an appreciation of what automakers were once able to offer and the lost recognition of the importance of craftsmanship as a lifelong pursuit. I liked Howard Gardner's[2] premise that people are born every day with differing combinations of intelligences. Some have the combination required to become great craftsmen. Today they are serving as auto mechanics or performing weekend overhauls because they enjoy the challenge. If the right business model were to offer them employment, they might just emerge from their fast-food jobs and return to a life of seeking continuous improvements in personal transportation.

I chose to study the Ford Motor Company because it was a leader in the evolution of auto making and because its documentation was the most prolific. I made side notes whenever I noticed the origin of something that had always bothered me. I wasn't sure what value these side notes might bring, but I knew that the turnaround of the steel industry by the mini-mills began with a side note. Nucor Steel got its start with a process for making stainless steel that had been pushed out to the back lots by the big steel mills because it was considered unprofitable. Maybe there was something equivalent that had become lost along the path chosen by the automakers.

---

1 Erskine Childers, *The Riddle of the Sands: A Record of Secret Service* (England: Clays Limited, 1903; New York: Penguin Books, 1978).

2 Howard Gardner, *Intelligences Reframed: Multiple Intelligences for the 21st Century* (New York: Basic, Perseus Books, 1999).

Back-of-the-envelope thinking is taught in business schools. Partners in a potential business are mentally exercised with case studies and asked to jot down what they sense are the key objectives for their venture. Five to ten high-level items are usually enough to test the compatibility of the partners and either set them off in a common direction or bring to the surface the reasons they should part. My experience in piloting the first scenario-planning activity in GM gave me a chance to get close to the thinking of an incoming Board chairman, John Smale. In essence, Smale was pushing his staff toward agreement on what should be on the back of their envelope. He defined what he was after as a list small enough to fit on the back of a playing card—and big enough in thinking to be a reference guide for making fifty-year-plan decisions. It was something his staff should be able to reference as they made decisions quickly, avoiding the tradition of forming of committees to study a situation and prepare proposals. My role had been to lead the development of a set of scenarios on the future of transportation on each continent. North America was first and would prove to be the most fruitful. I explained the scenarios in great detail to John Smale and Jack Smith early in January 1995. The following day I took their immediate staff members through the same scenarios. A designated facilitator then took over, and I left the room so they could let their hair down. The facilitator drew out their opinions on where the company should be headed, and although I wasn't there to witness them getting to consensus, the strategic moves in the following months made clear that narrowing the focus of GM to automobiles was a part of what was written on the back of their new card. EDS and the Hughes Defense Group, as well as many other segments of the business, were spun off.

I thought about this back-of-the-envelope planning process as I began piling my research notes into the areas of high-level objectives that I recognized from my days in the GM think tank. One thing became sure very quickly—Henry Ford was not following the traditional carriage maker's business model. The distilling eventually settled into just eight categories.

HENRY FORD'S BACK-OF-THE-ENVELOPE CATEGORIES

Product Design and Development
Growth
Organization Development
Sourcing
Equipment
Sales
Research and Development
Manufacturing System

As I worked with these eight categories, I sorted the material into time frames and included descriptions of the surrounding circumstances. The material on

Henry Ford in 1903 was very different from that on the other automotive entrepreneurs. Each of Henry's eight line items was brilliantly supported by the other seven.

A look at the material for 1908 revealed that Henry Ford was not at all apprehensive about altering the objectives on the back of his envelope. He recognized the importance of making adjustments, and when William Durant made his move to corner the auto industry that year, Henry stood his ground. Henry's logic was sound, his move unique, and his bravery decisive. Once again he forged a path very different from the other automakers, who chose to compete with Durant.

My reading led me to the origins of things that in my career I had always accepted as inherent weaknesses in America's automotive business model—things I had written off long ago as just part of the cost of doing business. Many of them had been targets for change in Roger Smith's dream for the Saturn Corporation, and finding their origins was enlightening. Aligning inherent weaknesses in today's auto business with early decisions began to reveal a path by which America's industrial sector could retreat from the abyss. The more origins I found, the more I became convinced that there is still a way for Americans to make a very good living in the industrial sector.

The chapters that follow track the evolution of business objectives at the Ford Motor Company throughout its first century. They describe the essence of what has happened to all US auto companies and most of the other segments of the industrial sector. The chapters begin with the chronology of adjustments to the envelope Henry Ford must have carried around in his pocket—his list of mental notes on direction and objectives. Each chapter ends with a pointing out of present day problems introduced or exacerbated by each adjustment. To illustrate the effects of some of the decisions, I have included some creatively reenacted personal anecdotes culled from my years of experience at GM.

CHAPTER 2. 1903 AND 1908: HENRY FORD'S INITIAL BACK OF THE ENVELOPE

Features and ease of use often serve to begin a conversation about automobiles.

1903—PRODUCT DESIGN AND DEVELOPMENT

Quickly develop prototypes in a full range of prices and sizes, while incorporating continuous improvements into models already in production.

Henry Ford's earliest product design and development objective was to blanket the market with every popular size in every price range. He was out to match the breadth of offerings of the competition. Automobile customers in 1903 were affluent and accustomed to the attention given in custom-design conversations with carriage companies. Henry offered them choices of color and optional features, like the rest of the automakers, but his primary focus was on reliability, durability, and ease of use. Automakers were not skilled enough to match the custom-build capabilities of the carriage makers.

With a competent component-supply-base at hand, and a handful of carefully selected assembly craftsmen surrounding him, Henry began to assemble vehicles for sale. Each year he added more models and improvements.

- 1903. The Model A was introduced at a price of $750, with options in seating and tops, and it remained on the market until replaced in 1906 by the Model N.[1]
- 1904. The Models B and C were added, selling for $2,000 and $850 respectively.

---

1 Early Ford History, www.ritzsite.nl/FORD_1/01_eford.htm, Accessed March 17, 2010.

- 1905. The C-delivery car and the Model F were added and sold for $1,000.
- 1906. The Models K and N were added at $2,500 and $500.
- 1907. The Models R and S were added, selling for $750 and $700.

In five years Henry's crew would prove to be the most prolific in the industry. His teams of former carriage craftsmen would design and build nineteen prototypes in those first five years, developing nine of them to the point where they were put into production. Henry began with his Model A. He assembled them in a rented building on Mack Avenue in Detroit in 1903. Twenty months later operations were relocated to a larger rented building on Piquette Street, where production continued on the Model A, supplemented by Models B and C. Some of these first models would remain in production at Piquette Street long after the Model Ts rolled out of Highland Park.

Henry's craftsmen were unrestrained compared to today's vehicle program managers with their entourages of hundreds of supporting staff members. Henry selected hands-on people who could complete a design and development with their own hands while intermittingly assembling cars for sale. The prototypes they developed were completed in months instead of years, while keeping expenses so low that sales of a few hundred were enough to recover the investment.

The assembly craftsmen area was the core of Henry's organization. Their roles were similar to those of the assembly craftsmen that the carriage builders had employed for centuries. The pace of continuous improvement from 1903 to 1908 was as astounding as the pace of prototyping. Draftsmen during this era busily put lines to paper while peering over the shoulders of the assembly craftsmen. Skilled hands put cars together and discovered refinements on the fly. Steady increases in durability, reliability, and ease-of-use put distance between Ford and the competition.

Centering product development and continuous improvement in the heart of the production environment ensured immediate implementation. In the eighties, I had a conversation with Ken Iverson, founder and CEO of Nucor Steel. Among other things, we talked about research and development and where and how to conduct it. Iverson's answer paralleled what I was reading about Henry Ford. Iverson chose to position R&D personnel in every plant rather than at a remote research center. Iverson hired the hands-on type with expertise in metallurgy and hot metal processing. He counted on them to solve the problems of meeting the daily production schedule while simultaneously inventing new and better products and processes. Iverson would more than double the varieties of chemistries offered in steel catalogs in one decade. Similarly, Henry established a new level of expectation for the number of models in showrooms.

The second item Henry jotted down on the back of his imaginary envelope was probably his plan for growth. It was a three-pronged effort.

1903—GROWTH

Keep employment below five thousand; leverage a line of credit from suppliers to keep the number of investors to a minimum, and buy out start-up investors as soon as possible.

Quoting *Horseless Age* magazine, "Beware of guilders [advocates of the system of craft guilds] with dreams of more than 5,000 employees in a single company."[1] Entrepreneurs wanting to expand their automotive ventures were wise to stay under the radar of these guilders and note other warnings by financial column writers. Growth beyond 5,000 employees under a single roof had a history of becoming unwieldy in the carriage business, and the same was expected in auto making. Oldsmobile's payroll would reach 4,000 in 1903, and 2,500 at Buick. Whether by choice or market forces, both companies stayed under the radar of financial column writers, and Henry Ford did the same. His fight for market share would come later.

The second point of Henry's three-pronged growth objective was to expand without selling more shares of stock. He entered into financial arrangements with his component suppliers; the price of components would include the cost of a ninety-day line of credit. Ford Motor counted on selling its vehicles to wholesalers in ninety days or less. The railroad's pursers had to complete cash-on-delivery (COD) transactions and return with the money before the ninety-day notes came due. Leveraging supplier credit was a big part of Henry's growth objective. A century later it is still a part of the growth objectives of most companies producing industrial goods.

The third prong was a focus on buying out initial investors at every opportunity. Henry was diligent in his monitoring of investor ambitions; when they wanted to cash out, he would buy up their shares. In 1907, Henry Ford began talking about some daring countermoves to the expected ambitions of William (Billy) Durant. Henry's bold plans would drive out all but two of the remaining shareholders. Only the Dodge Brothers with their 35 percent share and his financial officer James Couzens would remain.

This three-pronged objective enabled Henry to grow quickly. His leveraging of the supply base avoided the pitfalls of Wall Street schemes. His line item for growth was very different from what the carriage makers had relied on for more than a century. Carriage buyers were expected to make payment up front and wait ten months for delivery. Customers watching the moves of the new automotive entrepreneurs were leery. The media was filled with stories of them going out of business soon after they hung out their shingles, and an automobile was roughly ten times more expensive than a carriage. Henry gambled that his customers would be willing to choose an automobile off a lot rather than wait for a

---

1 *Horseless Age* (1904).

custom order. Auto companies today are still suppressing consumer interest in being able to order a customized design.

The third objective on the back of Henry's envelope set his course for building an organization.

1903—ORGANIZATION DEVELOPMENT

> *Evolve the role of assembly craftsmen from carriages to automobiles; bootstrap component-making skills in each new area of advancement in processing and design.*

The Midwest had attracted craft-oriented immigrants from Europe throughout the nineteenth century. They brought with them tried and true approaches to apprentice selection and development. Without the surrounding support of a nurturing culture, the Midwest would never have evolved into the world's finest carriage builders. A carriage apprenticeship was expected to take upwards of ten years under the watchful eye of a master craftsman. The goal of every apprentice was to become a certified craftsman and, if he was good, perhaps receive a master's position someday. The shops owned by masters were filled with apprentices of all ages, and some of them were eager. Key to Henry's early success was his ability to attract good apprentices away from the guild's system.

Only the guilds could certify a master in craft, and only a master could certify an apprentice had completed his training. The bottom line: the guild controlled the flow of apprentice certifications. Control kept income levels high for all craftsmen, which was the purpose of the guild. A very similar system is used today to control the income levels of dentists, doctors, and other professions. Controlling apprentice certifications meant the guild could control the rate at which the automotive entrepreneurs could grow and the rate at which they could in-source component production. Henry chose an organizational objective that would move his organization out from under the power of the guilds.

Henry's organization-development objective altered the course of craftsmanship in America. His division of the traditional craftsman roles into journeymen trades left behind the portions of the crafts no longer required. For example, he divided the blacksmith's role into casting, forging, heat-treat, and welding, among others. But he discarded the learning of how to handle a horse while fitting it with shoes. Henry's hands-on experience with building prototypes enabled him to select his protégés and invent their new roles. Henry's decision enabled a shortcut. Once again it was brilliant for the times.

The most thoroughly trained in Henry's crews were his assembly craftsmen. They became his clones. The assembly area was the heart of the organization—the wheelhouse from which all activity was ordained. The assembly craftsmen (journeymen) knew enough about how components were made to feed back direction to solve the emerging daily problems. The result was a natural flow of continuous improvement.

Henry's decisions regarding how to organize a workforce and how to short-cut the development of skills would both enable a fast-paced business expansion. When he added the demands of building multiple models, his new teams were prepared. His journeymen had walked away from the traditions of the craft culture, and their faith in Henry was so strong they did not look back.

My grandfather Max would sometimes mention the guilds on Sunday afternoons in conversations with my father about workmanship. The old masters who settled in Flint had built the finest carriages in the world. When Max arrived in 1919 and Buick's leadership discovered his background, he was handed a role in the development of a journeyman educational system. I know now that when Max was reverent in his discussions of the guilds, he was hinting that there was something missing from the education system for Flint's journeymen.

My grandfather Floyd's childhood career on the Saginaw Bay ferry had taught him how to assess the merits of a stranger. His peanut customers didn't pick up a bag of burgers and drive off. They spent time loitering around as the ferry made its journey. Floyd's interest in people and their merits made him a natural leader. He began as a wheelwright apprentice in 1908 but quickly transitioned from craftsman to journeyman and then to foreman. Floyd would sometimes describe the hiring process before World War I. It was little more than a foreman walking along an employment line looking for candidates. He would tap a few on the shoulder and lead them back to the job. By day's end, the candidate knew what was expected and whether he would be returning to the hiring line.

When I was sixteen, Floyd returned from Florida with plans for building a two-bedroom summerhouse. After five years in retirement, he had decided that summers in Florida were too humid; he wanted to spend them in Michigan. I was excited when he asked for my help and confident that my strength and energy would serve him well. It wasn't long, however, before Floyd proved he could run circles around me when the sun was blazing. One hot evening in June, when I sat down to dinner too tired to eat, my father explained, "Your grandfather is one of those people who have foundry sand in their veins. They like the heat." Then he added, "I once saw him carry a piano into a house all by himself. He is the strongest man I have ever met." Floyd and I would complete his summerhouse in less than three months. He had the skills of a mason, carpenter, electrician, plumber, tinsmith, and all the other trades, which was part of the reason we finished so quickly. We never sat down to wait for a subcontractor. Another part of our quick build capability was Floyd's organizational skill. The right material and the right tools were always at hand. The days were long but rewarding, and the three months flew by. What I didn't realize that summer was that Floyd was handing down his most valuable lesson. He could have hired a builder to erect his summerhouse, but chose instead to give me a private lesson in leadership. Six years later, I was assigned a production foreman's role. His lessons proved invaluable.

1903—SOURCING

Wrest the strategic automotive component business away from the craft shops that are giving away competitive advantages in processing.

Henry, like the hundred-plus entrepreneurs before him, began by assembling components purchased from the carriage makers' supply base. He ordered from the same suppliers that served his competition. These suppliers viewed the auto business as small but lucrative, a supplement to their income. Henry saw them as a threat to competitiveness. He began to in-source even before his first twenty months at Mack Avenue were complete. He began by in-sourcing the processing innovations his craftsmen were inventing, that is, cladding the wooden bodies with stamped sheet metal to protect the finish from stone chips and making improvements to chassis and steering components. He chose things that were on the leading edge in material and processing advancements, things he knew the suppliers would share with his competition if he showed them how he wanted them made. Henry's propensity for in-sourcing would change the basis of competition from salesmanship to craftsmanship. The only lag in development during Ford's first decade was in the design and build of a power train; that is, the engine, transmission, and differential. The Dodge Brothers were the leaders in power-train development in 1903 and were Henry's choice for a supplier. It would take Henry more than a decade to bootstrap capability in the design and development of power trains.[1] He chose to make the Dodge Brothers a 35 percent shareholder in the Ford Motor Company in exchange for a steady supply of power trains under the ninety-days-same-as-cash arrangement. The Dodge Brothers were well down the road in power-train development when Henry began and were already selling power trains to most of the new automakers. Henry chose to make them a major partner, thereby assuring they would become increasingly interested in the success of the Ford Motor Company, perhaps to the exclusion of competitors in years to come.

1903—EQUIPMENT

Acquire specialized equipment as fast as capital becomes available.

With each in-sourcing move, Henry was forced to spend more of his limited capital on equipment. He chose the most durable and accurate brands—equipment designed to be re-fixtured, retooled, and rebuilt for decades to come. While taking inventory of equipment in Happy Valley in 1966, I came across some pieces that been purchased in 1910. All the auto companies were choosing what would come to be called flexible equipment.

---

1 "Bootstrap capability" is an old term used to describe figuring things out for yourself. It stems from the expression "lifting yourself up by your own bootstraps."

The craft skills that had guided hand tools as they formed components for carriages fell by the way in favor of journeyman skills that guided hand tools as they formed fixtures and tooling that was mounted to this new flexible equipment. The equipment then mass produced the components. A drill press, for example, would be fitted out with multiple spindles that could be reconfigured to each new pattern of holes rolling off the drawing boards. The feed rate and drill extraction rate could be set to cycle automatically. Henry was making inroads in equipment design, encouraging builders of equipment to design something different than what they sold to the component suppliers.

1903—SALES

Focus on selling wholesale and recovering the investments in cost of goods sold in less than ninety days.

The sale of carriages had evolved in the nineteenth century to become a mail-order transaction with payment up front and delivery promised within ten months. By 1903, the media was pumping out stories of how the new automotive entrepreneurs were failing and how the average auto was roughly thirty times more expensive than the average carriage. Asking customers to gamble such a large sum of money on the delivery of a new automobile was too much. Ford set off on a new course. He chose to sell through wholesalers and began to assemble a network of bankers and bicycle shops willing to invest in his finished-goods inventory. The cycling fad had come to America in the late 1800s, and the entrepreneurs who had gambled on opening bicycle shops were vying to retail this new motorized form of personal transportation. The bicycle shop owners were familiar with teaching customers how to operate and maintain their purchase: which spots needed to be lubricated before each trip, which spots required a dab of grease each week, and which ones needed to be fine tuned periodically. An auto owner had to know how to crank the engine without spraining a wrist and how to keep the spark advance just right on these very temperamental motors, along with knowing the lubrication requirements. There was also a need for driving lessons over difficult terrain and lessons in who has the right of way in traffic. Selling autos through wholesalers familiar with mechanical things and customer training had real advantages over selling them through livery stables or general stores.

1903—RESEARCH AND DEVELOPMENT

Coordinate R&D efforts from the hub of the organization, the assembly area where all issues merge.

In the carriage industry, the assembly craftsmen gave direction to research and development efforts. Henry's choice of objective here was not brilliant but was simply a continuation. He expected his assembly craftsmen to guide advancements in component making that would enhance the performance of automobiles.

In the 1960s and 1970s, the steel industry's mini-mills followed in Henry's footsteps, placing the coordination of R&D in the midst of the foundry floor. The scientists (master craftsmen) of the steel industry added new metallurgical choices to their steel catalogs and new custom shapes to bars and blanks. Both Henry and the mini-mills made inroads into market share by counting on the production environment to guide their R&D efforts.

1903—MANUFACTURING SYSTEM

Adapt the carriage industry's staged assembly system to meet the demands of manufacturing the horseless carriage.

My efforts to exhaust the supply of old accounts of the auto business uncovered some fascinating explanations of systems for assembling automobiles prior to 1913. They were all variations on the carriage builders' tried and true staged assembly system. Carriages were traditionally manufactured in two stages by two different clusters of expertise. Cabinet makers guided the activities in the body assembly area, and blacksmiths guided the chassis assembly area. The cabinet makers would form and assemble the wooden body components. Painters stepped in to apply a custom-order color and perhaps a monogram. The leather and fabric craftsmen then stepped in to add the custom cushions, headliners, and curtains. The locksmiths assembled the hinges, door latches, steps, and other hardware that they had fabricated. Simultaneously in an adjacent area, teams of blacksmiths and machinists worked to fabricate and assemble the chassis on sawhorses. Painters added color to both the metal and the wood on the chassis, and wheelwrights added their matched assemblies of spokes, hubs, and rims. The final step was a joint effort that provided feedback to both groups. The chassis was pushed to a location near the body which was sitting on sawhorses. The teams would lift and place the body atop its mountings. The volume of production of carriages and wagons would reach 1.2 million per year without even the slightest hint of the need for an assembly line.

The Mack Avenue building was close to the surrounding carriage makers' supply base, and the components Henry ordered for his Model A were delivered by horse-drawn wagons. Henry's version of a staged assembly system had three working areas instead of two. The third was positioned between the chassis and body assembly areas. It was where the driveline was positioned atop the chassis and where attempts were made to start the new motor.

At the first stage of Henry's system, the chassis was assembled and the wheels were mounted. When a team of four was finished with the chassis, they pushed their work down the aisle and into a driveline assembly area. Then they hurried back to begin again on the next chassis.

In the second stage, a team of four of a new breed of drive-train assembly craftsmen would assemble the motor, transmission, and driveline components atop the chassis. They would attempt to start the temperamental Dodge Brothers' motor, and, whether it started or not, the driveline and chassis were moved down the aisle and into a body assembly and trim station.

This third and final stage was where four assembly craftsmen added the purchased body, seats, and trim components. When their work was complete, they pushed or drove the finished automobile out the back door and onto the rail dock.

There were twelve working stalls in the Mack Avenue building. The stalls allowed the simultaneous assembly of four chassis, four drivelines, and four bodies. The focus during the first twenty months of the Ford Motor Company was to hire and train more and more assembly craftsmen. The goal for each team became the assembly of one before lunch and one after lunch. Working two shifts, the teams accelerated output to sixteen cars per day within their first twenty months. Sales projections anticipated expansion, and Henry relocated his teams from Mack Avenue to a larger three-story factory two miles to the north at the corner of Piquette and Beaubien Streets.

The Piquette factory had forty-five stalls on the second floor, which allowed daily production to grow from sixteen to sixty cars. It was a move that brought renewed efforts to hire and train assembly craftsmen. At the same time came the quest to bootstrap skills to make components, which meant even more hiring. The earliest in-sourcing included the processes for forming sheet-steel cladding for the wooden body, the forging of new metals, and the machining of new designs for components. Cars were assembled on the second floor. A ramp down to the shipping dock allowed gravity to assist in the shipping of any cars that wouldn't start. As an industrial engineer, I can attest that Henry's choice of manufacturing system was more efficient than historians are recognizing and more efficient than the assembly line in the beginning.

As I studied the old accounts and photographs, I became convinced that in the first few years Henry Ford survived day to day on wits, happenstance, and luck like the rest of the automotive entrepreneurs. The documented early moves of the Ford Motor Company imply what must have been on the back of Henry's imaginary envelope. Henry did not follow the conventions of the carriage industry. He pioneered a very different business model for auto making that vaulted his company into a powerful position. It is little wonder that he enjoyed spending time with Thomas Edison. Both would be remembered for their genius.

The chapters of this book provide a chronology of the evolution of the business model of the American auto industry. They end with reflections on present day problems, more than a hundred of them. They are the problems that are making the United States uncompetitive in the new global economy. The sheer number of problems makes the search for solutions complex, but not impossible. The problems are listed at the end of their respective chapters to reveal the surrounding circumstances and show that these were not bad decisions at the time they were made. Rather, over the course of the 20th century, conditions changed and some of the early decisions became entrenched. Problems began to compound upon each other. Appendix 1 enumerates the problems in a discrete list and Appendix 2 offers a business model that addresses all of them.

LONG-TERM INEFFICIENCIES IN THE OBJECTIVES OF 1903

For all his genius, Henry Ford would set in motion six troublesome alterations to the carriage maker's business model in the areas of organization development, equipment, and sales. These six would become entrenched and inefficient, inhibiting American industry from thriving in the latter half of the 20th century. Attempts to correct them led to more and more problems.

1. Organization Development: Henry Ford's 1903 decision to divide the traditional craftsman's roles into silos of skill called "journeyman classifications" served to accelerate apprentice training but would later drive up the cost of doing business.

Dividing up the traditional craftsman's responsibilities shortened the length of training programs in the beginning, but it evolved to have a dampening effect on competitiveness. When Henry Ford launched his shift away from the guilders, he unknowingly began a narrowing of the problem-solving capability of his workforce. In generations to come, specialists took over for generalists and the cost of doing business went up while the pace of continuous improvement slowed down.

2. Organization Development: In 1903, the carriage builder's community was serving to steer youth with potential into apprentice programs.

This support culture began to disappear as the journeymen took over. A culture that did not understand journeyman classifications began to lose track of what was happening inside the huge factory fences. Cultural appreciation shifted to size of paychecks and pride in craft slipped away.

Changes in the carriage maker's culture were subtle. The aspirations they laid out for their youth changed slowly. Most of my uncles became journeymen and, thanks to my grandfathers, were capable of much more than they were ever asked to do inside the fences. But by the time the third generation of autoworkers entered the workforce, the concept of master craftsman was lost.

3. Equipment: Henry's pursuit of equipment builders that could offer complex mass production equipment would eventually lead to out-sourcing the design and manufacture of fixtures and tooling.

This handoff evolved slowly until the seventies, when equipment suppliers became the sole source for solutions to processing problems. The capital investment requirements then jumped to another plane as experience in the design and manufacture of equipment disappeared from within the auto industry.

In the 1960s, the journeymen skilled in fixture and tooling development began leaving the auto business to join the payrolls of equipment and tooling suppliers. Evidence of the damage caused by letting the American machine tool industry take over became apparent when factories in Asia and Europe did not order equipment from America. When Asian "transplant" assembly plants were built in Ohio, Indiana, Alabama, and Tennessee in the early eighties, Asian companies equipped their factories with manufacturing systems designed, built, and shipped in from Asia.

The eighties brought a wave of computerized numerically controlled (CNC)[1] machines that the American workforce was not able to operate. These new CNC machines demanded a return to a knowledgeable workforce experienced in fixtures, tooling, and the steps of metal removal. It also demanded accompanying skills in computer programming—not programmers, but craftsmen with programming training. The workforce in Japan and Europe was quick to pick up on the CNC era. But America continued down its path of hiring workers to stand in stanchions. America was expecting its machine tool industry to design and build equipment that could be operated by its low-skilled workforce that would compete with Asia and Europe.

4. Sales: Henry Ford initially offered a few options on his models, but he didn't strive to nurture consumer preference like the carriage builders.

With the volume of auto sales exploding, demand drove Henry and others to focus strategically on increasing the volume of production rather than the number of custom options. The attractiveness of "custom built" in the mid- and luxury-priced lines is still an opportunity today. The size of this iceberg is already exposed by the size of the aftermarket and up-fitter industries.

5. Sales: One of Henry's initial decisions was to sell automobiles through wholesalers, and this mode has outgrown its usefulness.

---

1 CNC machines are essentially the universal machines of Henry Ford's early days: mills, lathes, shapers, etc. The only real difference is that a craftsman programs this new CNC equipment and then a computer takes over to repeat the attentive movements of the hands of a craftsman to make duplicates. When the craftsman chooses to use Kentucky windage to increase the accuracy of the machine, the computer remembers and repeats the maneuver. The result is (1) more accuracy than the machine builder can promise and (2) the accomplishment of mass production using universal equipment.

Auto buyers today rarely take a test drive, and they don't need to learn lubrication details or need a lesson in how to turn a crank. Today's electronic banking has replaced the train's purser and allows for instantaneous collection of revenue. The carriage makers' system of selling direct and building to order should have reemerged. Today dealer lots are still carrying a hundred days of inventory to act as buffer between production and sales. It supposedly gives consumers selections to choose from; but with fewer choices of color and options being produced, consumers must pay the carrying cost on a hundred days of inventory with little gain in value.

Many entrepreneurs are already selling used cars on-line and delivering them direct to your door, and yet it is illegal for an original equipment manufacturer (OEM) to sell directly to the consumer. Legislation pulled together by the National Automobile Dealers Association (NADA) and pushed through state government houses in the fifties and early sixties made OEM direct sales illegal. Selling direct was once the preferred course of all carriage makers. Returning to build-to-order and custom work would make it difficult for imports to compete.

6. Sales: The decision to sell automobiles from a finished-goods inventory has all but erased a cultural memory of owning custom-built personal transportation.

"Custom built" did make a short comeback in the sixties and seventies. Customers were allowed to choose from lists of options and pay only for the ones they wanted. This comeback revealed that there is still an interest in custom-made personal transportation. (It must be an inherent part of human nature.) The number of customers choosing to place a custom order and wait two to three weeks for delivery grew to 11 percent in 1970, while I was leading an industrial engineering team at the Flint Truck Assembly. The plant was equipped to handle a much higher percentage, but dealers began to make strategic discouragements to keep the interest in custom orders from returning to prominence.

Recap 1903

Henry Ford's original decisions to (1) walk away from the guilds that controlled the flow of certified craftsmen and (2) steer away from the made-to-order approach to sales have never been reversed. It is amazing how decisions made a century ago would subsequently make it so easy for imports to gain and hold a beachhead on American soil.

1908—HENRY IS FORCED TO MODIFY HIS ENVELOPE

In media accounts of late 1907, I found hints of changes to the back of Henry's envelope. It was apparent that William Crapo Durant was setting out to corner the auto business. Durant had proven he could assemble the largest carriage company in America, and his investments in Buick made the rumors of his move on the automobile business seem like a foregone conclusion. While Ford was occupied with blanketing the market with multiple model offerings and leveraging the wealth of the supply base, Durant was stacking up his cash reserves and figuring out the steps he would take to leverage his holdings into a dominant collection of auto companies. In September 1908, Durant made his move. He formed the General Motors Corporation, pulling Oldsmobile, Cadillac, and Oakland under his Buick umbrella. From where Henry Ford stood at the corner of Piquette and Beaubien, it was clear Durant was out to amass a formidable position. Durant was not only going to collect auto companies but also a complete set of the leading component makers.

In 1908, Durant offered Henry a chance to sell out and walk away, but Henry chose to stay and compete. It was a daring decision to gamble the future on the newly-acquired skills of his crew; and it turned out that in just five years Henry had developed a workforce that would take the Ford Motor Company to a place where General Motors could not follow. Henry gambled that his crew could insource any component Durant would attempt to corner. A head-to-head competition between bootstrapped skills and acquired skills ensued. Win or lose would be the only options for Henry. Henry chose to make adjustments in four of the eight items on the back of his envelope.

> 1903—*Product Design and Development: Quickly develop prototypes in a full range of prices and sizes, while incorporating continuous improvements into models already in production.*

This was totally revised:

> 1908—*Product Design and Development: Focus on perfecting a low-cost entry. (The 1908 decision to build the Model T remained unchanged until 1921, when slumping sales of open roadsters forced Henry to rethink his product line objective. The Model T would remain in production until 1935.)*

Henry's decision to walk away from the carriage builders' supply base through in-sourcing served the company well when it set out to design and develop the extremely low priced, broadly accepted Model T. Henry's crew was already experienced with continuous improvement at a rapid pace, and the work on a durable low-priced entry for the masses became a collective goal. It was a move that Durant would not be able to follow. Durant was busy wrestling his newly acquired companies into agreements to trust one another and to accept his overarching decisions on how to share income and allocate capital. Henry's decision to bet the farm on a single market entry went against the advice of his investors, and he bought them out.

> 1903—*Growth: Keep employment below five thousand; leverage a line of credit from suppliers to keep the number of investors to a minimum, and buy out the start-up investors as soon as possible.*

This was totally revised:

1908—Growth: Grow quickly without restraints to avoid being shut out.

Henry had steered around the shadows raised by the financial sector. His decision to lean on suppliers for credit and avoid Wall Street's investment sharks had worked, but now he needed something more. Durant was bent on cornering the supply base, which would cut off both the flow of components and his ninety-day lines of credit from suppliers. The decision to launch a low-priced Model T was accompanied by a decision to build a huge factory. The architectural firm Albert Khan and Associates was contracted to design and build the Highland Park plant. The site, four miles to the north along Woodward Avenue, was expected to solve the elevator and other problems inherent in the Piquette plant. It was a leap in capacity from four thousand to two hundred thousand vehicles a year with enough floor space to manufacture all components. His capacity exceeded the combined capacity of the assembly plants Durant had acquired. Henry was setting up to grow faster than Durant.

Henry Ford's initial investors let go quickly when Henry gambled everything. Only the Dodge Brothers, who supplied the power train, and his financial officer, James J. Couzens, retained an ownership position. Couzens would soon bow out to enter the political arena. (He would be elected mayor of Detroit and then senator from Michigan.)

Growth, to Henry, was more about building a protected empire than elevating share price.

1903—Sourcing: Wrest the strategic automotive component business away from the craft shops that were giving away competitive advantages in processing.

Was edited to read:

1908—Sourcing: Develop in-house capability in all automotive component processing except the power train, and protect the company from outside interests in cornering the component supply base.

The few auto producers that chose to compete with Durant had to ensure that their links to suppliers could not be cut off. Henry Ford was ahead of this game, having made independence from the supply base a goal since day one. Henry strove for competence in all fields of component processing with one large exception, the driveline, which was supplied by the Dodge Brothers. The Brothers were 35 percent shareholders in Ford and the sole suppliers to several other automakers. Ford was confident they would not sell out to Durant. He believed the stories in the media hinting that the Dodge Brothers were going to launch a car with their own name on it someday.

1903—Organization Development: Evolve the role of assembly craftsmen from carriages to automobiles; bootstrap component-making skills in each new area of advancement in processing and design.

Was intensified:

1908—Organization Development: Train thousands of new assembly craftsmen quickly; focus on bootstrapping skills in all types of component processing.

Workforce development moved to a high priority while the Highland Park plant was under construction. The hundreds of assembly craftsmen at the Piquette plant began doing double duty, building cars and training thousands of new workers for Highland Park.

Recap 1908

The rewrites of objectives in 1908 would not cause problems in the century to follow. But this was the only era when Henry's decision making did not create cracks in the business model that would widen as the century unfolded. The next four years were a time of growth. Production volume swelled, and the Ford Motor Company became the largest automaker in the world. The new Model T was manufactured and assembled under a single roof. Nothing on the market could compare to its low price, reliability, durability, and ease of use. But then the Highland Park plant began to have trouble keeping up with demand. The staged system of assembly was struggling.

CHAPTER 3. 1913: THE ASSEMBLY LINE WAS A RELUCTANT MOVE

By 1912 it was clear that Henry Ford's shift to a single-model objective was brilliant. Sales of the Model T were nearing a pace of two hundred thousand per year as the year came to an end. William Durant's move to corner the auto business, on the other hand, had pushed backers to the verge of bankruptcy. They retaliated by banding together and pushing Durant out of his own company. Undeterred, Durant started over. This time he partnered with Louis Chevrolet and by 1913 was ready to launch a new low-priced entry named after Louis. Durant was still intent on giving Henry Ford some competition. Henry's Highland Park plant was struggling to keep up with market demand. Henry was under the gun, knowing that Durant would step in quickly to pick up the customer demand he was unable to satisfy.

With output exceeding that of any auto plant in the world, Henry's hand-picked and trained teams of assembly craftsmen were the first to reach the ceiling of staged assembly systems. They were assembling roughly 180 vehicles at a time, 60 in each of the three stages. The work areas were arranged in clusters rather than along an aisle. The clustering reduced the total distance that the chassis had to be pushed by teams of workers. Units were being pushed every two hours instead of at the beginning of the shift and right after lunch as they had been at Mack Avenue and Piquette Street. As the volume of production grew, the staged system became more and more inefficient. Sheer size was a problem and increasing production was only making things worse. Three shifts were working around the clock. The plant is described in media as chaotic and hazardous.

Frederick Taylor had published his recommendation that industry use "scientific methods"[1] in 1911, about the time Charles Sorensen and Charles Lewis, members of Henry's staff, urged consideration of an alternative to staged assembly. Henry was invited to demonstrations of the assembly line on the third floor of the Piquette plant, where a rope was used to drag the chassis along while workers assembled components. For two years Henry postponed the adoption of the assembly line. I like to think that Henry was reluctant because he sensed where the assembly line would lead.

In January 1913, Henry made the decision that would set a new course for the US industrial sector. He renounced his faith in the abilities of his assembly craftsmen and with a reluctant nod set the first assembly line system in motion. The craftsmen he admonished with that nod were the people who had worked side by side with him for a decade; some were there in the beginning at Mack Avenue.

Once it was clear that Henry was not going to reverse his decision, his well-trained assembly craftsmen began walking off the job. Thousands left in the first month. By the end of the second, only a handful had not yet found jobs with other auto companies. The magnitude of the exodus left Henry stunned for years. The decade he had spent selecting and nurturing assembly craftsmen was lost.

Ford Motor Company would hire twelve thousand replacements five times during 1913.[2] The replacements would verbally agree to stand in their stanchions while they were secretly making plans to find a better job. Henry offered a 15 percent raise and shortened the workday from ten to nine hours.[3] Still the mass exodus played out on paydays. In January 1914, Henry made another of his complex strategic moves. He authorized the doubling of the daily wage to $5. He attracted people who came for the money and not a career. The fabric of the organization had changed. With one decision he stopped the exodus but set adrift a raft of long-term problems that compounded over time.

The assembly line decision forced Henry to rethink six of his eight intricately linked objectives. He was forced to rethink the auto industry's basis of competition. It even changed the order of importance of the lines on the back of the envelope.

> *1903—Manufacturing System: Adapt the carriage industry's staged assembly system to meet the demands of manufacturing the horseless carriage.*

Was rewritten:

> *1913—Manufacturing System: Discontinue staged assembly. Divide the work into segments and spread them along a moving assembly line with feeding tributaries.*

---

1 Frederick Winslow Taylor, *The Principles of Scientific Management* (New York and London: Harper & Brothers, 1911).

2 Harry Barnard, *Independent Man: The Life of Senator James Couzens* (New York: Charles Scribner's Sons, 1958), p. 88.

3 Harry Barnard, *Independent Man: The Life of Senator James Couzens* (New York: Charles Scribner's Sons, 1958), p. 91.

Ford Motor Company was the first to bump into the ceiling of one of the many caves etched with variations on ox cart assembly systems. Ford was the first to find it impossible to build two hundred thousand automobiles a year in one huge staged assembly system. Ford was also the first to adopt the assembly line as a solution. Accounts written by people on the inside, including Floyd my grandfather, reveal that the shift to the assembly line was made with great reservation. It tore the heart out of every organization. The handpicked clones (assembly craftsmen) of the pioneers of auto making would not accept the yoke of the monotonous assembly line.

> *1908—Organization Development: Train thousands of new assembly craftsmen quickly; focus on bootstrapping skills in all types of component processing.*

Was edited to read:

> *1913—Organization Development: Reorganize Highland Park to run without a core of assembly craftsmen while continuing to focus on the in-sourcing of all component manufacturing.*

Fredrick Taylor's *The Principles of Scientific Management* prescribed the application of the "scientific method" to increase productivity. It called for optimizing the way tasks were performed and simplifying all jobs so that new workers could be trained quickly. Taylor's approach was to define a single best way to perform each task, making it possible for managers on the sidelines to direct activity. The advantage of being in touch with what was happening minute to minute was lost.

Today a twenty-first-century assembly line is most efficient when it is assembling a thousand vehicles a day. Highland Park was close in December 1912, with an output of 762 per day. A twenty-first-century assembly line employs roughly 1,700 on each of two shifts. Highland Park was employing roughly 1,500 assembly craftsmen on each of three shifts. All but 400 of the assembly craftsmen at Highland Park in 1912 had less than two years of experience. Henry observed as his organization grew in numbers and experience in 1911 and 1912. He hoped they would continue to figure out ways to build more and more Model Ts. But the confusion in the assembly area was compounding. His experienced assembly craftsmen were busy fixing assembly errors, training new workers, and trying to direct improvements back into the evolving component-making workforce, which was already busy dealing with its own set of problems. The year 1912 was an organizational nightmare, and 1913 brought new problems. The average worker was standing in his stanchion just long enough to find another job.

Henry proclaimed the wonders of his assembly line in the media in 1914. He had to attract new hires from beyond the local community that had become filled with disgruntled craftsmen. Midwest communities, accustomed to nurturing apprentices, were soon flooded with families holding very different values. In the midst of this fog of unrest, Henry refilled his ranks with people willing to row toward his elusive White Whale.[1] They came for the money and not a career, setting the stage for labor unrest in the generation to follow. The descendants of the people who came for the $5 a day did not nurture a new generation of craftsmen. They followed the example set by their parents.

Ford's success in volume of sales enticed the other auto companies to follow suit. They soon joined Henry in his embrace of the assembly line, and the basis of competition shifted from superior skills in craft to simply rate of growth.

> *1908—Growth: Grow quickly without restraints to avoid being shut out.*

Was edited to read:

> *1913—Growth: Invest in faster assembly lines and start making strategic moves to weaken the positions of fast-following competitors.*

Doubling the daily wage channeled profits away from the Dodge Brothers at a time when they were expanding their production of power trains for the Model T and making the final moves toward the launch of their own line of vehicles. Being a 35-percent shareholder in the Ford Motor Company had been lucrative, and they were counting on profits from 1912 and 1913 to put their own line of vehicles on the road. Henry's decision to distribute profits to his workers (in wages) bought time for the development of a Ford version of the power train for the Model T. Henry made a habit of timing his decisions so they solved several issues simultaneously. The $5-a-day decision was one of them.

> *1908—Sourcing: Develop in-house capability in all automotive component processing except the power train, and protect the company from outside interests in cornering the component supply base.*

Was broadened to read:

> *1913—Sourcing: Expand in-sourcing investments to defend the origins of all tributaries feeding raw materials.*

In 1912, Ford Motor Company became the largest auto producer in the world. Henry had forced the competition to double their wages in 1914 to attract employees, and he was receiving a lot of negative press. Being the largest made Ford a target. By 1915, the Ford Motor Company was refocused on insulating itself from a potential "DeBeers"[2] move; that is, a move by a competitor to block access to any of the required raw materials. Henry increased Ford's level of integration all the way back to the mines. He began construction of "The Rouge," a huge manufacturing complex with a canal accessing the Great Lakes near Dearborn, in 1917, and he even purchased a fleet of lake freighters. The freighters carried iron ore, limestone, and coke from Ford mines to Ford smelters. The Rouge became a self-contained automobile manufacturing complex. It employed one hundred

---

1 Herman Melville, *Moby Dick* (New York: Harper & Brothers, 1851).
2 Hedley Arthur Chilvers, *The Story of De Beers* (London: Cassell, 1939).

thousand people when it was complete and turned shiploads of basic raw materials into finished automobiles. Henry gave protection of his supply base a high priority.

Fifty years later, another brave entrepreneur appeared. His name was Ken Iverson. He walked away from his position among the giants of the steel industry and founded the first "mini-mill." He named it Nucor Steel. His vision of how to survive was surprisingly similar to that of Henry Ford. Iverson went after the entire value chain, from sorting scrap iron through the mixing, melting, pouring, soaking, rolling, and cutting processes, to loading for delivery. Iverson began with truckloads of reinforcing rod that had been cut and bent to meet the needs of each construction site. Iverson went on to capture more and more market share with superior quality in chemistry and with an expanding product line and on-time delivery in the quantities ordered. The media in the seventies quoted the giants of steel on several occasions. They proclaimed Nucor little more than a flash in the pan and said that it would quickly run out of raw material (scrap), the very thing that Henry feared in 1915. The giants were right, but then they didn't anticipate that the price of scrap would rise so high that it would stimulate the invention of better ways of rounding up scrap iron. Nor did they anticipate how a doubling of scrap prices would affect their own profitability and ultimately their grip on their own industry. Ford sensed that the supply base was an area of vulnerability and made the achievement of the highest possible level of integration one of his back-of-the-envelope objectives.

> *1908—Product Design and Development: Focus on perfecting a low-cost entry. (The 1908 decision to build the Model T remained unchanged until 1921, when slumping sales of open roadsters forced Henry to rethink his product line objective. The Model T would remain in production until 1935.)*

Had to be reorganized to still function without a core of assembly craftsmen:

> *1913—Product Design and Development: Continue to focus on improvements in the Model T, but by using engineers (a hands-off approach), rather than a core of assembly craftsmen, to direct designers.*

Assembly craftsmen had been the heart of Henry's product design and development function from the beginning. They performed both production and prototype build using regular tools and equipment in the regular production areas. The staged assembly areas were where all components came together, and the assembly craftsmen who worked there could keep their fingers on the pulse of the organization. They would feed back advice on the fine tuning of operations and keep track of progress on continuous improvements. They were the first to know when things began not to fit properly and were capable of directing adjustments through their runners who quickly passed information back and forth between the assembly and component areas. In 1912 every corner of the huge Highland Park complex was receiving direction from the assembly craftsmen at its core.

The skills of these assembly craftsmen led the continuous improvement cycles and kept the Model T ahead of the evolving competition. There are accounts of draftsmen looking over the shoulders of the assembly craftsmen. The role of a draftsman in the beginning had been to document the ingenuity flowing out of the minds of the assembly craftsmen and component makers.

Some of the earliest accounts describe Henry Ford interacting with his assembly craftsmen to find solutions to design, reliability, durability, and performance problems. He knew the importance of informal links between assembly craftsmen and component makers. His two years of reluctance in adopting the assembly line system was well founded.

As the roaring twenties got underway, customers started preferring enclosed sedans and coupes. The Model T was an open roadster, and sales of the Model T were falling. In 1922, with GM overtaking the role of largest auto company in the world, Ford Motor Company purchased Lincoln Motor Car Works and added an upscale brand to its product line.

Henry Ford's reluctance to introduce another model between 1908 and 1921 was due in no small part to the loss of his talented assembly craftsmen. Their disappearance took apart his vision for directing product design and development efforts. The assembly line had forced the separation of design and development from operations. It also eliminated the origins and natural tracking of continuous improvement. The system of product design, development, and manufacture that had made Ford so successful was erased.

I saw evidence of the importance of links between operations and design still around at GM in the early sixties.

THE DIE ROOM

> Remnants of the earliest designer-craftsmen interfaces were still in play when I began my required year of skilled-trade experiences in 1964. My first assignment was to perform the duties of an apprentice die maker. The new die build area in Happy Valley was in Plant 2, and the die design area was on the balcony above. It was the sixties, and the art of forming sheet metal had evolved into sweeping curves, fins, and intricate lighting configurations. The art of processing sheets of cold rolled steel was at its peak. The chemistry of the blocks of steel used to make the die tooling was evolving as well. That summer I was coached through putting a die together, and before I went back to my engineering studies I depressed a set of palm buttons and watched as a ribbon of steel feeding in on one side would pop out on the other side as a series of timing pointers. The rate was more than one per second. The blocks of steel I had assembled were of varying properties in wear hardness, malleability, shear, and compression strength. Surprisingly the prints sent down from the balcony were only sketches of what I had to make to exact dimensions. The skills and imagination of a die

maker were an integral part of getting from the blueprint sketches to formed sheet metal components.

During the summer I was surprised several times to see stark white shirts leaning in to talk with silver-haired die makers in dirty coveralls. The pristine white posed a stark contrast to the world where the machining of cast iron left a film of graphite on everything. The white was worn by some of the die designers who worked on the balcony above. I was an eighteen-year-old apprentice under watchful eyes and far too intent on proving my worth to listen. Still, from time to time, I would look up to see arms waving in the midst of a story, reminiscent of my uncles on Sunday afternoons. The white shirts were buying the coffee and sipping in silence while the silver-haired ones, with a coffee in one hand, explained something with the other.

Forming a coil of sheet steel into a fender with sweeping curves, headlight openings, and a curved break line to match a hood was an evolved skill. Especially when the sheet metal components from one plant would travel hundreds of miles by rail before their shape was verified by a mating component. The designers put lines on the huge sheets of velum to roughly define the sizes and locations of the dozens of blocks of steel. But it was the die maker who figured out the precise dimensions and doweled components into exact locations. Each die was part of a set of from three to fourteen dies. There would always be a draw, a trim, and a flange and pierce die in a set. Most components were more artistic and complex. A fender, for example, would require a combination of draw, redraw, restrike dies, together with multiples of trim, pierce, and flange dies. An auto body was comprised of roughly 250 sheet metal components. Each component had to be formed and trimmed by a set of dies. Die making was a big business in the midst of the era of drastic annual model changes.

The following year I spent the summer in the die design area among the white shirts. It was quiet up on the balcony; if anyone spoke, it was in a low voice as if it were a sanctuary. The white shirts leaned over their huge drafting boards or sat on their stools with chins resting on fists.

I had always assumed that the designers who drew lines on the expensive semi-translucent and low gloss vellum paper knew it all. What I witnessed in the die room below was that the silver-haired die makers in dirty coveralls were guiding the evolution in die making. They were pointing to where last year's design had worn out and where it was overbuilt. Their interpretations changed the thinking of these die designers. Die makers were actually altering the standards for lines on vellum each year. I learned that many of the designers began as apprentices and became die makers before qualifying to work on the balcony. I was also surprised to find that some gave up their white shirts and went back to wearing coveralls.

Die builders were learning year to year from die maintenance crews. Advances in metallurgy were sometimes significant enough to risk a change in die design practices. There were no absolutes in their experiences with material properties; it was a time of complex change and opinion. Creative thoughts were quickly put into practice. The white shirts I witnessed had asked what-do-you-think questions, knowing there was a design problem waiting for them on vellum upstairs. The sixties were a time of free-flowing information from the hands-on die maintenance crews, to die builders, to die designers, to component designers, and back again. It was a time of efficient hand-offs. The whole system is now buried in a landfill. America has lost its systems of melding the evolutions in thinking of (1) the hands-on people with (2) those who design and with (3) those who want to buy something new. Doing your defined task and passing it over the wall of a cubicle or sending it with the touch of a button does not link people who know the customer with those who understand evolving capabilities in materials, processes, and skills. The decade of the sixties was a time when the skilled-trades portion of American industry was still a global leader of the evolution in how things were made. What the assembly craftsmen once added to the speed of evolution was lost in 1913.

> *1903—Equipment: Acquire specialized equipment as fast as capital becomes available.*

Was expanded to read:

> *1913—Equipment: Acquire equipment that will enable the high-volume production of power trains, increase the output of the assembly line, enable the in-sourcing of raw-material processing, and continue to improve in-house component manufacturing capability.*

LONG-TERM INEFFICIENCIES IN THE OBJECTIVES OF 1913

The decision to adopt the assembly line required Henry Ford to alter six of the eight objectives. These alterations would later add fourteen more long-term problems to the six introduced in 1903.

7. Manufacturing System: The assembly line system is a very inefficient way to build cars.

Vehicle assembly lines are thought to be efficient, but if you corner an industrial engineer and ask the right questions, you will find most manufacturing lines waste labor, energy, intellect, capital, and profits. I stumbled upon this conclusion the first time I picked up a stopwatch and clipboard and set out to time-study a tailpipe line.

THE PIPE LINES

I was allowed to begin classes at GMI when I was seventeen, but could not work on the factory floor until I turned eighteen. My first job on the floor was as a fill-in operator in the tailpipe area in Happy Valley's Plant 6. The foreman, Max, assigned rookies like me to fill in wherever someone didn't show up for work. The lines were equipped with hydraulic benders, which would bend straight steel pipes into contortions that would allow them to be threaded along beneath the floor of an automobile or truck. The pipes were lifted in to the leadoff stations by an overhead crane that picked them up in bundles of two hundred from the nearby tube mills. Three tube mills roll-formed a ribbon of sheet steel and seam-welded the edges together in a continuous stream. The mills cut the pipe to length as fast as it flowed out of the straightening rollers.

The workstations along each line were equipped with hydraulic benders. A pipe would be passed down the line with each operator adding a bend. Near the middle of each line was a horizontal bender that formed the long sweeping bend that arched over the rear axle for both cars and pickup trucks.

On my first day I was assigned to the horizontal bender in the middle of a line. The relief man demonstrated how to position the pipe and depress the palm buttons to operate the bender. I stepped in and repeated his motions, and the wiping die grabbed and wrapped the pipe around the arbor like a wet noodle. When the die released, I lifted the pipe out and placed it on a chute leading to the next operator. I then turned to get the next one, and the whole line began to flow. It didn't take long to become familiar with the idiosyncrasies of the bender. It was the workforce that I wouldn't get to know. Production workers in our family often told stories of playing games with rookies; I knew better than to expect anything else. My father had told me to just do my best, and everything would be fine.

As the first hour neared its end, I noticed the crews on other lines began sitting down at about 7:15 a.m. We, however, kept working until 7:25, when everyone stepped away and sat down. I had heard that the labor contract allowed a five-minute break every hour on some jobs, and this must be one of them. I also deduced that I was the one who was holding up the line, though I was unable to make eye contact with anyone. I vowed to do better. I began the second hour focused on eliminating all wasted movement. By the end of the third hour, our line also sat down for ten minutes. By the end of the fifth hour, I was welcoming the breaks. I had played football and run cross-country but was not in shape for this. In the days that followed, I was placed on a different line every day, and a different set of muscles had to be engaged. The job was exhausting.

During my fourth year of engineering school, I returned to the pipe lines escorted by Pete Apperson, a senior member of the Work Standards Department, a wiry fellow of few words. His role was to instruct rooky engineers like me in the Chevrolet way to take a time study. What Pete explained was in fact quite different from what I had learned in the classroom.

"The pipe lines aren't studied until they are operating smoothly after rearrange," Pete began. "We inform the foreman that we are here to study the line. The foreman in turn informs his workers of our intent to set a standard. It's required by contract."

Upon reaching the familiar pipe-line area in Plant 6, Pete nodded a greeting to the foreman, and we followed him to the head of one of the lines.

It had been three years since I stood in the middle of this maze of benders, but it was all coming back. I knew that the standard would determine the length of the break for a crew for the rest of the model year. The standard was important to both the crew and the company. The crew we were about to study had been working fifty-five minutes out of every hour since the model year began in August. A good standard would provide a ten-minute break. A bad one would provide only five minutes, on one end of the spectrum, or more than ten, on the other. A twenty-minute break would lead to management problems, something about idle hands and the devil's playground. Five would mean they didn't get anything for their extra effort, and they would slow down.

The foreman leaned in to say something to the lead-off operator, and I watched as familiar glances rippled down the line in seconds and a chill came over the crew. It was the same reaction I had observed when a time-study man appeared three years earlier. I had been standing at a horizontal bender when the variations on a three-quarter-time mime performance began up and down the line. At the break, the crewmembers who had been ignoring the rookie brushed by and whispered in threatening voices, "Slow down, you're killing the job." They wanted me to perform like a mime as well.

"Watch the operators carefully," Pete explained, "and you'll begin to sense when they're in a rhythm and using a good method." Then he added, "Stopwatches tend to make performers out of everyone, so observe for a while before you begin. Wait till you see an operator lapse back into a normal routine before you start recording your readings."

I replied, "Okay." This business of sorting out the acting and the working was not something we had been trained to do in lab experiments at GMI.

"It takes more energy to slow the pace than to move in rhythm," Pete assured me. "Be ready and take your readings when you sense the operator is working at a normal pace. You'll need twenty readings, especially on the bottleneck station." After a pause he added, "You can get away with fewer readings on the rest of the line." Pete was passing along a shortcut.

"Let's begin with the lead-off," Pete instructed. As I took up a good position for observation, Pete peered over my shoulder. "Record the date and exact time and be sure not to leave any boxes on the form empty. Any time study we do can end up in the middle of a bargaining table during negotiations. They must all be complete and accurate." Pete coached me through the rest of the Chevrolet way on the first study, explaining the required level of detail. But when I got to the small box titled "Method Description," Pete said nothing.

I sensed he was waiting for me to take some initiative. I looked at the tiny box and thought to myself, *this is going to be brief compared to what was required in a lab report.* I wrote in small print: "Reach 40 inches to right, get pipe from rack." I skipped over the operator putting his thumb in the end of the pipe and jerking it up to brake the oil film attraction; I skipped his shifting the end of the pipe to the left as he jerked it so it didn't fall back into place during his re-grasp. Next I wrote, "Move C/L of pipe 96 inches to the left with four re-grasps and place the pipe into the tooling. Slide pipe to left against stop. Rotate to orient the weld seam 15 degrees beyond top dead center. Get and hold palm buttons. Grasp bent pipe as ram recedes and slide C/L 50 inches to left with two re-grasps to dispose." Brief by lab standards, it seemed to satisfy Pete.

"Now take out your watch and cradle your clipboard," Pete said. In the office he had already demonstrated how he wanted me to hold it. My left wrist, watch in hand, was draped over the upper right corner, and the lower left notch in the board rested nicely on my left hip.

I nodded a ready signal, and he said, "Start your watch the instant he releases the pipe to dispose. Snap the instantaneous reading each time he returns to the same release point. Record the time in the first box and continue recording for fifteen cycles." I began clicking and writing, finding I needed to use all of my peripheral vision skills. I focused mainly on the operator and performed both the reading of the watch and writing down of readings without real focus on any of the three things. Within fifteen repetitions I was comfortable with the routine, and my writing was becoming legible. Keeping more focus on the operator was important. Pete had explained earlier that I was going to have to explain why some of the cycle times were longer and would not be valid.

"Now for the next fifteen readings," Pete instructed, "if the operator pauses anywhere in the cycle, perhaps waiting for the next operator to catch up, disregard the reading and keep clicking off cycles without recording them. Wait until the pace of the line resumes." At first this required total focus on the operator's performance; reading the watch and writing were nearly impossible. Ten minutes later we moved on to the second operator.

Pete watched as I repeated the cycle, filling out the next time-study form and recording readings. This time I clicked off a long string without writing anything down. I sensed this operator was a very good mime. After a while Pete concurred, "This guy is a performer," he said. "Just move on and observe him from afar while you study the others. It takes a lot of strength to keep moving a fifteen-pound pipe at three-quarter speed all day."

As I took up a position behind the third operator, Pete leaned in and said, "Stay until you've studied all of the operations and then come back upstairs." With that, he was gone.

I spent the rest of the morning working my way down the line and looking back once in a while to take some readings on the mimes. Lapsing back into a normal routine was evidently hard to avoid. When they went to lunch, I went with them. I had eaten in their cafeteria every day when I was working on the lines and was familiar with unrecognizable food in steam trays. When I was a student running a horizontal bender, none of them had wanted to enter into a conversation. Now they didn't even want to sit at an adjacent table with a white-shirted time-study man. I had crossed over to the other side.

In the afternoon it was still difficult to sort out the acting. It was helpful to have had some hands-on experience. As the day progressed, I began to warm to the feeling of responsibility that came with my new profession. I returned to the office around 3:00 p.m., and Pete asked to see my studies. He looked them over carefully, questioning some of the highs and lows. He showed me how to document when a reading was being ruled out. He explained in a language he said was used around bargaining tables.

Next came the adding of the standard allowances. For example, the contractual allowance for job preparation and cleanup was eighteen minutes per shift. The overhead crane allowance for stocking the line was five minutes per bundle, based on some old delay study. The fixture adjustment allowance was fifteen minutes per shift, again based upon an old delay study. At the bottom of each time study form was a series of fill-in-the-blank calculations from which emerged the gross and net pieces per hour for each workstation. The number I entered in that last box on the bottleneck operation would be the "standard" that everyone was waiting for.

By 10:00 a.m. the following morning, I had finished the details and double checked my calculations. I was confident that I had captured the "normal" pace of the line and each operation. On a lined pad, I jotted down a table of the eighteen studies. My intent was to verify that together they made sense. But the summary revealed more than I had expected. The horizontal bender was clearly the bottleneck in the line. Now I understood why I had felt like I was holding things up no matter how hard I worked. I recalled my uncles' tales of their initiation of rookies and had to smile. Rookies were supposed to be given the hardest job, and I had been no exception. There was something else. Eighteen people may have been manning the stations, but there was only enough work content for eleven.

The summary bothered me. It was foolish to think about harvesting snippets of free time from the people along the line. What else could they be doing? And yet the idle time amounted to the wages of seven people. That was the day I began to question the efficiency of all operations and wonder how the company made any money or kept its component operations in-house. It was also the day I began to realize the power and magnitude of the information I had been trained to glean.

I set the standard at 394 per hour. Feedback through the grapevine the following morning told me that the crew on nights had already tested my first standard. They had given it the usual wholehearted up-to-four-hour effort. Night crews often tested a new standard. If they couldn't figure out how to achieve it in the first four hours, they would settle back into a routine of a 70 percent work pace and a five-minute break for the balance of the year. My standard of 394 was 30 percent higher than the output of the crew since the model year began, which made it a stretch. But the night crew achieved 394 in their third hour, which I was told was good. Meeting it in the first hour would indicate it was too easy, and idle time would become a management problem. Not meeting it by the fourth hour would lead to a loss of 30 percent in operating expense. My first attempt at setting a standard was acceptable.

To a casual observer, a pipe line looks like a well-oiled machine with elbows and pipes in fluid motion. It could be likened to a nineteenth-century bucket brigade. When a fire broke out, local people would instinctively form a line. They would pass full buckets of water from person to person toward the fire, and a line of smaller volunteers would pass the empties back to the watering trough. No training was required. Tailpipe crews were similar, in that training took only a few seconds. But my first study was proving that a pipe line was very different. The work assignments along the line were not even close to being equal. It was something that a casual observer would never see, and very few would ever quantify. Pete had tried to make the job easier when he told me in a whisper, "Just concentrate on the bottleneck operation and skip lightly over the details on the others." The imbalance in workloads was understood but was not being discussed.

The following year I began the required fifth-year project, which was to culminate in a hundred-page thesis—a requirement for graduation from General Motors Institute. GMI would not hand an engineering degree to anyone who had not completed the fifth year. It was a year with no classes but many hurdles, beginning with the selection of a mutually agreeable original engineering work sanctioned by your sponsoring division. My thoughts on a subject kept taking me back to the huge amounts of idle time in pipe lines. I couldn't believe that the people who had figured out how to avoid splits, kinks, and wrinkles while making extreme bends in steel tubing had never bothered to focus on how to improve the labor cost.

On a hunch, I went back to take another look. Armed this time with the lab version of a clipboard fitted out with three split-second stopwatches,[1] I studied a line at a level of detail I had read about in textbooks and experimented with in the lab. I put the three-watch board on my hip and began splitting each operator's cycle into three elements: (1) the time to get a pipe from the chute and bring it to the wiping dies; (2) the time to position and slide the pipe against a stop, rotate it against the fixture, get and hold the palm buttons as the ram cycled, and reach in as the ram went up to catch the pipe as the punch released; (3) the time to firmly grasp the pipe and dispose in the correct orientation. The three-watch board enabled me to split the seven-second cycles into three elements. What jumped out immediately was that the time spent handing off to the next person and the time spent getting the next pipe was greater than the time spent making the bend. My hunch was right; there was only enough work here for six people. The challenge was how to make all the bends on a single bender. The value to the company would be in reducing labor costs on pipe lines by a factor of three. It would be worth tens of millions of dollars in operating expense. It would be easier for line workers to lift sixty pipes

---

1 A three-watch board is an industrial engineer's tool. It simultaneously clicks three stopwatches on staggered settings, which is useful when studying jobs with multiple short-time elements. One starts, one stops for a reading, and one resets with each press of the lever.

an hour than four hundred. This could be a good fifth-year project, if I could figure out how to make it work and make the change palatable to an organization that had been hiring bucket brigades for years.

But as I said, there were hurdles. The benders along the line were fitted out with punches having different radii. A line changeover would include the setup man refitting each bender with the specified-size punch. In the weeks that followed, I engaged in many creative discussions and negotiations, winning approval for a test run with a single radius punch making all the bends. My goal for the thesis was to prove that a pipe could be made on a single bender and then project the significant gains in quality and cost reduction. One thing led to another, however, and the testing and validation idea got caught in a wave of exuberance. My projections of a 50 percent reduction in crew size and equipment requirements attracted too much attention. My supervisor Lloyd went to bat, and within two weeks the highest volume line, the B-Body, was being rearranged to run multiple cycle benders in parallel. The day before the rearrange was to be completed, a new general superintendent came to Happy Valley. Second in rank only to the plant manager, he stopped the rearrange and ordered everything back to its original state — without explanation. Lloyd, who had been so excited, suddenly shifted gears and informed me that I would have to change the topic of my thesis.

The following year the tailpipe and exhaust-pipe lines and even the tube mills were shut down and the equipment put up for sale. The business of making pipes was out-sourced. That explained why my proposal had been shut down. The decision to out-source the pipe business had already been made. The grooming of outside companies to receive the business must have been already underway when I came along with a fifth-year project.

A decade later the bending of tail and exhaust pipes was in-sourced for a short period. A new wave of computerized numerically controlled (CNC) equipment was in vogue and the bending portion of the pipe business was brought back inside. Product designers linked up with the process engineers to figure out how to take advantage of the full capability of this new processing equipment. The process engineers used the close proximity to launch a tooling and handling equipment-design phase that optimized CNC machines. Maintenance crews used the proximity to figure out how to program and maintain the equipment. For me it was proof that forming pipes using a single radius punch was possible and that a single machine and single operator could make any pipe. My fifth-year project would have worked, had not the pipe lines already been tossed like a chip on a bargaining table.

The sixties was a strange decade when labor savings and operating improvements were taking a backseat to considerations of a return to lower levels of integration. Through it all, the cost of doing business was going up. The threat of out-sourcing had begun in the fifties. What I had stumbled upon in 1967 was the UAW calling a bluff. The first areas to be out-sourced were those with highest labor content. They were areas where large numbers of workers were in close proximity, and the up-and-coming union leaders could win over a large enough portion of the workforce to win an election. My career had begun in the midst of implementation of the 1941 plans to fight the UAW rather than work with them. Had my original fifth-year thesis subject been published, it would have been a proof that out-sourcing was not about striving to reduce labor cost.

It would take three decades for component making to shift entirely to outside sourcing, leaving only power-train and body manufacturing in-house. Spinning off GM's DELPHI and then Ford's Visteon in the late nineties were the final steps. The management of component operations had migrated onto the shoulders of purchasing agents, one bluffing routine at a time. I will always wonder: had the pipes area been reconfigured and the bucket brigades discarded in 1967, would it have been the beginning of a movement back toward managing the "willingness" of workers, something not promoted since 1912, before the assembly line came to town?

Five years after the pipe-line fiasco, I would again find proof of the inefficiency of line operations. This time it was a much larger secret. Henry Ford's famous vehicle assembly line was no more efficient than a pipe line.

THE TRUCK ASSEMBLY LINE

In 1972 I was promoted to supervisor in an industrial engineering department at Flint Truck Assembly. There were eight experienced industrial engineers assigned to the truck line, and their job was to keep the number of stanchions along the line to a minimum. My experience with the work content in pipe lines had left me skeptical, and it wasn't long before my concerns were justified.

There were roughly 1,700 workstations along the pickup truck assembly line. The line ran at a pace of sixty vehicles per hour. Sixty was the theoretically ideal pace for a vehicle assembly line. Decades of building and operating assembly lines around the world had zeroed in on sixty. Running a line faster meant workers spent more time walking back to the next car than they did assembling components. Slower than sixty meant more time walking away from the line to get components than building cars. Sixty was the ideal.

For an industrial engineer assigning elements of work along an assembly line, the work begins with looking at the vehicle assembly drawings and the precedence diagrams. The drawings provide descriptions of the orientation and number of components to be assembled. The precedence diagrams outline the extent of freedoms in the order of assembly; that is, what must be already assembled before a component can be added. For example, the wiring harness must be positioned on the floor of the sheet metal body before the pad and carpet can be laid over it, and the carpet must be laid before the seats can be installed. Industrial engineers then define "time elements" for the assembly of each component using standard data.[1] The time elements together with the precedence logic are then loaded into a batch-run software program that spreads the work elements across the workstations. The software is supposed to solve for the minimum number of workstations required along the line. The industrial engineers then set out to define the arrangements of containers and subassembly equipment along the line that would accommodate the order of assembly defined by the printout.

The time elements for the assembly of a vehicle are in chunks. The software spreads them along the line, but it rarely adds up to sixty seconds for any workstation. I was shocked to find that the first printout for balancing work along a line produced an average work content of just 68 percent. To the industrial engineers, the printout was just a starting point. They set to work juggling work elements to increase the average toward a goal of 78 percent. The goal of 78 percent was an unpublished number much like "sixty jobs per hour." It was a figure handed down, something written on a cave wall somewhere in the Midwest. The engineers would have to eliminate 218 workstations to get from 68 to 78 percent. The juggling required years of experience and ingenuity.

It was hard to believe that Henry Ford's wondrous assembly line invention could include so much idle time. I got to thinking about the time spent getting and disposing of the pipe between operators. With an assembly line, it would be the time spent walking back to the next car. I headed out of the office and walked the line using the second hand on my watch to approximate the average time workers spent walking back to the next vehicle. It was close to eighteen seconds. I asked my team of engineers to sort out the walk-back-to-the-next-car time in their studies, and they confirmed it was eighteen seconds. With a goal of 78 percent average work content, the average line worker was idle for thirteen seconds every time a car went by. If I added the eighteen seconds for walking back to the next vehicle, the average assembly line worker was adding value only twenty-nine seconds out of every minute. This was almost as bad as needing just six of the eighteen workers on a pipe line. A bucket brigade forms when a fire breaks out because the participants can be trained in seconds. Both a pipe line and a truck assembly line are easy for inexperienced managers to oversee. Was ease of management really that important?

I spent a year with the industrial engineers on the truck line, learning they were worth their weight in gold. It was a year of discovering the other things that made the assembly line costly. Optional features were another problem. When customers were allowed to order optional features, like four-wheel drive (4x4) or air conditioning (A/C), the options put wrinkles in the uniformity of workloads along the line. Some stations received added work elements and others were reduced. The industrial engineers did their best to level the work elements and

---

1 "Standard data is a structured collection of normal time values for work elements . . . a means to establishing standards quickly." William K. Hodson, ed., *Maynard's Industrial Engineering Handbook* (New York: McGraw-Hill, 1992) p. 127

minimize the number of workers standing idle at any one time; that is, a line worker assigned to A/C component installation was expected to fall behind when a vehicle with A/C passed by and then catch up on the next one without A/C. But scheduling vehicles to run down an assembly line in a certain order is not always possible, and when two vehicles in row with A/C come down the line, it will push the A/C workers down the line and out of station. The further they are pushed down the line, the farther they are away from containers of components, their equipment, and their tools. The air hoses can be made longer, but they get more difficult to manage. Smoothing out the flow of options is part of the industrial engineer's job but is not always possible. The result is always an increase in the number of workstations for options and the average work content drops.

Then there were issues of seasonality, with more A/C ordered in the summer and more 4x4s ordered in the winter. The list of assembly line drawbacks goes on and on. The appearance of organization that comes with the wondrous assembly line is costly.

---

8. Manufacturing System: An assembly line system is a very poor solution for building vehicles with diverse labor requirements.

An assembly line system cannot efficiently accommodate multiple models, for example, a two-seater sports car and a sport utility vehicle (SUV). The assembly line was introduced as a solution for building two hundred thousand Model Ts per year in Highland Park. It was introduced at a time when you could get any color you wanted, so long as it was black, yet somehow the assembly line became the system of choice around the world. Many factories now use an assembly line system to assemble multiple models, not realizing there are more efficient alternatives.

BUILDING VANS

While I was working in GM's think tank in the late eighties, a note came down from the leadership asking for a review of plans for production of a new van. It had been roughly twenty years since the design of the large van had been upgraded. To refresh my memory, I set out for the old van plant in a small town near Toronto. It had been a decade since my last visit.

Toronto had been building the same four variations of the full-sized van for twenty years: (1) a fully trimmed vacation version, (2) a minimal unit to be shipped to up-fitters, (3) a stripped contractor version without side windows, and (4) a chopped unit with nothing but a chassis behind the front seat. Specialty shops were turning the chopped units into ambulances, delivery trucks, cantinas on wheels, and so forth. I walked in assuming that after ten more years of making the same thing, the plant would be finely tuned.

My walk-through quickly told me they were hanging onto people they didn't need. The chassis assembly and engine dress lines were pretty efficient; however, the body shop, trim shop, and the final line were not. There were roughly four hundred extra workers in the plant. People along the line were standing around reading books. Those working were more concerned with getting back to their books than building vehicles.

I talked with the schedulers and learned that they were trying to slot a fully trimmed recreational model in just ahead of each chopped unit. When workers fell behind on a fully trimmed model, they could catch up because the chopped version didn't have as much work content. The trouble with the scheduler's plan, however, was that the fully trimmed models were seasonal and very dependent upon the economy. Most of them sold in the spring and early summer, and this was December. Orders for fully trimmed models were running one in thirty, and chopped versions were selling at a rate of one in six. The schedulers explained that dealers were supposed to dampen the effects of this seasonality by accumulating a hundred days of inventory over the winter, but a forecast of a coming mini-recession was making the dealers drag their feet. Recreational vehicle spending was always the first to slow in a recession. On the inside, management was reluctant to lay off their workforce for a short time each winter, knowing that the low-seniority workers would be let go and that the young would be the most likely to look for work in the city.

I returned from Toronto and paid a visit to the new van development group. "How are you planning to deal with seasonality and blips in the economy?" I asked at one point. My host, a former industrial engineer from Flint Truck Assembly, danced around his answer, while being interrupted by phone calls. After a while it became clear that he didn't have an answer. The new van plant, already under construction, would be just the same as the old. It too would be unable to cope with the product mix inherent in making multiple models of vans.

---

9. Manufacturing System: An assembly line system blocks the natural flow of information through an organization.

The early assembly craftsmen and their runners served as a natural feedback system for all the automakers just as they had done for the carriage companies for centuries. But a moving assembly line only communicates to workers downstream. There is no immediate recourse when components do not fit or are the wrong color. Those that do not fit and all the components that must be attached to them are tossed into the trunk as the vehicle passes. By the time a single error reaches the end of an assembly line, the trunk is often filled to overflowing with a jumble of components. The simplest of problems can fill the yard (parking lots behind the assembly plants) with hundreds of trunks filled with components. Vehicles in the yard must wait until the corrected components arrive. They must also wait until a weekend, when catch-up crews can be called in to empty the trunks. Meanwhile customers and dealers wait for delivery. When sales are high and the assembly plant is working overtime, it is difficult to find crews willing to work on Sunday and still show up on Monday. The juggling of crews and shutting down the line for relief make it difficult to maintain high levels of quality. With today's out-sourcing to Asia, the time required to fix a problem can fill the yard and shut down the plant until planeloads of components can arrive. Fear of the consequences of mistakes in components today puts a real damper on product innovation and erases all thoughts of continuous improvement. It is little wonder that America began to fall behind in market share or that all cars began to look alike.

10. Organization Development: When the assembly craftsmen walked out, they took their handed-down knowledge and experiences with them.

My father's father, Floyd, called the leaders of his era the masters. "Better than any mechanic you can find today," he would say. "They knew how to make every component and who their runners should talk to when there was problem." Floyd would then add, "When the assembly line forced craftsmen into stanchions, they just picked up their tools and walked out."

There are people born in America every day with the right combination of intelligences to make them great assembly craftsmen. But there are few places where they can apply what comes to them so easily. Ferrari employs a handful of assembly craftsmen who work alone as they assemble an engine. In the 1990s, Volvo's Uddevalla plant employed teams of workers that trimmed out the painted bodies shipped from the Gothenburg plant. Uddevalla was recognized for the superior quality of the Volvos they assembled. They used a version of the carriage makers' staged assembly system rather than a moving assembly line. In Springhill, Tennessee, Saturn's assembly teams would trim out a vehicle while riding a hardwood platform they referred to as a skillet. The vehicle and a team with a cartload of components would ride the skillet through areas where they pulled down overhead tools as needed. When finished, a team would step off the skillet and refill their carts as they walked back to where they would step aboard their next skillet and start trimming out the next Saturn. Experiments with the advantages of using variations on assembly craftsmen instead of Henry Ford's assembly line have been going on for decades. Someone in the twenty-first century can be expected to try again. If that someone comes up with the right combination of items on the back of an envelope, he or she will outstrip the competition. I am getting ahead of myself.

11. Organization Development: Workers are no longer selected based on criteria that consider inherent craft intelligence.

In my grandfathers' era, workers with spatial, mathematical-logical, and body kinesthetic intelligences evolved under the watchful eye of a master craftsman. The implementation of the assembly line in 1913 dumbed down the workplace. This in turn watered down the cultural values that had nurtured young carriage builders and brought the craft culture to the brink of extinction. Author Ben Hamper captures the lingering misconception in the hearts of the young in the Midwest. In his book *Rivethead: Tales from the Assembly Line*, he articulates his discovery when he and his mother attended Family Night at the old Fisher Body plant.

> I was seven years old the first time I ever set foot inside an automobile factory . . . we found my old man down on the trim line. His job was to install the windshields using this goofy apparatus with large suction cups . . . Car; windshield. Car; windshield. Car; windshield . . .

> And here, all this time, I had assumed that Dad just built cars all by his lonesome. I always imagined that building adult cars was identical to building cars in model kits . . .

> I wanted to shout at my father, Do something else or come home with us . . . Thank God that, even at age seven, I knew what I was going to be when I grew up. There wouldn't be car windshield cha-cha awaiting me.[1]

Personnel Departments today are asked to sort out the potential white-collar candidates with interpersonal, intrapersonal, and linguistic intelligence. They pass over the intelligences that once mattered in the auto business. And yet there are people born every day with the right combination of intelligences to become great automotive craftsmen, but there are few jobs where they can apply themselves. Some of America's problems with its industrial sector are rooted in a cultural change that began a century ago.

THE APPRENTICE SHOP

> My earliest days in the auto business happened to be in one of the rare environments where masters (people with the rare combinations of the right intelligences) were still nurturing apprentices. I have never been able to trace how I got there, but I believe that the lingering influence of my grandfather Max had something to do with it. It was an experience that taught many lessons and introduced me to the fulfillment that comes with building something that others appreciate.

> My first semester at GMI began with six weeks of school. As a rookie freshman in a cooperative engineering program, I was peppered with warnings from older students. "This is a business, not a college." "Doing well in class will not be enough." "You need to accumulate a series of good performance reviews to ensure your scholarship." "Along with weeding out one third of each freshman class to meet the budget, there will be times when your sponsor will have to cut spending. Stu-

---

1 Ben Hamper, *Rivethead: Tales from the Assembly Line* (New York: Warner Books, 1986), p. 2.

dents are a luxury." I listened to their warnings, knowing some of it was true. I grew up with recessions and knew they were always just around the corner. There were sixteen work sessions ahead over the next four years, and I was going to have to prove myself in each one.

After six weeks of classes at GMI, I began a six-week work assignment. As I waited in the lobby of Happy Valley's Personnel Building, I thought back to high school and how I had avoided conversations about career plans. Just a year ago I was simply hoping to land an apprenticeship and a career in skilled trades. Now I was reeling from the pace of the first six weeks of classes and crouched in a second set of starting blocks marked "career start position." The cold, hard business side of this contract for a scholarship was about to weed out those who couldn't do the work.

Mr. Leonard, personnel's student coordinator, ushered me into his office at 8:00 a.m. and called in an assistant named Ted. "Labor laws do not allow anyone under the age of eighteen to work on the shop floor," Mr. Leonard began. "Freshman students are supposed to work production the first year, but you are still seventeen. We usually keep students under eighteen here in the Personnel Building for their first work section." There was a hint of curiosity in his next statement. "However, the apprentice shop has asked for you. Ted here will be your escort out."

Ted and I walked along the riverbank toward a small old brick building in the heart of Happy Valley. We walked to the threshold of an open doorway. Ted shook my hand, said good luck, and made a hasty retreat. Peering inside I saw young men hardly older than myself, and they were all peering back from around a collection of machines. A man in a white shirt with "Jim" embroidered on the pocket walked up. "Hello, I'm Jim Andrews." He said, shaking my hand. We walked down the center aisle, as he pointed out the lunch area, the restroom, and the lockers. We came to a fenced-in tool crib and stepped up to the window. I signed a log sheet that made me responsible for ten brass tags stamped "#87." Jim explained: "You will need to bring in your own padlock for the locker. Keep those brass tags in your pocket until you can lock them up." Just then someone came up to us, and Jim excused himself saying, "Wait right here."

It gave me a moment to look around. This place was like high school shop class, only better. The machines were bigger, and there were far more of them. Lathes, mills, shapers, drill presses, grinders, furnaces, hob machines, gear shavers, and some I had never seen—not even in textbooks. There was no woodworking or sheet metal forming equipment. This was a machine shop. A good one, well swept and with machines freshly painted and wiped clean.

Jim returned, and we walked up to a table covered with rows of neatly folded prints held down by blocks or bars of steel. He picked up one of the bars and the print under it and motioned for me to follow. We walked up to a machine lathe not unlike the one I had learned to use in shop class. Jim handed me the bar and the print saying, "You can check out whatever you need from the tool crib using your tags. Make the part exactly to the dimensions on the print, and watch the tolerances in the center. Bring the part and the print to me when you are done." I nodded, knowing this was a test and not a time for questions. Jim added, "You will not be able to check things out overnight until you have a lock for your locker, so be sure to return all items to the crib before 2:45 and clean up your machine before you leave. You have half an hour for lunch, and the shift is over at three." Short and sweet. It was time to go to work.

More than fifty pairs of eyes glanced at me from all sides as I studied the print and the lathe. The tool stand held the standard cutters, chucks, a drift, and turning dogs of every size. I was amazed to see tools in such good condition. I determined I wouldn't need much from the crib, so I walked to the window. The attendant was probably four years my senior, and I knew this was going to be my first sizing up. I began with, "I need a twelve-inch scale, zero- to one-inch mics, a ten/thirty-two tap, and a drill to match," and laid down four #87 brass tags.

"I don't match drills," he replied curtly. "You have to specify what you want." He slid a well-worn printed card through the window.

It was the standard drill/tap size table that had been on page 137 in my shop class textbook. It was also on the wall over my dad's workbench and hanging near my grandfather's drill press. I corrected myself, "A number 21 drill."

The attendant took the four tags and hung them on an array of hooks as he selected my requests.

I checked the micrometer before I left the window. Several in shop class were no longer accurate. This one was fine. It read zero when closed.

As I turned to leave, the attendant volunteered, "If you break anything, bring back the pieces to get a new one."

I walked back thinking, I was breaking drills and taps before I was ten. I know a lot about how much force and shock they can withstand. My dad's drill index and tap set had already suffered my learning curve. Not breaking something must also be part of this test.

I set to work, squaring off and centering both ends of the bar using a medium-sized chuck and centering tool. I installed a turning dog, fired up the lathe, and removed metal on several passes, turning the rough bar down to a .508-inch diameter. In the next pass, I set the depth of cut to just two-thousandths of an inch and the feed rate as fine as the gearing would allow. When the pass was complete, I checked the diameter in the center. Deflection had made the center two-thousandths larger than the ends. The tolerance on the blueprint called for not more than 1.5 thousandths along the length of the shaft. Jim must have known this would happen when he said "watch the olerances." He had given me a hint. I checked the progression of the variation along the shaft with the mics and judged when and how much Kentucky windage[1] would be needed to keep the shaft uniform.

---

1 Kentucky windage: The human judgment that once compensated for the wind on a bullet fired from the century rifles preferred on the American frontier. It is used here as

I had done this before in wood and figured it could be done in steel. The vernier on the lathe's tool feed dial read in tenths. I turned the tool feed in until it would remove the last two-thousandths at the end and engaged the feed. As the tool passed along the shaft, I gradually turned the tool feed in, reaching two-thousandths deeper at the center. I then backed the tool feed out again as the pass came to an end. I had to focus intently on this last pass, imagining the profile of deflection that I couldn't see. I checked the shaft again with mics while it was still on the lathe. It was nearly perfect all along its length. My attempt to counter the deflection of the shaft had succeeded. I chucked each end of the shaft and made the cutoffs, then carefully drilled and tapped each end without breaking either the drill or the tap.

At 10:25 I returned to the table with the print and the shaft just as Jim appeared from around a corner. Two hours seemed a reasonable elapsed time, though my grandfather would have done it in less than thirty minutes. If Jim asked why I took so long, I would assure him that I would be faster once I had a locker and didn't have to go to the crib to get tools.

Jim took the shaft, saying, "That was quick." He pulled a set of mics from his shirt and checked the diameter along the shaft. Finally he looked up and said, "Pretty good. Wash up for lunch and meet me back here afterward."

I had passed a test that was apparently familiar to many of the pairs of curious eyes. I had cleared the first hurdle along the path to proving myself worthy of Chevrolet's investment. In the weeks that followed I machined blocks and bars of steel to whatever was on the print under them. Jim doled out the jobs one at a time and checked them carefully. The combinations of lathe, mill, and drill press work became increasingly complex. Jim would point to the dimensions on the print that were critical, which signaled to me that a little windage would be needed. He never suggested the steps I should take, and I never asked. I had watched my father and grandfather make so many things to repair the farm equipment, appliances, and old cars that I felt confident the solution would come to me no matter what the challenge. I wanted him to know I had a few tricks up my sleeve. I wanted to be a good investment. As the days flew by, I came to the conclusion that if this is what co-op[1] work assignments were like, the next four years were going to be enjoyable. Little did I know how much more complex things would become.

I would be one of the last to experience the centuries-old system used by masters to nurture apprentices. Years later, when I was asked to lead the activities of thirty-six industrial engineering positions at GM's HydraMatic Division, I ap-

---

a machining term to indicate using human compensation to get machines to produce beyond their built-in accuracy limits.

1 Co-op work assignment: A work and study program where industry cooperates with academia in a year-round work-study program.

plied what I learned in the apprentice shop. I assessed levels of skill and handed out increasingly complex assignments carefully. I added selected words of caution in the right places and checked their work from a distance. As engineers evolved, I kept increasing the complexity and the expectation. The reputation of our Industrial Engineering Department spread and attracted highly skilled young replacements.

Today what is left of the American industrial sector counts heavily on Personnel Departments. The personnel staff is supposed to take over for the surrounding communities that once nurtured, selected, and steered members of its youth into apprenticeships. College classrooms have replaced the apprentice shops. The proofs of hands-on skill and common sense are missing. The gene pool is still stocking the population with craftsman capability, but there are shortcomings. The right people are not being steered into the opportunities in the industrial sector. Some potential assembly craftsmen find their way in auto service centers and some become weekend mechanics. But the real criteria for sorting out the craftsmen have dissolved.

12. Organization Development: Getting people to do mindless tasks along an assembly line has required higher wages to compensate for the boredom.

The workers who agreed to stand in stanchions in 1914 had to willingly sacrifice their pride and intellect for money. They were not the proud local descendants of the carriage builders' culture. Their values and sheer numbers soon overwhelmed the culture that had nurtured carriage craftsmen. Their craving for wealth overpowered ambitions for the satisfaction of craftsmanship. It was a shift to short-term gratification. By the second half of the twentieth century, the problems became evident. The disgruntled communities surrounding the auto plants were being whip-sawn by hiring and layoffs as the plants ramped up, ramped down, and then they sat idle awaiting the next allocation of a product line to slide off a bargaining table. Whole communities gambled their tax dollars on investments in new infrastructure in exchange for promises of high payroll infusions. Money may be the prime motivator of workers in the finance, insurance, and real estate segments of the economy, but it does not kindle the lifetime pride in workmanship that is required of the industrial sector. The skill levels of America's craftsman slipped and so did the standard of living in automotive communities.

THE PATH TO SOCIAL DECLINE

On my last day on the pipe lines in Plant 6, my intention was to have a short conversation with Max, the foreman. I hoped to round out his impression of me before he wrote my evaluation. But he wasn't around when I returned from washing up. I walked out that Friday without ever having a conversation with him. My parents had always said,

"Just work hard and things will work out." I had to hope that Max had seen what I could do to make a horizontal bender sing, because no other opportunities to prove myself had been presented.

There were no farewells to fellow workers along the line. I had found it impossible to talk with them at breaks. By the end of the first week, I became resigned to their ignoring me. I was an eighteen-year-old kid doing a job that it should have taken twelve years of seniority to hold. Their kids couldn't find a job, their friends were unemployed, and yet here I was working the day shift with them. The three o'clock whistle blew, and I walked out of Plant 6 and across the bridge. I placed my first Coordination Report in the appropriate in-box in the student co-ordinator's office but didn't speak to anyone. In eight weeks I had had two conversations with co-workers; both were a single sentence. My only gratification was in knowing the second of the required sixteen work sections was complete.

I exited the Personnel Building via the door that had let me into Chevrolet on my first day. As I walked the quarter mile to my car, I reflected on the plight of the people I was leaving behind. They would spend the rest of their lives in a place without conversation. They were expected to content themselves each day with striving to beat the standard and gain a few more minutes of rest before the next hour began. It was noisier in their environment than sitting on an Allis Chalmers pulling a double-bottom plow across a field. Their air was heavy with an oil mist from hundreds of cycling hydraulic cylinders, and it retained the faint smell of cresol that lingers above the sealed wood block floors beneath their feet. The lure of high wages and being able to borrow against a steady income had trapped them in a realm from which they would never escape. The sum of their challenges at work would be jostling with each other to forcefully reserve a good place to sit for a few minutes when the line stopped.

On a farm in the spring, summer, fall, and winter the chores are different. In Plant 6 there is only one season. Farmers gamble each year with choices of seed, herbicide, fertilizer, pesticide, when to plant, and when to harvest. In Plant 6 there are no gambles, no choices to get a person involved. Each spring a farmer gets to turn and look back to see how straight he has laid this year's first furrow. In Plant 6 there is no avenue for personal-skill expression; the chain gangs work along an endless road. The day they were hired, a setup man gave them the same sixty-second training session that I had received. At that point they had unknowingly reached the peak of their lifetime career development. Oh, they probably spent some energy on games with their foremen (keepers) in the beginning, but they would soon meld into a common mental stupor. The ones I worked alongside had to have twelve years of seniority to hold a job, and they were already past their life's "point of no return." They were just steadily paddling out to sea.

At family reunions I had listened to our family's production line workers over potato salad and hot dogs. The younger ones would vent their dissatisfaction with their jobs, their bosses, or their union representatives. The older ones were subdued. Each year's account from them was like a recording of the last, except they had a little less to say. Now I understood why.

---

13. Organization Development: The assembly line unplugged the hive-mind capability of the US workforce.

In 1995, Kevin Kelly introduced the concept of the power of the "hive mind" in his book *Out of Control*. He defined the "hive mind" in chapter 2 with a challenge to readers to explain which starling is steering the flock as they swoop through the air. He defies the reader to point to which starling will launch the flock back into the air once they alight. He draws analogies to ants, bees, and flights of bats. Somehow these collectives in nature do things that could never be accomplished individually. Henry Ford managed to assemble a hive mind in 1903 when he set out to produce automobiles. His hive mind had assembly craftsmen at its core, and in Highland Park he achieved a complete hive-mind capability for the first time. He gathered the manufacturing capability for every component of the Model T into one huge fully integrated factory. Highland Park was building more automobiles than any complex in the world. At its core were hundreds of assembly craftsmen using runners to direct the activities in every corner. For two years the volume of sales had risen, and Henry had kept hiring and training. Over and over he dodged his staff's recommendation to adopt the assembly line system. He knew what they couldn't see. The assembly line would destroy the hive mind that had made him so successful.

Just as Henry feared, when the original assembly craftsmen walked out in 1913, they took the hive mind with them. Their runners, who had once served as the vital link for continuous improvements, followed them, and so did the management culture. The new managers who stepped in to rebuild had to deal with workers refusing to stand in the stanchions. The challenge of meeting the rising daily build schedules and the new complexity of involvements made them unwilling to take risks for the sake of continuous improvement. Responsibility for the evolution of product and process disappeared into ever-larger circles of off-line indecision making.

THE V-8 VALVE ROCKER COVER[1]

> In 1970, I was pulled out of research at the GM Tech Center and reassigned to production on second shift in Plant 8. It was the second time I'd been assigned to the role of a front-lines production supervisor, and this time there were subtle overtones of it being a test of integrity. I had set the standard for this department in 1968, and it had

---

1 V-8 valve rocker cover: One of two covers placed over the rocker arms that control the opening and closing of valves on a piston engine (the upside-down sheet metal bread pans on either side of a V-8 engine).

never been achieved. Production counts for V-8 rocker covers were never much above eleven thousand per shift; I had set the standard at sixteen thousand.

My grandfather Floyd was helpful. His council on management issues and insistence that I continue to find ways to drain the swamp no matter how many encounters I had with alligators kept me on course. Early on, I encountered what was left of the naturally occurring hive mind on the production floor. My experience with delay studies as an industrial engineer was hinting at places to drain the swamp. One of them was the number of times the housings and baffles jammed. I asked the four load station operators to begin collecting the ones that jammed. Their collections were sadly deformed by the time they pried them out of the slide-and-ram mechanism, but the burrs were clearly evident. My experience with building dies told me that the burrs might be causing the jams, and the dull trim steels would be the root cause. In talking with load station operators, I learned they could often recognize the ones that would jam by the burrs. They were already trying to sort them out, because it was easier than prying them out after they jammed. They also told me that the bad ones usually came in spurts, and that sometimes they could run for hours without a jam. At that point I was confident that watching the wear on the trim steels in the progressive die was the problem. I set out to find the source. The presses that made housings and baffles were at the far end of Plant 8, and both presses were running when I walked up. I approached each press operator carefully, as I would one of my uncles. I entered into a dialogue and then showed them the burrs we thought were causing the jams. I learned that their requests to have the steels sharpened were sometimes ignored. The inspector and their boss often couldn't agree on when to shut down, and many times they were told to keep running. I then talked with the die makers and their supervisor, learning that it wasn't always clear when the steels needed to be sharpened. The roving sample inspector was supposed to make the request. Patiently I expressed my concerns to all parties and made clear my desire for more concern on their part. I began visiting all parties once a week to reinforce my sincere interest. I got to know them all by name. I even came in early once a week to have the same conversation with the day crew. The day shift was easier because I knew the die room people and the roving inspector. I also cruised the storage area, where I found forty-nine containers of housings and baffles with roughly four thousand in each one. It would take time to work through the inventory and determine whether my efforts would have the desired effect.

Finely tuned systems of continuous improvement maintained by craftsmen once made the industrial sector thrive. In their place we now have exorbitant expenditures on automation. The automation comes with a promise that it will make components to match the drawing, but it comes without features for adjustment, making it impossible to pursue continuous improvement. America's eagerness to walk away from reliance on craft-based intellect in the workforce has led away from reliance on the minds of the collective to improve on the drawing. The outcome of decades of struggling to get the automation to run at promised levels of quality and speed has been a steady decline in American innovation. There really are no perfect designs of products or automation; there is only the opportunity to evolve and the United States has forgotten how.

In the months that followed, the jamming ceased to be a problem. Daily production climbed. I was impressed that showing sincere concern would work in an environment of mindless tasks. What I hadn't realized till then was how hungry line workers are for any chance to become involved—any hive-mind opportunity. From then on, I looked for opportunities to involve all who were interested. It was also a lesson in the subtle values of higher levels of in-sourcing that would never be captured on a spreadsheet. I was the runner making the daily interface with the component makers, informing those upstream of the needs in the assembly area.

---

14. Organization Development: Pushing the task of problem solving and continuous improvement onto the shoulders of a supporting white-collar workforce in 1913 caused employment to swell.

During my stint as superintendent of industrial engineering at the Hydra-Matic Division, I asked an industrial engineer to study the cost of making the simplest change to a part print. I could hardly believe the answer. The cost of white-collar workers signing off on a part number change was $3,500, and the paperwork required a minimum of two weeks to circulate. The number of keep-trackers that had crept into the transmission business was astounding.

15. Organization Development: The supporting white-collar organization became top-heavy with far too many levels of hierarchy.

The top-down culture that developed to replace the assembly craftsmen filled offices with white shirts and maintenance cribs with blue ones. Without a system of self-checks and balances, the support staff headcount steadily grew, backed by arguments that more people were needed "just in case"; what's more, each time a problem arose, more subsystems were needed for more external checks and balances. The value of the collective hive mind had been sacrificed over and over for a quick increase in production, resulting in the upward spiraling of support staffs.

FIXING A CLUTCH

When I was a junior, one of my work assignments took me into the realm of the process engineers. I was assigned to work with Robert, who spent his day on the phone. At one point he handed me a letter from his in-box. "See if you can figure this out," he said, and returned to his phone conversation. It was an official notice from Chevrolet Central Office informing all involved parties that a growing number of warranty claims were surfacing due to early failure of manual clutch assemblies. The letter listed complaints of the clutch slipping, making scraping sounds, often accompanied by the unmistakable smell of burning clutch plates. Many of the complaints were occurring within the first twenty thousand miles. As I read the letter a second time looking for clues on where to begin, Robert cupped the phone, saying, "A shipment of failed clutches just came in from Central Office. They're down in the Quality Control Lab."

A guy in the lab seemed glad to see me. "Are you from upstairs?" he asked. I nodded, and he pointed to a skid. "These are the bad ones. Tore some apart and, sure enough, the clutch is nearly worn through."

Stepping into my newfound role as the guy from upstairs, I looked them over and commented, "The plates seem to be wearing through only on the inner diameter."

The lab tech chimed in: "Yeah, the plate's not meshing evenly with the flywheel."

"Is the clutch plate flat?" I asked.

He walked me over to a surface plate setup. He had already positioned a returned clutch face parallel to the table. He slid a dial indicator slowly across it to prove the plate was flat. "It must be the flywheel," he said proudly.

I nodded in agreement. "Did they ship back the flywheels with these?"

"No, just the clutch assemblies. The dealers pull and replace the clutch assemblies, not the flywheels."

I told the lab tech to hold the material; I would get back to him. I added a "thank you" for his initiative. I walked the half mile to the Manual Flywheel Department. It was easy to find. It was right next to where I spent a week welding ring gears on stamped steel flywheels for automatics. The flywheel for a manual transmission is made of cast iron and weighs roughly seventy pounds. They were machined on an eight-station Bullard.[1] I walked around to the back while the machine was running and watched the station that finish-turned the clutch plate surface go through its cycle. When the operator stopped for a break, I stepped in and peered up under the chip guard. The tool bar that passed across the clutch surface held two round ceramic inserts. One was cutting the clutch surface, and the other was cutting a clearance surface. As the bar moved across, it would finish cutting the clearance surface while it was still passing across the clutch surface. A little machining experience told me that when the inserts became dull, deflection forces would increase. As the forces increased, the cutter insert that was halfway across the clutch surface would dig in and cut the outer surface of the flywheel a little deeper when the clearance cut was finished. The person who had set up this Bullard should have anticipated this change in deflection and adjusted for it. A simple repositioning of the cutter bar would solve the problem. The result should be a longer-lasting clutch plate. I couldn't discern whether the tool designer or the setup man had made the mistake, but I was sure that any machinist worth his salt would have thought this through before he'd made the first flywheel. Someone must have altered the setup.

---

1 A Bullard is a machine that indexes components mounted in a fixture around a circle of stations. At each station a drive mechanism is engaged that spins the component while cutting tools pass over one or more of the surfaces.

On a pushcart I took a few flywheels back to the Quality Control Lab. The lab tech helped me document the degree of flatness on each. I could see without magnification where the tool was digging into the surface and could imagine how much worse it would become when the inserts became dull. In my write-up I explained that when the correction was made, (1) the torque handling capability of the outer diameter of the flywheel would be greater and (2) the clutch plate would have more surface area on the outer diameter. Both factors would increase the life span of clutch plates.

Robert had me fill out a Request for Change form on the Bullard and a second request to add a flat-checking routine to the roving inspector's role. That day I was the man from upstairs who swooped down to solve a problem. I was glad that I had enough experience to solve it. But it was the kind of problem that would have self-corrected in Henry's original hive mind.

———————

16. Product Design and Development: The long lead time to prototype a new vehicle and equip an assembly plant to produce it made the assembly line system vulnerable in times of rapid changes in style and interest.

Design solutions that try to address these rapid changes often resemble variations on vanilla and miss out on the more lucrative swings in fashion that the carriage builders once tapped.

17. Equipment: An assembly line is managed with an intense focus on keeping it running at all cost. Quality takes a backseat.

If the line stops, the losses are catastrophic. If one assembly line workstation has a problem, the entire line stops. Proposals to improve a design must often wait until the next model comes along. The few product updates accepted into an assembly line system in the midst of a model run are those that can be made on the fly with minimal risk of mistake.

18. Equipment: The mechanics of an assembly line channel vehicle designers into assembly processes that can be divided up into sixty-second increments.

Vehicle designers must consider ease of assembly. It must be possible to divide the tasks of assembling a component into 40 second increments leaving 20 seconds to walk back to the next vehicle coming down the line. Further, if the task requires sitting on the seat and then reaching up under the dash, and getting out from under the dash and out of the car, there may be as few as 5 to 10 seconds available to perform a task. If, for instance the task calls for loose assembly with two screws just to hold a component in place it might be impossible to assemble and keep up with the line. Designers must pay careful attention to both the order and ease of assembly.

When an assembly line stops, the entire line crew becomes idle. In a staged assembly system, only a single team is affected. The risks of assembly line stoppage caused by equipment breakdown affect capital spending decisions, and just-in-case thinking takes over. To make matters worse, the out-sourcing of design and build of assembly systems leaves buyers at the mercy of the equipment suppliers who set the price and project the capability. The tendency is to purchase whatever suppliers recommend. There are even breakdown crews paid to be on standby.

In instances where the cycle time must be longer than 40 seconds elaborate and expensive line tracking and retrieval loops must be designed. Transmission top-off (adding the appropriate amount of transmission fluid while the engine is running), and charging the cooling system—are two tasks that must be done with tracking systems. Vinyl roof installation used to be one of them as well. These loops of equipment increase the risks of breakdowns.

19. Equipment: Assembly lines must be accompanied by capital-intensive precautionary systems to minimize the impact of equipment breakdowns.

All assembly lines employ breakdown crews at the ready. Like a city fire department crews of skilled trades are on standby at all times, ready to climb aboard there breakdown wagon loaded with tools and race through the plant with lights flashing and a siren blaring. The cost of having these crews on standby is part of the cost of operating an assembly line.

20. Equipment: The equipment along the assembly line is not focused on allowing the phasing in of new models while phasing out the old.

When using the assembly line system, the production of one model ends abruptly. Before 1913 and throughout the carriage-building era, the phasing out of old models occurred only when customers stopped ordering them. The buying public today includes both early adopters and those who hang onto traditions. The assembly line serves neither of these tapering levels of interest.

Recap 1913

(1) Walking away from the guilds and (2) refusing to build to order were the right objectives for Henry when he was trying to take over an industry already dominated by carriage builders. (3) Choosing to adopt the assembly line was also the right decision when no other avenue for increasing output presented itself. But all three of these "right" decisions became entrenched and have since become problematic. The assembly line decision added fourteen more problems to the original six and they would all compound themselves as the twentieth century unfolded.

CHAPTER 4. 1941: THE UAW WINS FAVOR OF NEGLECTED LINE WORKERS

The 20th century dawned with the finest carriages in world rolling out of craft shops around Michigan, Indiana, and Ohio. The American Federation of Labor (AFL), founded in 1886 by Samuel Gompers, was on its way to becoming the largest union in the United States in the twenties. Gompers claimed 1.7 million members in 1904 and 4 million by 1920. The AFL was "the conservative alternative to working class radicalism."[1] It recruited only craftsmen, offering to promote their excellence and win higher wages and better working conditions for them. Gompers won over the business leaders with his belief in capitalism as the only path to the betterment of all concerned. The AFL was successful in small and medium-sized craft shops and steered clear of mass production industries, the places where new business leaders like Henry Ford were busy in-sourcing and bootstrapping new skills. Henry's operation was a hybrid of craftwork and mass production. When Henry made the reluctant decision to implement the assembly line, he moved the auto industry even further from the creed of the AFL.

The workers who came to man the stanchions along the assembly lines came for the money. They overran the carriage communities and altered their culture. By the mid-thirties, the streets surrounding the auto industry were filled with second generation assembly line workers, out of work and disgruntled. They were not candidates for the creed of the AFL. A new subcommittee of the AFL called the Committee for Industrial Organization (CIO) formed to address their interests. The creed of the new CIO was to pit workers in mass production industries against owners and win concessions in wages and benefits. By 1937, ten

---

1 Melvyn Dubofsky, *We Shall Be All* (Champaign: University of Illinois Press, 2000), pp. 5–6.

unions had formed under the CIO umbrella, including the United Auto Workers (UAW), the United Rubber Workers (URW), and the United Steel Workers (USW). The tactic of the CIO was to target one company in each industry at a time. Concessions won in the one company were then used to leverage concessions across the industry. In 1937 the first auto target was General Motors. The last was Ford in 1941.

The craft culture of Midwest was overrun in a single generation. Lifetime aspirations to become a master craftsman disappeared along the assembly lines after 1913. Union organizers began winning over the few masters who stayed to lead the skilled-trades segment offering to increase the number of journeymen on the payroll. The UAW offered much to gain and very little to lose. Organizers promised to pry wealth from the hands of shareholders, and members of my family attended some of the rallies. My mother remembers the National Guard coming to town in 1937; she and her father, Frank, watched as fights along the picket lines broke out and cars were turned over. Frank told her, "Look, those fools are ruining everything."

Two years later Frank walked out of Happy Valley for the last time. He gave up his role in the management of the paint shop. I was maybe fifteen when he explained why he had left while others had stayed. Frank explained that he grew tired of the outliers in his crew experimenting with just how much the committeeman could win on their behalf. He grew tired of teaching the young recruits that others were counting on them being on the job on time. He ended his explanation with, "There's too much to learn about how to paint cars to spend hours arguing over things people should know before they begin to look for a job."

The decision to adopt the assembly line turned the culture of the carriage makers into fertile ground for union organizers to plant their seeds. Shareholders decided to fight back rather than share what they had accumulated in a single generation. The original eight objectives on the back of Henry Ford's envelope increased to nine. One was added to give direction to efforts to counter the expected demands of the newly formed UAW.

> *1941—Unions (new objective category): Develop countermeasures to keep the ambitions of the UAW leadership in check.*

America entered into World War II during the year that the UAW hammered out a contract with Ford. The war would drag the American economy out of the Great Depression but at a terrible cost. Rationing and sacrifice in the forties would generate an insatiable demand for new automobiles and for places to live in the quiet suburbs. Demand was being created for second and even third cars in suburban driveways. America's auto producers began preparing even before World War II was over.

During the war years, strikes and the insistence that all workers join the union were put on hold. War production became the first priority. My mother served as a machine gun sight inspector while my father was away in the navy. Paying union dues was optional; she chose not to pay the ruffians, following the beliefs of her father. She truly believed they would all be ousted when the boys got home. Major shareholders did not, however, share my mother's belief. They worried about what might happen to their accumulated wealth when the war was over. The worrying led to shareholders making demands on Board members, which in turn led to new expectations for executives. Executives were instructed to prepare for a fight.

Ford Motor Company may have been the last strike-target for the UAW because too many in the community were still loyal to the memory of the founder. Stories of the wonders of Henry Ford were still being told. In the final months leading up to the contract agreement, members of the staff at Ford ushered the seventy-eight-year-old Henry away to Florida. He just couldn't grasp why his workers weren't happy after all he had done for them. He died six years later in 1947.

Perhaps the decade of World War II and the Korean War gave automotive shareholders too much time to worry. The newly appointed executive culture changed five of the original eight objectives as they prepared for battle against the unions.

> 1913—*Sourcing: Expand in-sourcing investments to defend the origins of all tributaries feeding raw materials.*

Was totally reversed:

> 1941—*Sourcing: Prepare to threaten the union with out-sourcing of component manufacturing wherever threats will be the most effective in dampening ambitions to increase wages and benefits. Develop a purchasing staff capable of controlling the supply base and blocking moves by the likes of Durant and Chevrolet.*

Threats of out-sourcing were threats to reduce headcount. Job protection was a fundamental responsibility of union leaders. Preparations for out-sourcing went so far as executive orders to prepare outside suppliers to take over component-making responsibility. My thesis project had stumbled upon one of them. Outside sources were already in the process of being groomed to make exhaust pipes and tailpipes in 1967.

The original objective of protecting competitive advantage through continuous improvements in operations was being moved to a back burner. Purchasing staffs were instructed to protect the company from attempts to buy up the supply base. Purchasing agents were expected to establish three outside suppliers to share the component-making responsibility. If the UAW pushed too hard at the bargaining table, the other side would call their bluff. Folders containing plans to outsource whole segments of component making would be slid across the table. Workers would be let go if the UAW didn't back off on a demand, and the folders defined how many and at which locations. If the threat didn't deter a union demand, the company would follow through. For some components, like wheels, a parallel in-house processing capability was retained for roughly 10 percent of the volume. Making them in house assured that suppliers did not jack up their prices over time. Still, collusion among suppliers was difficult to control. The number of components manufactured on the outside began to spiral upward as out-sourcing shifted from being a threat to being a goal.

> *1913—Equipment: Acquire equipment that will enable the high-volume production of power trains, increase the output of the assembly line, enable the in-sourcing of raw material processing, and continue to improve in-house component manufacturing capability.*

Was edited for the first time:

> *1941—Equipment: Seek out new fields of automation that will reduce headcount. Reallocate the annual funding for upgrades to the traditional universal equipment. Use the reallocated capital on experiments in automation.*

Henry Ford's original business model had sought universal equipment and counted on employees to aspire to the art of reconfiguring tooling and fixtures. The original intent was to choose equipment that could be easily reconfigured and maintained. This 1941 change introduced the era of seeking automation—and its attendant escalation of expenditures on equipment. America's machine tool industry began to flourish.

> *1913—Organization Development: Reorganize Highland Park to run without a core of assembly craftsmen while continuing to focus on the in-sourcing of all component manufacturing.*

Was edited to read:

> *1941—Organization Development: Replace up-from-the-ranks supervision with business-school-trained management. Increase the size of design and development staffs in preparation for an increase in the number of model offerings.*

Workers who could accept the mindless stanchions along the assembly line required a very different type of leadership than craftsmen. In time, workers expected their elected UAW representatives to step in and demand for them equal pay and overtime hours regardless of the amount of their effort, willingness to work, or ability to perform the task. Enter the era of Peter Ducker's professionally-trained managers. Major shareholders viewed these graduates as a solution: they could reduce the risk of workforce empathy for anticipated union ambitions and ease the resentment of shareholder wealth.

> *1913—Product Design and Development: Continue to focus on improvements in the Model T, but by using engineers (a hands-off approach), rather than a core of assembly craftsmen, to direct designers.*

Was edited to read:

> *1941—Product Design and Development: Increase number of offerings to keep up with expected post-Depression and war expansion and the expected changes in lifestyles.*

The Great Depression had driven consumers to low-end showrooms, and market forecasts were telling automakers that all of that was going to change. Ford Motor Company broadened its model offerings, adding the Mercury in 1939. Perceived at first to be a "gussied up" Ford, by 1945 the Mercury was upgraded and relaunched as the "Junior Lincoln." At the same time General Motors began working on a multiple-model move in the opposite direction. More than 70 percent of the GM customer base was purchasing the low-priced Chevrolet. As the thirties came to a close, Alfred Sloan authorized a shift in car product programs.[1] Buick, Pontiac, and Oldsmobile began working together on new lower-priced entries. Adding models introduced a new level of complexity to product design and development. The age of defining market segments was born, and with it came the risks and rewards of huge investments. The Edsel would be Ford's first major misstep.

> *1913—Growth: Invest in faster assembly lines and start making strategic moves to weaken the positions of fast-following competitors.*

Was edited to read:

> *1941—Growth: Focus on increasing market share. Spin up the scale race by adding an increased number of model offerings and making drastic annual model changes to drive out competitors that do not have deep pockets.*

A scale race in the auto business is about taking risks to achieve a higher volume of sales. Spending more capital on a new model introduction than the competition can result in a more attractive offering, which in turn can lead to higher sales. If you spend a billion dollars and sell a million cars, the investment recovery requirement is only a $1,000 a vehicle. But if you sell only 250,000, the recovery cost per vehicle will jump to $4,000. In a scale race, the leading competitors try to advance consumer interest in materials, components and features that can only be produced at high scale. The outcome of the scale race in the auto business was the Big Three: GM, Ford, and Chrysler.

At the same time there are risks. A wave of new technology can sometimes erase all high scale advantages. The handful of winners of the scale race in the U.S. steel industry suffered a 65 percent loss in market share in the seventies when a wave of daring entrepreneurs began launching a low scale business model that delivered better steel at better prices.

---

1 Alfred P. Sloan, Jr., *My Years with General Motors* (Garden City, N.Y.: Doubleday, 1964), p. 179.

LONG-TERM INEFFICIENCIES IN THE OBJECTIVES OF 1941

The 1941 adjustments to objectives were course corrections for the changes made in 1913. Adopting the assembly line had caused many problems. Another seven problems were added to twenty already brewing.

21. Unions: The decision to engage in an adversarial union-versus-management relationship filled the union electorate with watchdogs wearing spiked collars.

Wage and benefit concessions were won with threats of strikes and unwillingness to settle despite the entire membership being out of work. The majority that had voted to accept the union to represent them did not show the same fervor for electing the actual union leaders. In years to come, fewer than 2 percent of the workforce made the trek to the union hall to participate in elections. As with most democratic systems, the silent majority did not participate. The faction that did vote tended to support friends and relatives. The issues demanded at bargaining tables by heavy-handed union leaders were often slid off to the side in exchange for personal favors.

A CRANE OPERATOR'S DRINKING PROBLEM

John worked for me as an overhead crane operator. He revealed his dangerous side in early March, five months after I became his foreman. I didn't notice him coming back from lunch that day, but then, I rarely saw him on the ground. His first lift after lunch—a wooden crate filled with four hundred clutch cover blanks—bumped the corner of a press while moving at a good pace down the high bay. The blanks rained down on workers below like nine-pound knife-edged Frisbees.

After checking to see that no one was hurt, I motioned for John to move his crane to the far end and come down. I had never penalized someone before and stopped in the office to check with Rosy, my general foreman. I wanted to verify I was within my rights to write John up and send him home.

"Sure," Rosy answered, with the hint of a smile around his cigar. He then added, "Check with Jerry. I think John's up to four weeks."

"What?" Four weeks meant John had been penalized many times before.

Jerry, the clerk, had been listening and piped in, "John's up to four weeks. You can fire him if you want."

I headed for the far end where John would be waiting. I was determined to make my expectations clear. A safe work environment is the highest priority. Away from prying eyes, I began, "John, how could you have made such a mistake? You endangered the lives of a lot of people."

He smelled of whiskey and slurred his answer, "I jus' mis't the corner a little."

"You've been drinking!" I exclaimed in disgust, and John hung his head. Clearly he had been browbeaten on this subject before. His penalty record now made sense. I tried the shaming approach. "I can't believe you would so carelessly endanger everyone," I said like a father. "You know I am required to send you home." I stared at him in silence. "Four weeks without pay is going to be a very long time. Your time stops now. If you drink at lunchtime again, I am going to have to fire you." I walked him to the clock and had him ring out his time card. He turned once as he got to the doorway to see if I was still watching, and I decided to follow him out to the gate. I told the security guard not to let him return.

Rosy called me into his office four weeks later. A smile appeared around the cigar. "John's coming back on Monday," Rosy began. "He's coming back from that four-week paid vacation you authorized."

"What?" I exclaimed.

"Yep, put him to work," Rosy mumbled and went back to his paper work.

As I stepped into the outer office, Jerry explained, "John's brother is the president of the local. He can do whatever he wants around here. Some sort of deal was struck, and John's four weeks have been expunged. He will be receiving a large paycheck next Friday, covering the entire four weeks." I walked out of the office stunned.

I waited for John at the foot of his ladder on Monday. He was sober and ready to go to work. In a low voice I said, "If you ever again feel the urge to drink your lunch, have the decency to go home and not come back in here."

It was surprising to discover that the silent majority was choosing to work under threats of falling clutch plates. I say choosing, because they were paying dues to feed the watchdogs, and they were not voting in union elections. The silent majority in America's auto plants hasn't realized what they are trading away in exchange for the expunging of records of a few friends and family. There is a much larger role for unions; it will require the election of a different type of leadership. But I'm getting ahead of myself.

---

22. Unions: The political maneuvering in local union elections is not much different from that in any election. The local plant management sometimes gets involved.

MANAGING WHO GETS ELECTED

Late in 1967 my supervisor, Lloyd, received a phone call and abruptly directed me to go down and study a truck tailpipe line. "Stay until you have it fully documented," he said. "Take extra time on this one to be sure." His caution was usual; I always stayed until I had it right. I returned to the office late in the afternoon with the watch readings and details on the eleven studies. I was completing my calculations when Lloyd walked over to my desk and said in a low voice, "I want you to come in at six tomorrow to finish up on this one." I glanced over at Bob, my co-worker, who gave me a shrug with a slight narrowing of the brow.

I arrived before six the next morning and switched on the set of four fluorescents over my desk—a single spot on a dark stage. I set to work, finishing my calculations, and was busy checking when I sensed I wasn't alone. I looked over my shoulder and discovered the plant manager and general superintendent standing behind me. I knew the general superintendent from his challenge of my fifth-year project. The plant manager I knew from his oil painted portrait in the Main Office lobby. The general superintendent asked in a low voice, "What have you come up with?"

Unsure of what was happening and not daring to ask, I replied nervously, "It looks like the fifth operation will be the bottleneck." The words came out of my mouth before I realized that I'd assumed they were asking about the truck tailpipe line.

The general superintendent insisted, "What is the line rate *you've* come up with?"

"It looks like 122 per hour."

The plant manager then spoke in a similar low and knowing voice, "Show us the time study on that bottleneck operation."

I handed it over, and they quickly questioned my judgment calls. "You have a .12 reading here. Why is it so high in relation to the others?" And, "Why is this low reading not being allowed?"

My replies were far from convincing: "The operator fumbled a little with the rotation, and because this is a long pipe I believe the operators will always fumble with it from time to time." And, "I anticipated the end of the cycle and clicked the watch, but the pipe hung up and the cycle was actually a moment longer."

The plant manager came back like one of my grandfathers. "Don't you think that when the operators become more experienced, this fumbling will disappear?" He handed back the study.

I nodded obediently and began erasing judgment calls.

After what seemed like an eternity of recalculation, the general superintendent asked, "What is the line rate now?"

"One hundred thirty-nine per hour," I replied.

The plant manager spoke once more, "Get this ready for signatures as soon as possible."

I knew Lloyd would not accept erasure marks and pulled out a fresh study form for the fifth operation. One hand on the calculator and the other on filling out the time-study form, I raced to complete the study and mark up the routing sheet with all eleven. At some point I sensed I was alone again. I turned to find nothing but a cavern of pre-morning darkness behind me. As the sun came up, I began to wonder if they had ever really been there.

I finished the eleven studies and placed them, along with the marked-up pink routing sheet, on Lloyd's desk before seven. To my surprise when he came in he skipped his morning coffee ritual and immediately checked my figures without looking up. When Jerry the clerk arrived, Lloyd handed him the routing and cover sheet for typing. Lloyd carried the signature package out of the office before 8:00 a.m. He returned in less than ten minutes and set to work on other things without looking up.

Lloyd and I never talked about what had happened that morning. I figured the reason he didn't tell me why I needed to come in early was probably the reason I shouldn't tell him what had happened. I went down to Plant 6 that afternoon to begin a study on another line and could see both the general foreman and the superintendent observing the truck tailpipe line. When the shift was over, I walked over to the foreman to ask how the standard had been accepted.

The foreman's response was cryptic. "The crew wasn't able to meet your new standard."

I looked at the hourly counts in his notes as he posted the total to his production sheet. The day had begun with 101, 103 and then jumped to 114, 117, 120, and 122 followed by a 91 and a 93 the last two hours.

"They tried and won't try again," he said.

I knew what he meant. For the rest of the year, the crew would be resigned to fifty-five minutes on and five minutes off and would make no contribution to keeping the line running. They would produce 30 percent less than their capability.

My hunches on my study had been right. How could I have been persuaded to alter my judgments? If I was going to succeed as an engineer and advisor to management, I had to be firm in my convictions. I had buckled the first time the heat lamp was turned on. My succumbing to pressure would cost the company the wages of three people for the balance of the year. This demonstration of lack of courage of my convictions was a blemish that would be hard to eradicate.

My studies of the remaining pipe lines brought me in close contact with one of the setup men. At some point he nodded toward a rather hostile-looking fellow on the truck tailpipe line and said, "That guy over there was running for president of the local yesterday and he lost." He looked at me smiling and asked, "Can you tell?"

After a pause, the setup man continued. "He's a hot head, and he was challenging Bobby, who's been president of the local for years. Some say he might have won with his promises to fight management on every issue, that is, if he had had more time to campaign."

Everything suddenly added up: the reason I had been asked to come in early, the reason I had been approached in the dark. It all made perfect sense. My guilt was lifted.

My uncles often told tales of union elections and sergeants at arms who carried baseball bats. There were reasons why less than 2 percent of workers went to the union hall to vote. This hostile fellow probably had a following of rabble-rousers. Five-minute breaks had not allowed him time to travel far enough to reach enough voters.

---

23. Sourcing: The purchasing objectives would prove to be no match for the financial ambitions of the suppliers.

Along with a change in objectives, from in-sourcing to out-sourcing, came a supporting objective of seeking three suppliers in every field of component making. This was supposed to allow or encourage the suppliers to share processing innovations among each other to advance the capability of all three. It isn't hard to imagine that the three would also work together for the benefit of the collective rather than cut each other's throat in price wars. Purchasing agents could not control component prices, and they began to climb.

24. Organization Development: The well-compensated executives who appeared soon after the union won the right to represent the workforce may be the price that had to be paid to ensure that the interests of the represented workforce remained under control while the shareholders harvested profits. But high-paid executives are not the right choice for building a competitive industrial sector.

During the war years, the founders and major shareholders passed the batons of leadership to tough CEOs. They were paid well to keep the ambitious UAW leadership away from the latch on the chest holding the spoils of war. Peter Drucker cautioned in the fifties against pay differentials of more than twenty times the lowest paid worker. But his cautions went unheeded. In 2008, the Institute for Policy Studies documented that the average CEO pay was 344 times the pay of an average U.S. worker.[1]

In Europe, executive compensation is roughly one-tenth that in the United States. An important element of Daimler's struggle to manage a merger with Chrysler in 1998 was the difference in compensation, as well as the difference in levels of participation by government and union representatives in Board decisions.

25. Organization Development: The 1941 decision to manage the front lines with professional managers (business school grads) would steer America's Big Three into a vulnerable position. Decreasing quality levels accelerated the decline in sales. Japan's auto makers gradually increased their U.S. market share.

By choosing to disregard employee aspirations of eventually rising through the ranks, management squelched a fundamental motivator. The impatience and

---

1 Sarah Anderson, John Cavanagh, Chuck Collins, and Sam Pizzigati, *Institute for Policy Studies Report on Executive Compensation*, August 25, 2008.

lack of hands-on knowledge of these "professional managers" also squelched the flow of long-term continuous improvements originating from the front lines. The front lines had once been a place where you walked a mile in the other man's shoes before you rose through the ranks. Its real value is hard to quantify for a spread sheet.

WHEN WORKERS HAVE A CHANCE TO CONTRIBUTE

On October 1, 1970, when my research project came to an end, I was reassigned the role of foreman over the forty-five employees making valve rocker covers for all Chevrolet engines. A rocker cover is bolted on top of an engine to keep the oil pumped over the cam and valve lifters from spraying all over the engine compartment. They were made of stamped sheet metal and look like an upside-down bread pan. A V-8 engine required two of them. The two large automated welders at the heart of the department were producing eleven thousand V-8 covers a shift and the standard called for sixteen thousand. I knew because I was the time-study man who had set the standard three years earlier. When I learned that several foremen had tried and failed to reach sixteen thousand in the previous three years, there was little doubt in mind as to why the Rocker Cover Department was waiting for me. The management at Plant 8 was like an elephant. They had a good memory when it came to the people who set their standards. They remembered who had made their lives difficult.

During my third week, one of the two automated V-8 welders stopped. I looked up from the desk to see the crew walking away. I hurried toward them, intent on finding out what they knew about what was wrong. I got nothing but shoulder shrugs, until the housing station operator said, "Needs a welder repairman." I all but ran to the maintenance crib and filled out a pink AVO (Avoid Verbal Orders), writing in the problem line: "welder stopped, there may be a problem at the housing station." It took five minutes for the welder repairman to arrive. All the while the welder was down, I circled around making it abundantly clear that I was anxious. I watched the repairman reach in and clear the jammed covers, then tighten the mounting screws on a limit switch. He reset the control panels and signaled to the lead-off operator that all was in order once again.

As the welder repairman packed up his tools, I asked him what had gone wrong.

His answer was flippant. "Oh, it jams from time to time."

I gently inquired further, as if I were asking one of my uncles. "Does the shuttle-down indicator often move out of position?"

Realizing I knew something about his role in all of this, he smiled and said yes. "I've told them they need to shut it down so I can get in and tack weld that block in place, but they never have time."

Now I smiled. My glee was in finding my first long-term opportunity; this was the trailhead I was looking for that led to the trench that would drain the swamp. I looked at my watch and made a mental note.

I had just lost twelve minutes of production due to that block. Twenty people were idled—equivalent to four hours of wages. Experience told me that it wouldn't take the welder repairman fifteen minutes to set up and weld the block in place. It was time to get to work on my own long-term agenda.

In the fifth hour, the welder stopped again. As I approached anxiously, one of the workers, who had always shrugged whenever I looked to him for a sign, now offered a quick, "Needs an electrician."

Another worker then stopped me, saying, "Needs a welder repairman."

I headed for the crib again at a near run, deciding to try the electrical route, in support of my eager new volunteer.

When the electrician took a quick look, he said, "You need a welder repairman." I walked away doing a little frustration pantomime, glancing at the guy who had said it was an electrical problem. "Accuracy when you have a suggestion" was the lesson I tried to impart. I headed back to put in an order for a welder repairman. The problem this time was with the weld sequence, which was out of sync. The same welder repairman told me there were several relays that needed to be replaced, but there was never any time to get in and replace them. I smiled again, another opportunity . . .

I walked to the Production Office at the end of the night to turn in a count of just 5,300 V-8 covers. The counts of the others, the L-6s and Mark IVs, were okay, but the total was not nearly enough to pay the wages of the forty-one people who came to work. The following Monday, I got things going and deliberately avoided running one of the two V-8 welders although the daily build schedule called for both. I made out some AVOs and headed for the maintenance crib. I talked with both the electrician and the welder repairman, asking how quickly they could recruit a welder and gather the relays and components needed to fix both welders. We mutually agreed on a plan of attack that would begin right after the 4:55 p.m. break. I dropped the proper Request for Work in the proper slots and then asked Woods, my fork truck driver, to clear stock away from the idle welder to provide access before 5:00 p.m. The welder repairman and electrician appeared on time with a welder, a millwright, and a pipefitter in accompaniment. They locked out the power panels and set about their tasks. They finished in less than thirty minutes and cycled the welder a few times to make sure it functioned properly. I publicly thanked them for their efforts and walked them down to the coffee machine, where I dropped four dimes, saying, "You can have the other welder in about fifteen minutes." I walked back to my V-8 crew and told the lead-off operator to start the next hour on the other welder. I motioned to the rest of the crew that they would be moving down. Woods was already busy resetting the stock and shipping racks around the newly repaired welder without my asking. I filled out another set of AVOs and dropped them off. I knew enough about maintenance to know the foreman needed signed records of what his crew had been doing if he was to get his budget reimbursed.

Fixing things permanently went on for the rest of October and November. Anything that had a tendency to jam or jump sequence was being fixed. The maintenance crews were happy to do the work, knowing it would lead to fewer frantic short-term fixes. My crew seemed to get into the shifting around, as if we were cleaning house. During the first week of December, relations took another big step. An operator on the first V-8 welder walked past as his five-minute break began. With no one near and without looking my way, he said, "The lift arm on the shuttle is coming loose. You might want to get someone over to tighten it before it breaks." My heart jumped. My grandfather had been right. Your employees will help you meet your goals if you show an interest in theirs, and you are patient and determined. Shift counts on the V-8 began climbing through the 13,000 barrier that week. My line on the Daily Efficiency Report that was circulated to all members of management was beginning to look like a Wall Street darling. When workers begin to want to contribute, many subtle things begin to happen.

The supervisors who had preceded me in the Valve Rocker Cover Department were professionals, and they had not been able to get eleven thousand a shift out of the V-8 system for three years running. I was already making progress on increasing the output. I still had a long way to go, but I could already see the value of the hive mind of a collective. Whether my part was knowing enough to ask the right questions, or having enough experience to recognize extra effort when someone offered it, or having the experience to suggest a series of steps involving many different activities, or having the patience to guide self-discovery rather than preach, or having higher expectations—I am not sure. But I do know that line workers who have been chained to monotonous activities since their first day on the job can be rekindled, and leaders with hands-on experience can lead in areas where professional managers struggle.

---

26. Organization Development: With the UAW came enforced delineation of journeymen trades. Maintenance and construction projects suddenly required full complements of trades on standby.

To win over the skilled-trade workforce, the UAW needed to deliver something. One of the earliest moves was to support fair treatment of all journeymen. The union leadership insisted on strict lines of demarcation between trades, which led to tradesmen standing around while others worked.

Also the UAW insisted on equality in offering overtime to all journeymen and insisted on published logs of hours worked. When a weekend project required six electricians, a foreman was required to refer to the log of overtime hours. The electricians with the least number of logged overtime hours had to be the first to be offered overtime. In the real world there are electricians who are unable, untrained, uninterested, or unwilling to perform all jobs. Usually more than six had to be offered overtime to get to those on the list who would get the job done. Management added special journeyman classifications in attempts to isolate those who had specific skills and were willing to work. The number of classifications expanded over the years, but so did the numbers of journeymen standing around because the work was not within their classification. Standing around doing nothing became one of the new measures of stature in the sixties. My grandfathers shook their head in disgust when my uncles told stories of workers bragging about doing nothing all day.

The number of workers brought in just in case their classification might be needed grew. The days of the generalists and striving for innovation in any field of craftsmanship had disappeared.

27. Organization Development: Further separation of blue and white collars in 1941 drove up the cost of both. (A carriage company that valued its intellect and brawn equally could avoid the inefficiencies of class structure.) The UAW was broadening the cultural gap between office and floor workers and between skilled trades and both floor workers and contractors.

THE SUBTLE TRUTH OF THE FIVE-MINUTE DIE CHANGE

For me, the demo of the famous five-minute die change in Japan revealed the tip of a huge iceberg. The five-minute die change had been talked about for a couple of years before I went to Japan in 1983 and witnessed several for myself. Bottom line, it was a well-choreographed performance, a version of Cirque du Soleil but with very heavy objects. The ballet troupe consisted of the crew running the press line being joined by the crew from the adjacent press line. Before the last fender had cleared the last press, the performers were already hurriedly bottoming the rams and unclamping the dies. The overhead crane operator dropped his hooks as the draw die operator turned to grab them. Some of the crew from the adjacent press line jumped on two waiting die trucks and drove them into position on presses 2 and 3. Twelve people in all, the performers pulled out the seven dies and slid in seven replacements in minutes. The dies were rehooked to rams, and the line was back running fenders in less than the advertised five minutes. The lines of demarcation in responsibility in the Japanese workforce were blurred. The idea in America that only die setters were qualified to change dies didn't apply in Japan.

On the way home, I tried to sort out the logic of what I had seen. The die-change performance was occurring four times a shift with or without an audience. The press lines were not more than a hundred yards from the body shop where four different vehicles were being welded together. At Truck Assembly, we were building one model of pickup truck and had to switch railcars every four hours because there wasn't room in the building for more than four hours' worth of sheet metal. The Japanese auto plant didn't have any more floor space than we did, and they needed to bank eight different front fenders in the space where we had stored two. In Japan there were no buffers of fenders sitting in railcars in a nearby rail yard. The press lines, the dies, and the die changes had to work flawlessly. The lines were running at more than 250 units per hour. Nowhere near the 700-per-hour goals of fender lines in GM, and their tooling and handling equipment was much less expensive. The Japanese chose to make stamping operations integral to the assembly plant and use very little automation. They had no ambitions to become the world's fastest producer of fenders. I also had a hunch that their third-shift workers were polishing and sharpening the dies in preparation for the next day's performance. Japan's choice to tune the flow of components to the rate of sales rather than run at the highest possible speed had all the makings of the race between the tortoise and the hare.

I came to the conclusion that the Japanese production system was all about a well-run household. I was sure there were demarcations for trade skills, but their workers all came together when needed. It was like the summer rearrange in Happy Valley when line workers joined the skilled-trade crews. Ingenuity in America was making operations more and more channeled, complex, and expensive. The Japanese, on the other hand, were devising better ways to minimize capital investment and increase the use of their total workforce. It was the kind of thinking that did not follow the paths of either management or the UAW in the United States—a place where equipment is placed on a pedestal to perform, and workers are subservient. In Japan, workers perform on a pedestal, and the equipment is subservient. The trip helped me to understand why my grandfathers had been looking down and shaking their heads.

I wished one of my grandfathers were still alive. I needed someone to listen and help me sharpen my assumptions and prepare arguments for what America was going to need to do to compete. We needed a huge cultural transition. I tried to imagine how similar what I had seen might be to what my grandfathers had created in the beginning. They had to have had great respect for apprenticed skills. I had marveled at how they could organize my uncles into well-disciplined teams. Everyone had had a good time at our family's version of barn raisings. There were always words of encouragements, peer recognition, and demonstrations of skill and ingenuity.

I couldn't fathom what my grandfathers might say about the differences in the rank and file between Japan and the United States. They had witnessed the introduction of the assembly line and had watched the ranks fill with the unapprenticed. They had seen what happens when a workforce no longer strives to better its skills and there is nothing worth passing down to the next generation. They had witnessed the division of the craftsman's culture into skilled and nonskilled. The transition must have been a management nightmare and tension must have boiled over many times. From what I have observed, it seems that the

Japanese have assembled some of the respect for all workers that my grandfathers had described. Could Japan be the new model of an unfettered, self-motivated, striving-to-improve-skills culture that once gave American industry a leg up in the auto business?

Recap 1941

The 1941 adjustments to objectives on the back of the Ford Motor Company envelope were conjured by an appointed leadership that gently took the reins from Henry. He died at age eighty-four in 1947—just as the postwar battle over sharing industrial wealth began in earnest. The creed of the newly formed family of CIO unions was to unite nonskilled and skilled workers into one voice and take the wealth of American industry away from its shareholders. For sixty years, the millions of workers in the AFL's trade unions had complemented the interests of business owners assuring them they were hiring the finest of skilled workers at a time when craftsmanship was the basis of competition.

Henry Ford walked away from the creed of AFL in 1903 with his decision to develop his own journeymen. It was the right decision for the times. He was attempting a takeover of an industry already being claimed by the carriage builders and their traditional tradesmen. A decade later Henry would make his reluctant assembly line decision because he saw no other avenues for increasing output. But "right" decisions became entrenched and problematic. The company's response to the aggressive posturing of the UAW in 1941 would prove to be another bad decision.

CHAPTER 5. 1950S AND 1960S: COUNTERING UAW AND NADA AMBITIONS

As 1941 was a time of making plans and rewriting the backs of envelopes, the early fifties was a time for confrontation. The coffers of the auto companies were full; war-time production had been lucrative. The union leadership was eager to drill holes in the bottoms of war chests. Residents in new suburbs were looking to fill their driveways with second and third vehicles. Frontline management positions were filling with college graduates pumped full of Peter Drucker's theory of professional management. It was as if the business schools were handing out mimeographed diplomas that read, "Ticket to Try Your Luck on the Front Lines of the Auto Industry. Who knows—you might become CEO by the time you're 30."

Henry Ford II led these decades. He focused on financial criteria as he struggled to fill his father's shoes. Every objective on the back of the Ford envelope was altered during these decades and toward the end a tenth was added.

> 1941—Unions: Develop countermeasures that will keep the ambitions of UAW leadership in check.

Details of the plans began to unfold:

> 1950s and 1960s—Unions: Negotiate labor agreements using threats of automation, outsourcing, and the shutting down of hometown operations to keep union demands in check. For the long term, begin cutting back on apprentice development.

The war years had given the UAW time to sort out priorities and elect a leadership that could unify the rank and file of all auto companies, both line workers and the tradesmen. These were people who had survived the Great Depression. Their strength was in their numbers. The war years had given shareholders time to sort out new objectives and hand the reins over to high-paid executives. The

executives were chosen for their aptitude in affairs that would keep union demands from hurting the shareholders. The executives knew that the key to the
executive washroom could be revoked at any time. The stage was set for a major
test of wills.

Few Americans realize that the fifties launched a model of collective bargaining that enabled both sides to win concessions, while leaving the future of the
industrial sector in peril. For executives, collective bargaining afforded opportunities to out-source and automate and to throw whole groups of union rabble-
rousers out in the street. For UAW leaders, the model provided opportunities
to win high wages, great benefits, and the favors necessary to get them reelected.
Missing in all of this was any real concernfor the future of industry in the United
States.

Executives began collecting proposals to automate and to out-source. They
symbolically placed the proposals in folders and stacked them strategically along
one side of the bargaining table. Reducing headcount and closing plant sites
were naïvely thought to be good counters to the proposals of aggressive union
leaders striving for a new social order. The fifties and sixties were the decades
of strikes and concessions, closings, and cutbacks. The number of journeyman
positions dwindled as budgets for apprentice programs were cut back. Whereas
the assembly craftsmen had been wiped out in thirty days by a single reluctant
decision in 1913, the journeymen were weeded out slowly as outside contractors
performed more and more of the support services.

In the sixties, union organizers from the International Society of Skilled
Trades (ISST) attempted to draw the journeymen across the auto industry away
from the UAW. My uncles talked positively about the ISST, contrasting it to
the UAW, which they were beginning to conclude was not acting in their best
interest. There was too much "trading away of the journeymen jobs." But the
ISST would never rise to prominence. The Big Three would remain married to
the UAW.

> 1941—*Organization Development: Replace up-from-the-ranks supervision with business-
> school-trained management; increase the size of design and development staffs in preparation
> for an increase in the number of model offerings.*

Was edited to read:

> 1950s and 1960s—*Organization Development: Continue filling front-line management with
> professionals; adopt statistical quality control procedures along the front lines; avoid Edward
> Deming's path toward greater reliance on the workforce; cut back on apprenticeships in
> anticipation of the shifts to automation and out-sourcing.*

The stanchions along the assembly lines promoted the separation of thinking
from working. The selection criteria for management along the front lines shifted
from up-from-the-ranks to business school grads just starting their careers. A
decision was made around 1960 to deploy another layer of middle management.

This one was staffed with statisticians and given the title of Quality Control (QC) Engineering. QC replaced the requirement of experience in sorting out acceptable quality levels. Overnight, quality control statistics became the caretaker of the quality of workmanship. QC served up decisions in black and white that would be easy for an in-experienced leadership to follow. Work Standards Departments were established to set goals for these young college grads inexperienced at judging a fair day's work. The individual performance of each frontline supervisor was monitored on a Daily Efficiency Report.

Before World War II, Edward Deming[1] had peddled his fourteen points to industry. They were peddled under the heading of "quality" but were really avenues to "continuous improvement." At the time, industrial leaders were trying to figure out how to counter a radical splinter group of the AFL (what would become the CIO) that was intent on organizing the entire workforce and not just the craftsmen. Deming's message pointed to the cultural importance of striving for continuous improvement and the need to empower the decision making from the bottom up. It did not sell in the midst of a union takeover.

When the war with Japan came to an end, General Douglas MacArthur invited Edward Deming to join his postwar recovery team in Japan. There Deming found an audience that would listen as he spoke of the importance of continuous improvement as a way of life throughout the workforce. Deming preached like the masters of a craft had done for centuries. Each generation of apprentices was expected to make contributions to the continuous improvement of the culture it was joining. Deming would lead Japan into an understanding of fundamentals, while American business leaders were busy trying to build a wall between recently acquired shareholder wealth and a CIO that was organizing the workforce into a mob.

The Japanese industrial complex evolved quickly during these decades, while America's supporting craftsmen were being summarily dismissed. Japan quickly became the world leader in cameras, consumer electronics, and a host of other industrial segments. The Japanese and German assault on America's automotive segment had begun.

During the fifties and sixties, outside contractors were increasingly called in to perform nonproduction support tasks in the U.S.: the building renovations, the cleaning services, the shipping rack repairs, and so forth. Support staff headcount dropped with an attendant loss of hands-on knowledge of how to keep the old equipment running and a loss of experience-based judgment when selecting replacement equipment. Compounding the issues were the short-term interests of young business school grads along the front lines who seemed intent on laying the groundwork for their next promotion. Managing one's personal career

---

1 Kenneth T. Delavigne and J. Daniel Robertson, *Deming's Profound Changes: When Will the Sleeping Giant Awaken?* (Upper Saddle River, N.J.: PTR Prentice Hall), 1995.

took precedence over managing the long-term careers of supporting staff members who kept things running. American was beginning to walk away from its competitive edge.

The preponderance of business school grads evolved to include all levels of management and eventually even the board rooms. In 1959 the final judgment in a federal antitrust suit against GM was handed down in Detroit. It called for the resignation of five representatives of the DuPont family from GM's Board of Directors. Pierre DuPont had used his wealth to bail General Motors out of its financial crisis in 1921. He unseated William Durant and placed Alfred Sloan in the role of chairman to guard his family's wealth. This 1959 antitrust ruling unseated the five representatives of the DuPont estate who were said to be bringing undue influence to bear on the selection of a paint supplier for GM. The five seats were refilled with financial officers. Decision making that focused on near-term quarterly earnings displaced the long-term decision making once debated by representatives of operations and finance, and coached by the DuPonts. Ford Motor Company made a similar shift to financial-criteria-based decision making under the leadership of Henry Ford II.

Pushing the DuPonts out of the board room at GM left a vacuum in the real ownership thinking at the highest levels. The DuPonts had weighed in on long-term decision making for forty-eight years. They had insisted on receiving input from both operations and financial officers as they came to consensus. Ostracizing operations from board rooms affected the long-term health of the company.

The court ruling left only financial officers in charge, and the participation of operations in strategic planning was summarily dismissed. Alfred Sloan is quoted in the media after the ruling: "The operating issues will be increasingly subordinated to financial criteria." And he was right. Robert Freeland, in his book *The Struggle for Control of the Modern Corporation*, concurs:

> On the operating side — the new structure disrupted divisional consent — division managers were unable to participate in strategic planning — the decision-making process was dominated by men with little or no operating experience, and just as Sloan had feared, operating issues were increasingly subordinated to financial criteria. — General office and divisions soon became openly critical of one another, — pervasive contestation and an inability to cooperate, — was the source of GM's long decline.[1]

The out-sourcing of the manufacturing and assembling of auto components began in earnest in the 1960s. Decisions to bolster near-term quarterly earnings led to decreased investments in onsite operations. These decisions served to increase investments in a supply base that could take over component production and in turn weaken the position of the UAW.

---

1 Robert Freeland, *The Struggle for Control of the Modern Corporation: Organizational Change at General Motors 1924–1970* (Cambridge and New York: Cambridge University Press, 2001), p. 271.

The antitrust ruling was handed down in an era somewhat defined by President Eisenhower's warning, "beware the mighty military–industrial complex."

> *1941—Equipment: Seek out new fields of automation that will reduce headcount. Reallocate the annual funding for upgrades to the traditional universal equipment. Use the reallocated capital on experiments in automation.*

Was edited to read:

> *1950s and 1960s—Equipment: Solicit proposals for automation to displace the universal equipment in production environments.*

The high cost of annual model changes during these two decades was kept to a minimum by the use of universal equipment and custom tooling. The equipment in body shops, paint shops, and component operations was rearranged and retooled for each new model rather than purchased new and installed by the contractor, as it would be in later decades. During the fifties and sixties, the maintenance crews would shift gears each summer and take on the responsibility for rearrangement and reconstruction and installation of any new equipment. Using the maintenance crews as temporary construction crews saved time and money. The crews were fortified with temporary assistance from line workers with skilled-trade aspirations. The Plant Layout Departments in the Big Three were striving to shorten the downtimes and keep the run-ahead inventories to a minimum.

The strategic moves of the Big Three during these decades included drastic annual model changes, which were difficult to emulate if you were not a competitor with deep pockets. Studebaker would close its doors and American Motors, Jeep, and International trucks would be weakened to point where they would fail in the following decade.

When I was a teenager, my uncles told stories of the new waves of automation arriving with each annual model change: how expensive it must be and how ill equipped the contractors were to install it. I sensed their excitement as they described the big segments arriving on railcars and how the contractors struggled to unload and move it into position. More than once they had to step in and rescue a rigging company that was falling behind. Some of their stories continued into the "hooking up" phase. Huge new panel boxes would be swung open for weeks, revealing the thousands of numbered wire terminals awaiting a numbered wire to be pulled into the box. The crews furnished by the machine tool builder would then struggle for weeks to connect the wires and test all the subsystems. Some of the automation was so large that more than one machine builder would be involved. When that happened, the arriving segments were totally untested. My uncles would grin as they recounted the last part. After what seemed to be an eternity, someone would declare that all was ready. That someone would ask everyone to step back and then push the start button. Their accounts of things flying through the air and things being crushed were hilarious.

Once the huge Rube Goldbergs had been cycled a few times, the outside crews would hurriedly pack up and leave. The journeymen would then have to take over and get the machines up to speed. Some would take months of around-the-clock effort, and some would never run at the advertised speed. The people in operations would say the machine builder was at fault; the machine builder would blame the workers and the poor quality of the components. As the decades progressed, the automated systems got bigger and less reliable. In the early nineties, the body shop in GM's new Hamtramck plant was never able to achieve the daily output promised by its supplier. In Janesville in the same time frame, the new SUV body shop was so complex with its mix of models that consumers had to cancel their orders and choose another manufacturer.

> *1941—Sourcing: Prepare to threaten the union with out-sourcing of component manufacturing wherever threats will be the most effective in dampening ambitions to increase wages and benefits. Develop a purchasing staff capable of controlling the supply base and blocking moves by the likes of Billy Durant and Louis Chevrolet.*

Was edited to read:

> *1950s and 1960s—Sourcing: Out-source component manufacturing at the direction of labor negotiating teams and follow up with strategies that will keep prices from rising.*

Whole stacks of out-sourcing proposals began to appear on Detroit's bargaining tables. Business school grads were hired into purchasing roles. There they orchestrated a supply base to support the divesture objectives. Plans called for them to set up three suppliers, to (1) keep prices in line through competition and (2) prevent a single competitor from cornering the market. But problems with strategic out-sourcing slowly emerged. Advancements in manufacturing capability began to dry up for lack of funding and lack of focus. Suppliers would soon be forced to dance like puppets for a share of the volume allocations, but their clients could not force them to spend their dwindling profits on nurturing continuous improvements. America began to fall behind in component innovation.

At the same time, America's auto industry was becoming an imposition on highways and rail systems. People didn't seem to realize they were stuck on freeways in truck traffic or sitting on rail sidings while freight trains went by because auto components were being shipped back and forth across the country.

> *1941—Product Design and Development: Increase number of offerings to keep up with expected post-Depression and war expansion and the expected changes in lifestyles.*

Was edited to read:

> *1950s and 1960s—Product Design and Development: Proliferate model offerings to meet the demand for second vehicles in suburban driveways and begin to proliferate the number of options offered on each model to increase the strategic value of a shift to build-to-order.*

Between 1950 and 1969 Americans saw a proliferation in models, nameplates, and options flowing out factories in the Midwest. Some models were offered with four different drive trains. The American automakers were on a path back to the days of the carriage makers and catalogs filled with choices in models and options. It was an era of rekindled consumer interest in ordering something unique—not having to settle for what was on a dealer's lot. It was possible for several years to sell a million of the same model and have no two of them be identical.

> *1941—Sales: Focus on selling wholesale and recovering the investments in cost of goods sold in less than ninety days.*

Was edited for the first time:

> *1950s and 1960s—Sales: Continue selling wholesale but accelerate the return on investment from ninety to sixty days; develop counter threats to an emerging national automobile dealers association.*

This sales objective had not changed since the auto industry began, though it had evolved from the original cash on delivery (COD) at the railhead when pursers on trains would collect a bicycle shop owner's money before authorizing the unloading of automobiles. The bicycle shops had evolved into dealerships owned by individuals who had purchased franchise agreements. The agreements forced owners to subscribe to many things that assured a certain image for the car company. Owning a dealership was lucrative, and the auto manufacturers exacted a heavy toll from those privileged to land a franchise agreement.

In the 1930s, when the auto companies were struggling to keep their factories open, they ran ads in local papers. The ads would typically notify communities of opportunities to save money if they hurried down to their local dealer. Henry Ford was famous for running local ads notifying the community that their local Ford dealer was going to be cutting his sales margin over the weekend from 14 to 12 percent. Henry Ford was known for stopping into a dealership unannounced and deriding any salesman caught with his feet up on a desk. He expected them to be out selling cars door to door.

When World War II was over, America's auto dealers banded together and pushed through legislation that would protect them from maneuvers of the auto producers. In 1953 the National Automobile Dealers Association (NADA) was formed. It hired lobbyists to push legislation through the state government houses. While the word *National* appears in the name, the NADA leadership chose to use their closer relationships with state governments to get legislation passed. It soon became illegal in many states for manufacturers to advertise prices on behalf of the local dealer or orchestrate tent sales to sell off excess inventory.

In most states the NADA lobbied for laws making it illegal for manufacturers to rent temporary showrooms and sell off their excess production at reduced prices. It is now referred to as dumping. Manufacturers can no longer sell directly to retail customers if the same model is also sold at dealerships in the same state.

Major shareholders viewed the unchecked ambitions of the new NADA as a threat much like the rising ambitions of the UAW. The assignments of auto executives expanded to include erecting threats to the NADA. The threat they assembled was a shift back to the days of selling carriages. The design and development staffs were instructed to create as many option offerings as possible on top of the proliferation of models. The option lists included a full palette of exterior and interior colors with some in two- and three-tone combinations, long lists of power-train variations, long lists of choices in trim and accessories, and variations in suspension including several choices in tires. Option prices were printed on lists, giving buyers the sense of choosing the design and price of their own custom car. This ramping up of made-to-order increased consumer ties to manufacturers and lessened consumer interest in buying what they could find on the dealer lots. In time it could have become an affront that took dealerships out of the new car sales business.

Dealers were instructed to promise delivery in three weeks if there were no published part shortages. Assembly plant systems were altered to respond to this expanded number of options. Assembly plant build schedules were tuned to give precedence to custom orders over orders to fill dealer lots. I remember ordering a Blazer through my local dealer, and it was delivered in four days; but it took another two days for the paperwork to catch up and for the dealer to install the wheel covers.

In 1908, Henry Ford began Model T production with bold refusals to placate carriage buyers seeking their first automobile. "Any color you want, so long as it is black," he would exclaim. His factory was designed with room for only so many cars while the paint was drying. Lacquer dried the quickest, allowing more Model Ts to be built each day. Lacquer came in colors but only the black could be counted on to be uniformly opaque. The fifties and sixties were a time of proving that the auto companies had overcome obstacles to offering what the carriage makers had once thrived upon—semi-custom and custom build-to-order.

There were other things that made the manufacturer's counter threats to the NADA very real. An automobile was no longer a novelty item. Buyers were no longer kicking tires. Buyers no longer needed lessons in how to lubricate before each trip or every week, or lessons in how to crank the engine, feather the choke, and retard the spark. Carriage buyers were once willing to pay ten months in advance to get what they wanted. Car buyers would only have to wait three weeks for delivery from the time they made a financial commitment. And they were beginning to remember how their grandparents would ponder and formulate the perfect design for their family's carriages.

The strategic push to increase customer interest in direct links to the factory sent a subtle message to the NADA. A return to carriage makers' factory-direct shipments was possible. The inventory on dealer lots began to move more slowly. The NADA had to curb its controlling ambitions.

The long lists of options and delivery in three weeks faded as the sixties came to an end. Some sort of agreement was reached behind closed doors, and the NADA thirst for new state legislation was appeased; the fire under the build-to-order system went out. The long lists of individual options were bundled in packages and offered at discounts. Dealers could then carry the most popular option packages on their lots. The assembly plants began to lessen the priority given to special orders placed by customers through their dealers. Also a new "dealer trade" network was activated. A car in inventory in any participating local dealer could be moved overnight to another, free of charge. The network increased the selections available at all dealer locations. Of course it was not exactly "free of charge"; the expense of a dealer trade network was woven into the price of all vehicles. The automotive business model went back to selling wholesale, and customers went back to buying from inventory.

Late in these same two decades, the steel industry's mini-mills were born. They would climb to prominence by pulling together a highly integrated manufacturing capability that could build to order quickly. The capability made it impossible for traditional steel producers and for foreign steel makers to hold onto customers. Within a decade, over 60 percent[1] of all steel sold in America was being shipped out of local mini-mills. The Big Three began a similar move and then backed off. They could have cornered dealer margins and shut out the imports before they established a beachhead.

> 1941—Growth: Focus on increasing market share. Spin up the scale race by adding an increased number of model offerings and making drastic annual model changes to drive out competitors that do not have deep pockets.

Was edited to read:

> 1950s and 1960s—Growth: Continue to narrow the competition and strive for increased market share with each exit of a competitor.

As auto sales climbed, the assembly of the highest-sales-volume models was shifted out of hometowns including Detroit, Flint, Lansing, and Pontiac. The assembly work was assigned to remote sites around the country. Assembly work filled some of the plants idled when war production ended and newly built ("green field") sites with an equally green workforce. The freight traffic on trains, trucks, and airplanes grew exponentially. Each assembly site had to be linked to the component plants by a cushion of four or more weeks of rolling inven-

---

1 Donald F. Barnett and Robert W. Crandall, *Up from the Ashes: The Rise of the Steel Minimill in the United States* (Washington, DC: Brookings Institution, 1986).

tory. Parts were shipped in returnable containers, often with returnable separators specific to each component design. So many containers in the network demanded vast increases in the number of railcars and truck trailers on sidings. In my grandfather's day, shipping sheet metal was as simple as a fork truck move within the perimeter fence—very similar to what I had seen in Japan. In America, spreading jobs around the country was taking precedence over logic, and it was increasing the cost of doing business.

> *1941—Manufacturing System: Discontinue staged assembly. Divide the work into segments and spread them along a moving assembly line with feeding tributaries.*

Was edited to read:

> *1950s and 1960s—Manufacturing System: Adapt assembly lines to accommodate the build of infinite combinations of options; modify assembly line scheduling systems to ensure an order placed by a customer through a dealer can be produced and shipped in five days or less. Shift high-volume assembly operations away from emerging union strongholds.*

Despite its being ill suited for the emerging needs of the proliferation of models and options, the 1913 assembly line decision was now too entrenched to be disbanded. The assembly lines across the country had to be shut down and modified every summer to handle design changes and new options.

Along with tuning for major model changes and many proffered options, the revised vehicle assembly objective called for setting up new assembly lines in remote locations away from the old hometowns that had fostered the craft skills of manufacturing. The body-shop and paint-shop equipment suppliers had to step up their ability to furnish something close to a turnkey system, that is, a system that could be shipped and installed by locals with minimal skills and then started with a simple turn of the key. Bargaining tables were stacked with executive threats to counter UAW ambitions. There were threats to cut back on volume allocations and close down the hometown operations. The threats served to counter UAW demands for higher and higher wages and more and more benefits.

In all fairness to those considering the moves out of hometowns, the demand for automobiles was rising quickly. Annual car and light truck production for the Big Three rose from 6.8 million to 9.7 million in these decades,[1] which was more than the hometown assembly lines could handle. The original automotive complexes had already expanded to touch the surrounding picket fences in all directions. Local cultures were disenchanted with the lack of intellectual demand of an assembly line. The UAW locals were spreading dissent. It is not hard to imagine executives making decisions that would steer the added business away from southern Michigan.

The most popular models were the natural choice for the first relocations to new assembly sites. High volumes of sales in these decades meant more than one

---

1 *Automotive News* (December 1950); *Automotive News Data Book* (1969).

plant could be dedicated to building a single model. The machine tool industry took this opportunity to propose more costly and more complicated automation. The higher cost of manufacturing systems was to be offset by higher volume capability through automation and a further reduction in the number of UAW-backed workers. Spreading assembly plants across the country would require more trucks on highways and more railcars in the system to carry automotive components. In short, the cost of doing business in America was going up, and the public was taxed to build unnecessary infrastructure.

Chevrolet's standard-sized model, the B Body, would reach a sales volume of 1.2 million in the late sixties and require the output of five assembly lines to keep up with sales. The sites were so nearly identical that it was difficult to remember which plant you were in once you passed through the front lobby. Auto companies were on a mission to find the one best method and implement it across all lines. Local innovation was frowned upon.

> *1941—Research and Development: Coordinate R&D efforts from the hub of the organization, the assembly area where all issues merge.*

Was edited for the first time:

> *1950s and 1960s—Research and Development: Shift away from the practice of directing R&D from a briefcase carried by a visiting master. Build attractive research parks where the masters in different fields will interface as if still on campus.*

For nearly half a century, Henry at the Ford Motor Company and Charles Kettering[1] at GM steered the research in small laboratories around the Midwest. They carried little more than checks in their briefcases and wisdom under their hats as they made their rounds. Priorities were set on technical advancements, and the individual labs were synchronized to arrive on common ground at appointed times. The number of fields and complexity of automotive research exploded during their tenure. In the forties, the batons were passed. The monitoring of all fields of research had become too extensive to be carried in a single briefcase, and the founders were too old to continue. By the end of the Korean War, a new objective was already in place—a central campus approach. Architects were called in to compete in the design of these new research centers, and American versions of the Taj Mahal were erected. Called Technical Centers, the sites were meant to attract leading intellectuals to a common campus. Amassing a critical number of the brightest minds became the next move toward technical leadership. Each campus was charged with assuring its sponsoring corporation was out in front. But with limited hands-on research capability on campus, and located far from the processing on the production floor, the Technical Centers were limited to researching issues like crash safety and fuel combustion. The mo-

---

1 Charles Kettering was the founder of Delco and headed research for General Motors for twenty-seven years, from 1920 to 1947.

guls in the Taj Mahals seemed to settle for monitoring employees' technical developments in other companies and jockeying to acquire the rights to their most promising developments before the cost of the stock went up. In theory the Taj Mahal at each of the Big Three were supposed to steer the world's vast research networks.

> *1950s and 1960s—Imports: Develop countermeasures to the threat of imports (a new item on the back of the envelope).*

After fifty years of auto making, a tenth item appeared on the back of the Ford envelope. The addition was triggered by American consumers who had begun choosing imports, at first from Europe. Perhaps out of nostalgia—perhaps postwar ethnic support, perhaps a soothing touch of the old country, or perhaps attracted by lower prices and more exciting styling. The most popular imports were the two-seat sporty versions that were competing in road races across Europe. Their total market share was less than a percentage point. Still GM and Ford countered with their own versions of two-seat sports cars—the Corvette launched in 1953 and the Thunderbird in 1955.

There was one import that did not fit the sports car image. The Volkswagen Beetle that appeared in 1953 served many purposes. For some Americans it was a statement of frugality. As a kid, I did yard work for a banker. He purchased a Beetle and mounted a large wind-up key on the back. The dairy products executive next door purchased one as well. Our family saw Beetle buyers as people who did not appreciate the beauty of styling and the feel of performance. We did not fathom that these Beetle buyers were refusing to compete with neighbors caught up in a trumped-up annual model change race meant to drive Studebaker, American Motors, International, and Jeep out of the market. In 1953 the Beetle would sell just twenty-three thousand. But annual sales quickly climbed to half a million and then surprisingly leveled off throughout the sixties.[1] GM countered the Beetle with the Corvair in 1959, which was also a rear-engine, rear-wheel-drive (RWD) design with an air-cooled engine.

Japan's foray into the American automotive market began in 1968 with the Corolla after a brief attempt to introduce the Toyota Crown in the late fifties. Japan's automotive lineup would flourish in the seventies when oil shortages spiked demand for cars even smaller than the first and second generations of small cars in America. (The Ford Falcon had been followed by the Pinto and the Chevrolet Nova by the Vega.)

Behind the scenes in these two decades there was something much bigger than a simple product competition—something that few in Washington like to discuss. Both Germany and Japan were receiving international support for their postwar recovery. In July 1944, at Bretton Woods, a conference center in New

---

1 *Automotive News* (December 1953); Automotive News Data Books (through the 1960s).

Hampshire, representatives from forty-four Allied nations had signed agreements to set up the International Bank for Reconstruction and Development (IBRD), the General Agreement on Tariffs and Trade (GATT), and the International Monetary Fund (IMF). The agreement included wording to the effect that exchange rates would be fixed at a level that would encourage American and European consumers to purchase industrial goods from Japan and Germany. The yen was frozen at 360 to the U.S. dollar for twenty-seven years and would taper off from there through the seventies and eighties. The yen–dollar exchange rate finally dropped the last hundred points in the early nineties and is currently hovering around 90.

When the Toyota Corolla entered the U.S. market in 1968, it was priced below the Ford Falcon and Chevy Nova. In the fifties and sixties, America was flooded first with cheap plastic goods from Japan, and soon semiconductors, computers, consumer electronics, cameras, and telecommunications equipment, among other manufactured goods, began to follow. The U.S. consumer appreciated the low prices, heedless of the number of jobs being lost in Middle America.

The economic tide turned on the Midwest and its industrial sector after World War II. Sixty years later America's financial sector is on the brink of collapse, due to reckless lending, and the jobs that rebuilt the economies of Japan and Germany are desperately needed in the States.

As the fifties and sixties came to a close, 86 percent[1] of all cars and light trucks built in America were built by the Big Three. The imports, American Motors, and International Corp., controlled the balance. America's Big Three were formidable but busy finishing off their costly scale race, which had already driven Studebaker, Kaiser Motors, and Packard out of business. At a time when America's auto producers should have been seriously preparing for the import threat, the Big Three threw a few dollars into the development of two seater models and were making plans to harvest the value of their winnings from the scale race. American cars started to look more and more alike as investments for new model developments were cut back.

LONG-TERM INEFFICIENCIES IN THE OBJECTIVES OF THE 1950s AND 1960s

The adjustments to all nine objectives and the adding of a tenth to address imports more than doubled the number of inefficiencies facing the Big Three in the 21st century.

28. Unions: With the rise in numbers of outspoken union loyalists came a rise in the numbers of workers holding back in quiet eddies. A silent majority emerged that never bothered to vote in union elections. The union

---

1 *Automotive News* (December 1969).

did not represent their interests beyond fighting for wages and benefits. Management was struggling to counter the union leaders and failed to engage this silent majority.

I was introduced to the silent majority five months after receiving an engineering degree. Yanked out of a research project, I was pushed onto the front lines in Happy Valley. The department where I was assigned was populated with second-generation union supporters and third-generation line workers. Blind faith in what a union could do for them had subsided. They equally distrusted the management and the union. It was a culture that governed its own work environment and had an uncanny ability to keep the ambitions of both management and the UAW in check. The definition of a fair day's work was somehow understood, and they were accustomed to policing themselves. They certainly knew all about rooky supervisors.

THE RADIATOR SUPPORT DEPARTMENT

Immediately after getting my diploma from General Motors Institute (GMI), I was sent off to the Corporate Tech Center in Warren to work on a research project. Five months into the eighteen-month assignment, I was instructed to return to Happy Valley. The director of the project was told: "Chevrolet Flint Manufacturing is terminating its participation in the Manufacturing Standard Data Development Project effective immediately. Thomas Crumm is to report to the Chevrolet Avenue entrance to Plant 2A at 6:30 a.m. on Monday, February 3, 1969." I couldn't fathom why this was happening and did my best to conceal my feelings. Respect for your benefactor and a stiff upper lip were important.

My reoccurring dream that weekend was of being tossed into a choppy sea a hundred miles from the nearest land. I never recognized who pushed me from the deck but could see people at the rail far above me discussing whether I knew how to swim and taking bets on whether I would survive the long haul to shore.

By Sunday afternoon I was resigned. I had to do this and do it well. The magnitude of my future livelihood would depend on the outcome. My deliberations settled into believing that there were some experienced observers watching, and I wasn't going to disappoint them. This would be my first rung on the climb up the management ladder.

A walk on Sunday afternoon brought more confidence. I had spent many years at GM in many roles. Perhaps production management would be a good job for me. After all, the front lines are the bread and butter of automotive business, and its tough-love culture had more to do with savvy than education. All three of my grandfathers had been successful in operations. They had all been well-respected men in their community. A summer spent building a house with Floyd had brought understanding of how to manage people. I was about to learn that Floyd had given me a very special gift.

As a GMI student, I had met some of the obnoxious members of production management. They would boast that "operations" is the foundation of the auto industry. They would proclaim that there are engineers who design, and agents who purchase, but it is the leadership in operations that takes the risks, spends the real money, and gets the product out the door each day. It is operations that can demand a redesign or the repurchase of anything. It is operations that sits in judgment of all new system proposals. There are people who arrange finances and product sales, but it is the operations people who get the product into the customers' hands. They were right. A production foreman in the auto industry is a small business owner by anyone's measure. It would take a very rich uncle to set you up in an equivalent role.

I hadn't wanted to believe the obnoxious fellows when I was their servant, yet I had to marvel at their power in meetings. When they talked, people listened, and the big decisions were made in a hurry. I remembered the plant layout meetings during rearrange when people without operations responsibility would fall silent. A serious disagreement would lead to a production manager's threat, "If you're so sure this will work, maybe we can arrange for you to come down and run it yourself." The threat would include a statement that a replacement for an engineer, a bean counter, or a purchasing agent could be found in an instant. The intimidation was usually enough to carry the day, and the meeting would end with operations carving another notch in the grip of its pistol, while observers peered through conference room glass. In a few instances, however, a non operations executive would step out in the street to counter the challenges. The ones who did would find themselves assigned to operations the next day or by the end of the month. When the old gun fighters flexed their trigger fingers, someone's career path was altered. The wiser members of groups other than operations survived by staying clear of doorways that led out onto the street.

On Monday, I drove the familiar twelve miles trying to muster good thoughts. In my five years of cooperative education, I had observed many production foreman styles. They all faced the same performance requirement but approached it very differently. Key to survival would be making decisions that assured the department met its production requirements day in and day out. Missing the quota for more than a day or two would mean I was out, especially if I drew a large-part, high-volume, component department. The smaller miscellaneous components meant less pressure. There would always be a sizable inventory of small components between you and the assembly line. The inventory gave you time to solve problems. Then I remembered that fifteen years of seniority were required to hold a job. It was 1969. The people I would supervise would be as old as my parents. They would already know more than a rooky engineer. A few of them would be old enough to have been around when the National Guard cleared out Plant 2A with fixed bayonets in 1937. I couldn't fathom how this test of my character was going to unfold.

To muster confidence, I told myself that this really couldn't be screwed up. The union was always at the ready to step in and protect the rights of the workforce from any unruly new supervisor. I was reminded of something my father once said about being a production foreman, "Don't worry about administering the work rules fairly. The union will help you if you get something wrong." He had smiled and added, "When an experienced workforce asks for a [union] committeeman, you can be sure it is you and not them who is out of line. Supervisors who fail are those who lose their heads in the midst of pressures to meet deadlines. Under pressure they tread on too many of the people they should be counting on."

I arrived a little before six. The close-in parking lots would not open for another hour when office workers arrived. I didn't belong in those lots anymore. I parked up on the ridge and started down into the valley. I told myself the damage to an engineering department caused by a bad supervisor could be costly for years to come. This might be just a step toward a career as an engineering supervisor.

I stood just inside the Plant 2A entrance looking out through the steel-mesh-embedded glass. This was the doorway the National Guard had passed through thirty-two years earlier in their assault on the deer rifles inside. Nervously, I checked my watch. More and more workers were flowing into the circle of light at the entrance. They had to pass through a narrow opening, filing one at a time, past the dark glass of the security booth. They flashed their badges from under heavy dark coats. After a minute or two, the scene through the window became a loop of film from a black and white movie—replaying over and over.

I had all but forgotten how this place resembled a naval shipyard. Everything painted a battleship gray. I remembered joking about how the navy's surplus gray paint must have been bought up by Chevrolet. I was about to learn that the managers of foremen here were very comfortable in this color scheme.

I looked into the faces of the people filing past me—they looked old. Most of them were hired before I was born. My apprehension returned. How could I possibly step in to lead these people? They knew I was some young hotshot being given a temporary pass into their day-to-day existence. These were people struggling to support their families and their laid-off relatives and friends. I was a college kid who had never stepped on the deck of anything painted gray. My apprehension increased.

Somehow I was going to have to figure out how a rookie engineer was going to fit into this military management scheme.

At 6:20, the screeching of drive belts began to call, first from one direction and then the next, as the huge press lines came to life. The collective sound of hundreds of electric motors and pumps escalated into a roar. When the time clock indexed to 6:30, the noise jumped another level as if a checkered flag had been dropped. The mechanisms painted gray behind the yellow guards began to cycle, but I could no longer distinguish one sound from the next. Six months at the Tech Center had erased my memory of the noise.

At 6:35, my greeter appeared and introduced himself. Cliff was in his late forties. Although I had never seen him before, I was quite sure he was a general foreman. His stature said experience, and his demeanor was one of control. I could tell by the look on his face that I was not someone he would have selected for the yoke he was bringing to my shoulders. My slim hope that he might be looking for advice from a young engineering graduate was clearly foolish. I was about to become a foreman, being an engineer was over.

Cliff began to shout to make himself heard, "You're going to run the Mid-Sized Radiator Support Department." *Great,* I thought, *a large part with a high daily requirement.* If I sneezed, there would be all sorts of attention focused on why I wasn't keeping up with the schedule. The Daily Efficiency Report would broadcast my errors into every office every morning. I guessed Cliff wasn't quite sure what level of experience he was talking to. After five years of success without admitting any lack of experience, I wasn't going to volunteer anything. Cliff gave me a once over when I didn't reply and probably put me in the category of "fodder for the cannons." I thought of challenging him with a question of my own, *Why was I being yanked out of my first engineering assignment?* but stopped short. Cliff had no interest in where I came from or what I had accomplished thus far in life. He had had no part in selecting me for this responsibility. He was just doing a job.

We took off at a brisk pace with him shouting explanations of my new responsibilities. There was a series of do's and don'ts, of which I might have caught half. In a moment when the noise level dropped, I picked up, "The guy you are replacing did not show up today." I would find out later this wasn't quite true. His departure had been some mutual combination of quitting and being let go.

Cliff's pace increased, as if he was hoping this new stray dog wouldn't follow him home. The trouble was, the closer we came to the press lines the more difficult it was to catch one word in five over the din.

I could feel the pressure building. The outcome of this day was going to remain a part of my career history. This was a required course, not an elective.

At 6:50 Cliff reached the A-Body Radiator Support Department near the back of the plant. It was not a layout I had ever studied or something I had ever stopped to consider as I raced around looking for fork truck drivers during a delay study. I knew Cliff was pointing out the boundaries of my responsibility, though I couldn't hear a word. I watched Cliff's lips and body language. What Cliff knew, and I didn't, was that the comfort of this initial hand holding was best kept to a minimum if I was going to capture any initial respect as the new foreman. I began to sense that people within line of sight in all directions were watching intently. Cliff knew that a simple routine handoff would be best, and he was putting on a show for them, not me.

The department was required to fill two railcars with A-Body radiator supports every day. No matter what happened, we had to ship the quota. There were tens of thousands of people downstream from here and hundreds of millions of dollars inextricably linked to this operation. The system that manufactured mid-sized cars would grind to a halt if I failed. There could be no acceptable excuses.

I began to think about escape. The leader of the research project had made it clear on Friday that this was a one-way ticket. Cliff was making it clear there were no alternatives waiting for me. The auto industry was in a recession, and most people my age were out of work.

Cliff pointed to seventeen people. No introductions. His lips simply read, "That one and that one and those people over there." He paused to emphasize something, and although I couldn't hear the words, his body language was saying, "If you're not vigilant, these seventeen will find great satisfaction in drawing a paycheck for doing nothing all day." He could have been introducing a county chain gang. He would not have done it any differently.

Within five minutes Cliff was gone. He had handed me responsibility for $4 million worth of capital equipment and tools, an annual operating budget of $4 million, and simply walked off. This was now my segment of Chevrolet. All I had to do was keep it running.

As Cliff reached the main aisle, he gave me a backward glance. Maybe he sensed I was contemplating taking off for a cup of coffee and never coming back. I watched as other foremen in white shirts approached him. They all performed the strange ritual of heads together, each with his lips at the other's ear. Some of the conversations seemed to elevate as Cliff acted out his instructions. He was clearly a force to be reckoned with.

I decided to do a little settling in to make it clear to my observers that I was planning to stay. The desk didn't prove to offer any secrets or comfort, a few forms and papers on top and an empty drawer and cabinet below. I must have looked like a substitute teacher trying to get a grip. One of the papers was a list of names. I took a guess these were the people watching me. A quick glance around told me that I had struck upon something that attracted attention.

I had always imagined that I would introduce myself to the people I would lead someday. But here, without concert amplifiers and speakers, there was no way anyone could be heard. I decided to go around and introduce myself anyway. I began at the lead-off operation and worked my way through the system. I found the system was so inextricably linked, that each introduction stopped the whole crew. It took only a moment for an operator to slide off a glove, shake hands, and say a word or two, but that was enough to cause a fifteen-minute loss of production. I was cordial to each, despite the deadpan faces and limp handshakes. A few shrugged off my extended hand.

As I walked back to the desk, I reminded myself of the obvious. These people are not engrossed in a chosen career. They have not signed up to work in this department or these stanchions. These people are not proud of what they do for living, and they have no say in the method or procedure they use. There is no reason for them to make a contribution that would improve their lot. They need a paycheck, and they are doing what it takes to get one. I wondered if attitudes were any different for people in orange jumpsuits making license plates. These people must see me as the latest wonder boy passing through, so busy with my own career path that I would not begin to grasp their plight. My taking time to shake hands may have been viewed as naïve and foolish. I hoped it told them I was approachable.

I pulled out the only pad of paper and jotted down the things my industrial engineering education would tell me about my surroundings. This was a system of equipment, tooling, containers, conveyors, and people—a system conjured by an industrial engineer, like myself. That engineer, whoever he was, had to have abided by the fundamental rules of balancing work across all stations. Somewhere here there would be a bottleneck that determined the pace of the overall system. This was not such a foreign land after all.

At 7:25, everything in the department came to a halt. My new charges walked off in all directions. My first thought was something had broken. I stood still and did my best to act nonchalant. I looked around hoping someone would come up to me and identify the problem. Then I realized that this was not the motor plant, which never stopped. These people were taking the allowed five-minute break. Then I remembered Cliff had pointed to the bottom edge of his watch and his mouth had formed the words "five minutes." I stood firm and continued my act, like a professional.

Cliff had tried to say something else when we passed by the last welder in the system. His lips seemed to say "record every—." It was 7:28 when it dawned on me to walk over and look at the counter on the last welder. I returned to the desk and wrote down 7:25 a.m. and the number 142. Without realizing it, I had made an important first move. I had acted out concern for their output each hour. For someone as green as I, Cliff had to have known it was a good first step. My crew was smart enough to know that Cliff would be back to see what I had written down. A list of hourly production counts sitting atop my desk would tell him if they were dawdling under the nose of the rookie.

As hoped, at 7:29:30 my seventeen charges began reappearing. At 7:30:00, the system began cycling again. My second hour had begun without event. With a huge sigh of relief that no one could possibly hear, I stood fast. Maybe my future in operations wasn't going to be so bad after all.

The second hour was again uneventful. The counter read 333, which meant 191 had been produced in the second hour. But fifteen minutes into the third hour, everything stopped. I caught the gaze of a half dozen of my new charges, and they all shrugged off my questioning hand motions. The rest were already nestling into their favorite resting place. In one brief instant of eye contact, a crewmember gave me the sign of a breaking pencil. The welder he attended was the third in the system. It spot-welded two headlight rings to the radiator support. I hurried down the aisle to the maintenance department and approached someone who looked like an electrician. I foolishly shouted, "The A-Body radiator support has broken down."

Slowly, without the least bit of pace, my choice of electrician pointed to the maintenance desk and said, "You have to fill out an AVO (Avoid Verbal Orders) and then put it in the slot, pointing to a matrix of labeled steel slots on the wall. The stick-on labels down the side described the trades, "Electrician, Pipefitter, Welder Repair, Tinsmith, and Other." Across the top were headings, "Request, Working, Waiting for Parts, and Complete." There were blank AVO forms on the desk which asked for the bay location and brass tag number of the machine. I had neither. I wrote down "Electrician," "A-Body Radiator Support Welder," and 8:45 a.m., signed and pushed it into the slot marked "Electrician/Request," and hurried back. I figured standing there and staring while a tradesman decided to pick up his tools would not be a good thing. My uncles wouldn't jump up for a rookie, and I knew these guys wouldn't either. I did notice that a red light went on when I pushed my AVO into the Electrician/Request slot. I hoped somebody somewhere was keeping track of this "one-if-by-land" system and would be concerned about how long it took for the light to go off. I headed back to see if I could ascertain what might be wrong and get the bay number and brass tag number on the machine for future reference. Totally unfamiliar, I could see nothing wrong with the welder.

It took five minutes for an electrician with an attitude to saunter up and say, "You need a welder repairman and probably a millwright. The transfer is jammed." He pointed to where the transfer mechanism was slightly askew and added, "Looks like it has been coming loose for quite a while."

To me, his comment meant that one of the operators could have seen or heard something that would have signaled that the mechanism was coming apart. Stopping before it broke would have made the fix easier for the welder repairman. His comment was telling. My employees apparently had a reputation for not giving advanced warnings. My run through the gauntlet of gaining respect with crew and maintenance had begun. I thanked the electrician for the tip and headed back to the maintenance crib. I made out another AVO, this time for a welder repairman, adding the bay number, brass tag number, and a comment, "a millwright will probably be needed." All the while my crew was settling in for a long rest. I hoped the word *probably* would indicate my respect for the welder repairman's judgment *and* allow me to suggest a way to save time. Production had been stopped for eighteen minutes when I returned and stood over the jammed transfer, trying to figure out the problem. Diagnosis is something I had done with my father. Prying the transfer mechanism back into place and resetting the welder was the essence of what had to be done. When maintenance arrived, my guess as to the steps they would take proved correct.

It took forty minutes to get things going again, and five minutes later everyone walked off. I inquired, and this time was given the tap of the wristwatch. It was 9:25 and time for their five-minute break. It seemed ridiculous after sitting for forty minutes and watching the maintenance crew sweat. I walked over to the counter. It read 373. The net output of the third hour was only forty.

My father had demonstrated many times when we were out with our family beagle, "The woods and the dog will tell you many things if you watch and listen carefully. So will a car or a machine." He had taken me on many "listening" journeys, often trying to surmise what was wrong with a car or appliance. If I was going to survive here, I would need to discern the abnormal sounds of my department and pick up the signals my crew was sending.

The remaining five hours were uneventful, and I turned in a count of 1,352. Cliff didn't look up as I laid my first signed production sheet in his inbox. I think he already knew what had happened. My sheet would end up in the key punch room that night and tomorrow morning would be a line item in the Daily Efficiency Report. It would publicize that I had not done well on my first day. I knew the extent of the readership and that my drop in efficiency would not go unnoticed.

Before I left the production office, I asked the clerk for the Plant 2A Routing Book and where the production reports were filed. The Routing Book revealed that the standard had been set in October, at 2,400 pieces per eight-hour shift or 300 per hour; my best hour had been 195. Checking the production reports all the way back to September, the department had never met the standard and was clearly locked into producing 1,600 per shift. My crew of seventeen had been standing at their posts for fifty-five out of sixty minutes each hour since they came back from the summer rearrange. This crew's only reward had been drawing a paycheck for the past five months.

Over the next three days, the count rose slowly from 1,352 to 1,450 and then 1,520. I was not making the 1,600 per day that my predecessors achieved. The Daily Efficiency Report would show my performance climbing but not acceptable.

On Friday, I ran out of radiator supports flowing from the press room. The monorail flowing past the lead-off operation was empty. I hurried upstream to find out what was happening. A hundred yards upstream the monorail rose up through the floor above. On the balcony I found an area filled with radiator supports standing on edge on the wood block floor. The empty monorail was flowing silently through the area and no one was around. As a freshman I had stacked and unstacked six-cylinder heads between transfer stations. This was a similar bank between the pressroom and my department—except there was no one around. I nosed about and flushed out a napping attendant. He jumped up and began filling every other hook. I watched him for a few moments. When he glanced at me, I frowned and moved my head back and forth slowly. I decided not to seek out his boss and complain. For now, this was between him and me.

That afternoon I wasn't getting enough containers from the shipping dock. Again I took the issue directly to the person involved. I had performed a work sampling study on these drivers a year earlier. I had already recognized the man delivering my empty racks from the rail dock, but I didn't know his name. I figured it was another test of my determination. When I found him off his truck and talking to one of his buddies, I again frowned and chose to not bring up his boss. I wanted to establish that as problems arose I knew who was responsible and where. Besides, it seemed to be entertaining to my employees. For them, it was a break from the monotony. I was also making it clear that I was determined to stay.

On the second Monday, I was standing at my desk when the plant manager suddenly appeared. He smiled but did not say a word. He placed his hand on my shoulder, shook my hand, and left. *What was that all about?* As I glanced around for an answer, I could see many eyes trained on him as he walked away. The white shirts were framed in reverent poses, as if the pope had paid Plant 2A a visit.

After lunch one of the welders jammed again, and I hurried into the crib to compose another creative AVO. To my amazement a welder repairman stood and asked, "What do you need?"

Taken aback I replied, "It's the bracket welder, on the left side this time. The lights on the control panel suggest the weld heads are not coming up."

He grabbed his tools and hurried out. I wrote the AVO and slid it into the Welder Repair/Working slot. I knew his boss would want to know what he was working on.

As I turned the corner heading back to my department, the welder repairman was already stepping back and giving a thumbs-up signal. The crew stepped in, and the line started up again before I reached them. I thanked the repairman profusely. He leaned in to shout in my ear. "The weld points are loading up. Tell your setup man to clean them off at the next break." One visit by the plant manager and things had turned a corner.

The 1968 A-Body radiator support assembly consisted of seven stamped steel components, all spot-welded together, and twelve projection-welded nuts. The nuts had to be positioned over a peg on an electrode with the projections facing up. Then the proper hole in the radiator support had to be positioned over the peg. The operator would then press and hold two palm buttons while the electrode came down to clamp the support on the nut and a surge of current would weld the nut in place. The nuts held headlights, horns, and other components in place when the car was being assembled along a line. Ten different press welders, each with successively more brackets and combinations of weld nuts, defined my department. The second hand on my watch indicated each of the ten was capable of making more than three hundred per hour, and I needed two hundred to keep up with my predecessor.

I also knew what it was like to stand in a station for fifty-five minutes out of every hour. I remembered how much I had preferred joining a pipe-line crew that strove to reach the standard each hour with the immediate reward of a longer break. It was a simple thing, but it made you part of a team and provided an opportunity to be in control of something. The question was how to get to the standard of three hundred per hour and give the crew a longer break.

The welders were stopping every ten to twenty cycles, and crew members were constantly tapping and wriggling the tracks to get the nuts to feed down to the weld tips. The setup man would often climb up and unjam the tracks when gravity failed to feed the nuts down from the overhead platform.

I turned in a count of 1,610 that Friday. As usual, Cliff didn't look up when my first respectable production sheet landed in his in box. Over the weekend I told myself that I was going to have to overcome the grip of thinking that it was impossible to meet the standard. On Monday I would begin my assault on finding an avenue to the gratification of meeting the standard for my crew. The weld nuts jamming in the tracks were definitely a problem. They may have caused just a minute of delay each time, but the minutes added up. If the tracks were worn out, I would order new ones. If the problem was with the nuts, then there were recourses for that as well.

I wanted to find out why the nuts were jamming in the tracks. Weld nuts were a high-use item. In my department alone, we were assembling twelve into each radiator support, which required a supply of 38,000 per day, 192,000 per week. There were roughly 7,000 in a box. If purchasing was following procedure, there should be a three-week supply on hand. There would be eighty boxes on hand somewhere just for my department. Standard procedure would also call for three or more suppliers to be involved. There was risk in all of this. If the only supplier of radiator supports shut down, then the four assembly plants pumping out 3,400 A-Body cars per day would have to shut down. On two occasions I had witnessed the escalation pressures that come when a component threatens to shut down an assembly line. Higher and higher levels of management begin to appear, and the master electricians begin to camp out in tents nearby. At some point in the escalation, heads would begin to roll. The foreman was usually the first to go. I would have to be careful about making changes to the system. Yet improving things was what I had been training to do my whole life. It was time to get to work.

I began climbing the oil-coated steel ladders to the overhead platforms every time the setup man did and a few times when he didn't. I watched as he struggled to keep the welders running as if I were an industrial engineer doing a delay study. The most prevalent problem was definitely the jamming of weld nuts in the feed tracks. It took less than a minute to get them unjammed and the operation going again once he was up on the platform. But there were eight platform ladders to climb. He was a busy fellow. Each jam left the entire crew standing in their stations. I collected the weld nuts he removed from the jammed tracks. I strung them on a wire, tagging them with the time and the supplier name printed on the box sitting on the platform.

The nuts were made from a narrow band of quarter-inch steel. The band passed through either a warm or a cold form progressive die that pierced and tapped the hole and then formed the weld projections. The nuts would have to be tumbled for a few hours to remove burrs. The tumblers were probably large, and one of them could keep up with the output of several presses, which meant poorly formed nuts would easily become mixed in with good ones. When a progressive die becomes worn, the burrs become larger and the weld projections shorter. The longer the nuts were left in the tumbler, the less height on the remaining burrs, but also the less the height there would be on the weld projections. If the manufacturers were not vigilant, nuts with burrs too high or weld projections too low would be distributed throughout their product line. My quality control experience told me that a good supplier should ship less than one bad nut in ten thousand. A bad supplier might ship one in one hundred. At a rate of one in one hundred, the setup man would spend his entire day climbing ladders.

The stringing of nuts on wires revealed that only one of the three suppliers was making poor quality. I prepared a Quality Control Problem Report similar to what I had done as a student. I slipped the report and my tagged samples of bad nuts into a manila envelope and took it up to the purchasing department when the shift was over. The purchasing agent I had worked with as a student promised to call the supplier and go over my findings.

I began my fourth Monday with instructions: I told the setup man not to stock the platforms with boxes from the bad supplier. He smiled, which told me he already knew it would lead to fewer trips up the slippery ladders. I asked my fork truck driver to round up all nuts from that supplier and take them back to the receiving dock. That week we still had breakdowns and stocking problems, but our daily count began to rise. We did not reach the standard rate of three hundred per hour, but I was confident that once my crew got a good whiff of a longer break, it would be just a matter of time before attitudes would come around.

Attempts to begin a conversation with peers or Cliff were to no avail. I couldn't blame them. They had their own day-to-day struggles and no time for conversation. Their employees were striving to work less, the maintenance crew was trying to get by with easy fix, purchasing was forcing them to use the cheaper supplier, and the shifting emphasis from upper management was unrelenting. The shifting was in the form of campaigns: higher quality, less scrap, lower maintenance cost, safety improvement, housekeeping, and reducing overtime, to name a few. Peace-time military leaders were dreaming up new challenges to keep them off balance every week. I couldn't really expect them to welcome a newcomer. I had not yet proven I could survive.

Daily counts climbed to 2,050, 2,090, 2,110, and 2,150. Our line on the Daily Efficiency Report was now 25 percent higher than my predecessor's. The crew reached 300 and got a longer break on several occasions. I looked to Cliff for signs that I might not be just fodder for the cannons. But he didn't say a word. I resigned myself to believing that his network was feeding back all that he wanted to know about me. On Friday, the count was 2,210. I filled out the Production Sheet and headed for the office. Cliff was sitting at his desk as usual and for the first time reached for my sheet as it landed in his box. He turned to the general foreman in the fish bowl next to his and shouted, "2,210 on the A-Body today. How'd you do on the B-Body?"

His peer grumbled, "2,205."

Cliff added, in a joking manner, "Thought you said the B-Body always ran more than the A?" His peer frowned, looked at his watch, got up, and walked out of the office.

Cliff grew serious and turned to me. "On Monday, you are to report back to wherever you came from." He quickly went back to his paperwork. That was it, the sum total of our conversations.

The 3:00 p.m. whistle blew as I walked out of Cliff's office. I knew my crew was already at the time clock a quarter mile away and hurriedly punching out. There would be no farewells. Maybe it didn't really matter to them. Cliff would bring them another rookie to study on Monday.

As I walked past the B-Body Radiator Support Department, I noticed two white shirts in the midst of the maze, cycling welders. It was Cliff's peer and the area foreman. The B-Body crew had already headed for home. While cleaning out my desk, I heard the B-Body finish the welder cycle six times, to bring their count to 2,211. They were making sure that the A-Body had never out-produced B-Body. The significance of what Cliff had said came to light. It was his way of passing out a compliment. My first stint on the front lines had turned out well.

Both the Tech Center and Cliff had been convincing in their roles of insinuating that the A-Body Radiator Support was where I was going to spend the rest of my days. If they had left any hints that my assignment was temporary, I would have probably acted differently. My employees would have sensed that I was thinking like a temporary foreman.

Why I was sent back to Chevrolet became apparent a few weeks later. There had been an argument over who was going to pay my salary and expenses during the research project, Chevrolet or GM. It is amazing how a bookkeeper's entry can be more important than the task or the people involved.

Now I understood why business school grads working in operations boasted about "operations"; it is the foundation of the auto industry. I could grasp their proclamations, "There are people who design and people who purchase, but it is the people in operations who take the risks and spend the money every day . . . It is the people in operations who create value." I now had to admit they had been right. Operations is where everything happens, and everything else is a supporting role. For twenty-eight days I had been in charge of more capital and a bigger budget than most new business owners, even the ones with very rich uncles. I had not only survived, but also produced more than the B-Body on my last day, though the records would keep that hidden. The thrill of taking the reins and making the minute-to-minute decisions is captivating. The work had also been humbling and a test of the fiber of my commitment. As thankless as it seemed, it would become an essential building block in my understanding of the course of the American auto industry.

There is a silent majority working in America's auto factories. They tolerate the shenanigans of the union radicals they choose not to vote for, and they do not snap-to when a manager in a white shirt passes. They have their own sense of a fair day's work for a fair day's pay and strive to achieve it in private circles of peer expectations. As radiator support output climbed from 1,600 to 2,200 in eight hours, there were no complaints. Their exchanging the frustration of momentary delays, while the nut tracks were unjammed, for the handling of more radiator supports was accepted. For Cliff and his peers, it was a private game. They too strove to accomplish in their circle of peer expectations. The needs of the company are always somewhere in the background. A silent majority runs America's factories day to day. It is too bad that their jobs are mindless. Back in the days of carriage craftsmen, my crew would have been expected to contribute their thoughts as well as their energy; they would take home the satisfaction of having done a good job each day.

29. Unions: Many of the out-sourcing decisions were made at a time when true cost was not as important as putting threats on Detroit's bargaining tables.

My fifth-year thesis topic was overturned during these decades by plans already afoot to out-source exhaust pipe and tailpipe production. An outside supplier had already been chosen and was being groomed by coaches from purchasing to assume the responsibility. The change in system of manufacture that I had proposed must have upset the justifications already presented and approved. The pipes were a hotbed topic of union loyalists. Moving the pipes to the outside was more about union abatement than the cost of pipes.

30. Organization Development: When the 1959 antitrust ruling dismissed the DuPonts from GM's Board Room, it allowed financial officers to take control of long-term decision making. Moving component manufacturing to the outside where wage rates were lower (on paper) became a short term avenue to increased quarterly earnings. How to compete using a common supply base became a concern for the new Board.

31. Organization Development: The value of a supporting community was erased when culturally led aspirations around Detroit shifted from recognition in craft to recognition of ability to rise through the ranks.

32. Organization Development: When the front-line managers with hands-on experience began to disappear in the fifties, the informative link between line workers and maintenance crews began to break down.

The old-line management had the ability to empower maintenance workers by passing along the recent experiences of the line crews. They made a hive mind function in ways that the new business schools were not teaching. The era of taking the time to fix something just once has been replaced with layers of bandages placed on high-priced equipment until the equipment builder's fly-in expert arrives.

33. Organization Development: The shift to quality control procedures during these decades wiped out a parenting culture—inspectors—that kept a workforce on its toes in mind and spirit.

Think of the value of the beat cop in New York; though it is hard to quantify on spreadsheets, it is very real. In industry the roving inspectors and line inspectors were important. Quality control employees making studies replaced them in the sixties. It will be difficult to rebuild beat-cop expertise without handed-down knowledge.

When I was a foreman in the Rocker Cover Department, the two inspectors at the end of the V-8 lines picked up covers four at a time and stacked them in shipping racks. They didn't have time to look at every feature on every cover; they didn't need to. Their role was much like that of a master craftsman guiding the moves of apprentices. They had a sixth sense that told them where to look when a sketchy night's rest or the poor attitude of a member of the crew might cause a problem. Inspectors served as a measure of the pulse and blood pressure of my entire crew. When I shifted workers around, or added employees from other departments, these inspectors could be counted on to watch carefully for missteps and to dress down a culprit not doing the job properly.

34. Organization Development: America has lost market share for many reasons; one of them is the slowing rate of continuous improvement.

Henry Ford's assembly journeymen dealt face to face with designers every day. Assessments of cost and feasibility were instinctual. More important were durability and functionality. Evolutions in vehicle design were happening quickly, which made the early Ford Motor Company a success.

35. Organization Development: Frederick Taylor's 1911 goal of taking the intellectual and skill contributions of craftsmen out of the workplace was expanded in the fifties and sixties to begin taking away control of the pace on all operations.

To counter union demands, threats of automating and reducing headcount were placed on the bargaining table. When workers walked out at the direction of their union leaders, waves of automation followed. America's factories began to fill with more elaborate and expensive automation than the world had ever seen. The new automation took over, setting the pace of operations much like the assembly line; that is, workers were there simply to serve the needs of the equipment. The boom years of the American machine tool industry began. The complexity of the automation demanded that dedicated engineering teams from the machine builders be on site during the startup. The design and pricing of the automated equipment and its justification lapsed into the hands of the machine tool industry. America was now on course toward ever larger and more expensive automation.

THE PRICE OF RUNNING THE FASTEST FENDER LINES IN THE WORLD

In 1973, I was assigned to lead a special project for Chevrolet. Starting as a team of six representatives on assignment from three of the six divisions, we set out to pull together a comparison of the staffing at the twenty-six Chevrolet manufacturing locations. There were more than thirty vehicle assembly plants using a "Green Book" to compare headcount from one assembly plant to the next. The Green Book defined every expected workstation in every assembly plant no matter what kind of vehicle or line speed. Our job was to do the same, but we were comparing a combination of five stamping plants, five engine plants, four transmission plants, four axle plants, three foundries, and five miscellaneous plants (e.g., two forging plants, two assembly plants, and one catch all operation). It seemed a little preposterous at first, but then it wasn't like we were being asked to compare apples and oranges.

Our first workforce comparison proved to be a good one. We chose the shipping dock function and easily defined variables, such as the number of railcars and trucks loaded and shipped each year. We asked for the number of workers assigned to each of six carefully defined shipping dock activities, for example, fork truck drivers assigned to the shipping department; shipping dock supervisors. We invented our own version of multivariable linear regression mathematics to handle our limited twenty-six data points. We used a teletype system tied into a mainframe via phone line. The task for the mainframe was to sort out the most important variables in determining headcount and to plot the graphs.

We found one location didn't fit into the regression analysis of the other twenty-five. It was a large-stamping location using 450 fork truck drivers to load large stampings into railcars and trucks. Our regression analysis justified just 250. The operating cost for an extra two hundred fork truck drivers and their trucks was staggering. We headed back to the plant to take a closer look at the operation. On our first walk through, we agreed to roughly count containers, railcars, and trucks, and to judge the work ethic and count the heads. We compared notes afterward coming to agreement that the fork truck drivers we encountered were all very busy. We also agreed that the number of entries in the shipping log matched the numbers they submitted. Everything seemed to be in order. It had to be something else to explain the anomaly. On our return pass, each of us chose his own route. I considered the bigger picture. The plant was proud of its reputation for making fenders, hoods, quarter panels, roofs, and so forth, faster than any location in the world. They were able to run some of the world's largest press/welder lines at speeds in excess of seven hundred cycles per hour. Several of the lines were so long they ended at the edge of the rail dock. I found one of the lines ended so close to the railcars that there wasn't room to move the dock plates out of the way when it was time for a railcar switch. Dock plates were the aluminum gangplanks that bridged the gap between the railcar and the dock. The plant lay-out solution they chose was to open the doors on the opposite sides of the railcars and load them from the back. This meant fork truck drivers had to drive around the end of the string of twenty railcars and load every shipping rack from the other side. I followed the parade of fork trucks around the end and down the backside discovering an unlit off-ramp halfway down leading outside. In the back lot I found more fork trucks driving across to an inflatable Quonset hut. Inside people were unloading stampings into wooden racks. Others were loading stampings from the wooden racks back into shipping contain-ers. The Quonset hut was being used to manage the difference in press line speed and the pace of the assembly lines. Some of the lines pro-ducing seven hundred per hour were feeding assembly lines building fewer than fifty vehicles per hour. There were not enough returnable shipping racks to store the level of inventory they were generating.

Checking further when we returned to the office, the corporate Rack Control Committee had repeatedly refused to purchase the number of racks they requested. Our attempt at a Green Book had just quantified one of the penalties of a myopic focus in manufacturing operations. Running the fastest stamping lines in the world did not take into ac-count the overall impact. Our findings raised questions; how much excessive equipment and excessive tooling and excessive automation had been purchased. The size of the checks being made out to Ameri-can machine tool industry companies had to have been staggering. Being the fastest stamping plant in the world came at a price.

We put together a presentation and arranged a meeting with the stamping plant's manager and his staff. Though my team members were eager to accompany me, I declined their offers, knowing the meeting would not go well and wanting to protect them from the witch hunts that might follow.

I used a projector to display charts and graphs; I explained how we had arrived at our conclusion: two hundred extra fork truck drivers. The plant manager sat mute as I rolled out the story. At first all eyes focused on the Shipping and Receiving Department superintendent. A man of slight build and a soft voice—I sensed that he took a lot of abuse for not keeping up with the outpouring of the lines and that he had been begging a long time for more headcount in his budget. My showing up and saying he had two hundred extra employees must have been nerve racking. Then I showed slides documenting differ-ences in fundamentals between their location and others. This quickly kindled the ire of the master mechanic, a burly University of Michigan grad. His challenges escalated to, "Who the hell are you to question what I do?" It was fair because our discoveries really were challenging his decision making. I was sure he truly believed he was doing good work as he spent money to make the lines go faster every year. The reality of the bigger picture was hard for him to accept. I finished, saying, "I came to you first to let you know what we've found. I am now required to present this material in a general manager's meeting on Monday."

My first meeting had been with two of the six general managers in Chevrolet, Fred and one of his peers. Fred was the one I had been told to report to. It had been little more than an explanation of a proposed plan of attack and suggestions in the first meeting. The second meeting was quite different. This time three general managers sat in a conference room in Flint and were already discussing something else when I arrived. The Stamping Division general manager had joined Fred and his peer. Somebody had told him what we had discovered in his division.

I used a projector and handouts. I presented our shipping area results with compassion for the plant's decision making and the challenges this plant must face to reverse its pursuit of being the fastest stamping plant in the world. The fix required could not happen overnight. Fred let the others do the questioning. He then placed his copy of our handout in his briefcase as he got up to leave. There was just a glint of a smile in his face as he shook my hand. The meeting was over in twenty minutes.

Before noon I received a call from the Warren Tech Center. It was the secretary to the manager of Chevrolet. I gulped as I ascertained who was calling. "A special staff meeting is being called for tomorrow at 8:00 a.m.," she said. "You will be the only one presenting. What type of equipment will you need?"

I stumbled with a reply, "A transparency projector."

She suggested I arrive at seven to make sure everything was set up. I thanked her and hung up. I had never met anyone who had presented something to the Division Manager of Chevrolet, much less made a presentation to him in his conference room.

As I walked into the lobby of the Chevrolet Headquarters that morning, it was clear that security was expecting me. They guided me toward the conference room. I verified the transparency projector was working and in focus and then left the room and waited outside, as the secretary instructed. At exactly eight, her phone rang. "You can go in now."

There must have been a secret entrance; there were now seven men in gray suits around the room with at least one empty chair between each of them. They were clearly not close friends. I knew Fred and three of the others. I assumed the Division Manager was the man sitting at the head of the table. On cue I presented my material carefully, trying to be factual and without judgment. All questions came from the head of the table in a friendly voice, and my few minutes grew into ninety.

It ended with a polite thank you from the Division Manager who continued, "Would you be willing to come to my monthly staff meetings?" For the benefit of his audience, he added, "You'll be first on the agenda. Just bring updates on whatever you're working on."

I replied with a simple yes, and the room fell silent. I gathered up the slides. What went on after I left, I can only imagine. The next day our phones were ringing. Three more engineers from the three formally nonparticipating divisions joined us in our hunt for data. Our pursuit of a version of the Green Book began in earnest. Blind faith in automation from the American machine tool industry was about to be challenged. The practice of reducing headcount in one corner only to have it multiply in another was being drawn into the spotlight. The study took two years and it revealed that investments in automation were not always serving the best interests of the company.

———————

Twenty-four more long-term problems were set in motion by the shifts in objectives in the 1950s and 1960s.

36. Organization Development: "If you give anything back, you might not get as much the next time": such statements in budget discussions indicated that America's business model and staff goals were not aligned.

37. Organization Development: The shifts toward automation began eliminating journeymen from the rank and file. The machine tool industry began taking over, wiping out the remaining pockets of supporting skills that had once built the world's finest carriages.

It is hard to explain just how important even the few remaining craftsmen were as they kept America's industrial base competitive.

FOLLOWING CLARENCE

September 28, 1964, while I was sophomore at GMI, an assignment letter instructed me to report to Plant 7, one of the smaller buildings in the center of the complex. Although I had never been inside, I knew it was home to the construction crews filled with tinsmiths, pipefitters, millwrights, welders, electricians, painter/glazers, laborers, and even a saw sharpener. It was also the home base for the maintenance superintendent. I had observed trains of steel toolboxes racing out of Plant 7 around 6:30 a.m. on several occasions. The toolboxes were towed by a stubby engine they called a mule. Each was marked with the badge number of its skilled-trade owner, and the boxes were being towed out to the next assignment. Tradesmen would amble out behind the trains and catch up with the fast-moving tool boxes long after they were on the jobsite. On bigger projects the toolboxes would remain at the site for days; the tradesmen would report directly to the job site and not to Plant 7.

In the Plant 7 office that morning I found myself spellbound by a character type that would later be named Radar in the movie *Mash*.

He was the clerk in the front office, the brain stem of Plant 7. He was more in tune with what was happening than anyone in the complex. He was bald on top with long hair on the sides, combed up and over. He had a pencil over his ear and another in his hand, and the speed with which he spoke was astounding. Production offices were chaotic at this time in the morning with shouting and running. The chaos in Plant 7 was confined to a single desk with six lines leading into a tan phone and another four into a black phone. If someone needed a construction crew, it went through this desk. As I listened, I realized that Radar was keeping a running mental account of all requests on the six blinking phone lines. He knew the status of every skilled-trade crew at all times and the remaining amount of budgeted funds for all projects. He would as likely scream yes as no into the tan phone. The black phone was for outgoing calls. He picked it up only when he had reached a decision about who should be headed where. Even as he talked, he was typing orders for construction materials.

When a lull came in the flurry, he locked his focal length on me for a second. "You're Tom Crumm," he said, not really asking but merely thinking out loud. He shifted his gaze to beyond the office window, "That guy over there in the green checkered shirt. That's Clarence. You'll be working with him." In an instant, he was back into his own reality.

Clarence was a wiry fellow, maybe fifty years old. I introduced myself and asked what we would be doing.

"Well," he replied, "we'll be doing whatever comes up." It was 6:40 a.m., and Plant 7 was settling into silence as everyone left. Clarence sensed I was eager to start earning my keep. "Relax," he said. "When they need us, they'll call." As we talked I learned that he had hired in just after World War II and that he had eleven children, nine of whom were still at home; two of his sons were my age.

When the black phone next to Clarence's elbow rang, he picked it up. I could see Radar looking right at us through the glass, and their conversations were in sync. Radar was our source for assignments, like everyone else in Plant 7.

Clarence hung up and grabbed a well-worn screwdriver and channel locks and jammed them in his back pocket. We headed out into the faint morning light, crossing the railroad tracks, and on toward Plant 6. Our objective was the number-one tailpipe line, the B-Body line. Quite a crowd had gathered, people in white shirts and journeymen in blue shirts, all standing around something in the middle of the forest of Pines Benders. It resembled a large octopus. It was actually a horizontal bender with mechanical arms added to load and unload the pipes. This new automated equipment was doing the job I had performed as a student. There were two guys at the center whom I had seen earlier leaving Plant 7. They had electrical diagrams and repair manuals spread out in all directions and all the electrical panels open. Clarence stepped around the crowd inconspicuously and peered into the octopus. He reached in with his channel locks, did something, and stepped back without making eye contact. Then he walked slowly around to the electricians from Plant 7 and leaned in to say something to one of them. I could read his lips, "Try it now." Clarence then motioned for me to follow, and we walked into the time office where he picked up the phone and dialed.

I guessed right. He was calling Radar to get the next assignment.

Through the time office window, I saw the journeymen close the panel boxes and undo their safety locks on the power disconnect. One of them shoved the control lever up, and the control lights came to life. The setup man stepped in and pushed a few reset buttons, and the automation returned to a ready position. The crowd of support people retreated, and the production crew stepped in. Pipes began to flow again. It was not yet seven o'clock, and already Clarence had saved the day.

We walked out and headed east toward Plant 10 and one of the gas tank lines. Again, Clarence waded around a sea of blueprints and manuals and reached in with his channel locks. We left again before anyone realized Clarence was even around. On the way back, the railroad signals at a crossing on Chevrolet property were incessantly flashing and clanging. There were no railcars in sight. Clarence stopped, opened the signal box, and reset a relay. "We need to turn in an order to have someone fix that when we get back."

I asked, "Aren't railroad people supposed to do that?"

Clarence smiled. "Not inside the gates. Our millwrights laid this track and built that bridge over the river. It all belongs to us."

I was getting the idea there was nothing Clarence couldn't magically heal. He was one of those people my family aspired to be. "Someone who could overhaul the combine at the far end of the field with spit and bailing wire."

In our days together, Clarence would always deliver thoughtful answers like a coach. On the other hand, he never seemed to have time for idle conversation with tradesmen, though they all knew who he was. When he appeared on a scene, the tradesmen would part without greeting him. Clarence never asked what they thought was wrong; he always knew. He made a special effort always to hand off the credit. He clearly wasn't there to harvest congratulatory remarks. We just kept walking. Radar kept us headed in new directions as we covered both the Motor and the Pressed Metal side of the complex and everything in between.

I once told Clarence about the only time I had ever heard my father grumble about my mother. It was when she had torn the washing machine limb from limb and expected him to put in back together. I then asked, "How do you always know what is wrong?"

Clarence said, "It's simple, really. I was around when all of these machines were put together." I believed him at first, which rekindled my faith in my father's unlimited genius. But as the weeks went on, my admiration for Clarence increased. In my sixth week I challenged him again to reveal his source of so much knowledge about so many things. "How do you always know where to look for a solution?"

He began with a variation on his previous answer. "I've fixed them before."

"I don't think so," I replied. "We've fixed too many things and never the same one twice."

"I was around when these machines were built," he repeated.

"Okay," I replied, "but that horizontal bender automation you fixed the first day wasn't built here."

Clarence was quiet and then tried again. "I know how to fix them because," he paused, "I've fixed other things that that machine design-er has put together in the past." I came to the conclusion that Clarence was able to think like the automation designers and intuit where there might be flaws in their designs. Clarence was a dedicated employee, and he was taking responsibility for the entire complex as if he were the owner.

The masters still in the auto industry in the sixties were the ones who knew the processing requirements of components and could keep all varieties of equipment running. They are gone now. So are the ones who knew how to develop ideas into producible prototypes that could be integrated into an existing product. They were people like Clarence who could keep the business of making automobiles going.

––––––

38. Equipment: Rising sales volume led to buying vehicle assembly and power-train capacity in increments and installing it in factories across the country. This practice led to costly underuse of equipment, factories, and personnel.

As the fifties began, the hometowns of all GM brands but Chevrolet were as-sembling all available models. When the wave of new smaller and cheaper mod-els hit, the hometown assembly lines were cobbled to accommodate them. When sales climbed above one thousand units a day, second assembly lines were built inside the old picket fences in Michigan cities including Lansing (Oldsmobile), Pontiac (Oakland/Pontiac), Flint (Buick), and Ford, Chrysler and Cadillac (De-troit). Assembling multiple models on multiple lines had the hometowns thriv-ing. But when sales rose even higher, vehicle assembly and power-train manufac-turing had to expand beyond the fences; the assembly and manufacturing was expanded into other communities and new green-field sites from Framingham, Massachusetts to Oakland, California and from Janesville Wisconsin to Arling-ton, Texas. The lack of experience in the new sites was solved with assignments of a single high-volume model at each location. The volume allocations followed optimal guidelines: vehicle assembly lines, 1,000 per day; engine plants, 1,600 per day; transmission plants, 2,000 per day. Over time, the sales of a model and a power train tapered off as new and better developments appeared. The result was increasingly poor utilization of capital investments, down time for factories, and layoffs. The old model of adapting a site to produce whatever was selling disappeared, and with it went steady employment that was a result of an adapting and adaptable workforce.

39. Equipment: The new automated production systems were "all on," or "all off." They were designed to run at the pace of the forecasted peak sales volume, and they required a worker to be at every station before they could be started.

As a newly introduced model outlives its flash of opportunity in the marketplace, the production schedules drop. Partial crews cannot run the automation. The result is a juggling of full crews that is never efficient and goes on for years. The fifties and sixties were decades when America filled its factories with inflexible automation in the spaces where the out-sourced work had once occupied the floor space. The result was plants filling with idle equipment that was rarely used. Focus on the cost of building cars had been overshadowed by the cost of adapting inflexible automation. The spreadsheets that justified the investments in automation used peak-volume forecasts that avoided the life cycle profile. The race was on to automate and get to either lights-off factories (factories without workers) or factories that could be operated in developing countries without the support of three generations of handed-down skills.

RUNNING AUTOMATION AT SLOW SPEEDS

My evening crew on the V-8 rocker cover welder began to hit the standard day after day in late February and early March. Even the foreman on the day shift was nearing the standard of sixteen thousand per shift. I could only imagine the pressure cooker he had faced in getting there after three years of running eleven thousand and telling his boss that sixteen thousand was impossible. But my next major lesson in operations was about to unfold.

During the third week of March, we began having problems getting enough shipping containers. The dock supervisor was sending his checking clerk to the rail yard on the west side of town. The clerk would take a pry bar and open railcars, searching with a flashlight for more 108-inch shipping racks. He would return with a list of car numbers, and the foreman would call the yard and have them switched into Plant 8. We were also down to our last few coils of steel. The real show stopper came when we ran out of orders. On Wednesday of that week Bob, the superintendent of Plant 8, called me into his office. As I walked in, he motioned for me to leave the door open. Leaving it open meant the conversation was going to be all business. It also meant he wanted the rumor mill to spread a message. He began with, "You're going to have to shut down the V-8 job next week."

"What am I going to do with my people?" I asked in shock.

He was cold and matter of fact in his reply, "Find them jobs or send them home."

I knew if I sent them home for a week, they would not get paid. They could not draw unemployment unless they had been out of work for more than five days. The reward I would hand them for working hard was going to be a cut in pay. I had to find them jobs. On the phone with the clerk's help, I managed to convince fifteen departments across the complex to accept one or two people for a week. I needed jobs for twenty-seven. Twelve were going to have to be laid off. Those laid off would be chosen based on seniority. They would be those least likely to have money set aside for such a layoff. The clerk handed me a list of employees based on seniority; apparently he had such a list at the ready for occasions like this. I jotted down the twelve lowest-seniority names and headed back to my desk, catching a group of people on their way to lunch. I told them I wanted to talk to everyone around my desk when they came back. Thinking back, it is amazing how I could count on the grapevine to disseminate a message inside a factory.

At 7:30 my crew of forty-four was gathered around my desk. With a long face I began, "I have to shut down the V-8 welders and presses next week." I explained the facts and withheld what had caused them. I was sure they already knew. I had not intended to put them out of work when I began this crusade to meet the standard. I felt Plant 8 was more competitive as a result of their efforts but doubted that fact mattered to them. "I have called around and found jobs for twenty-five people in other departments." I continued, "But twelve of you will have to stay home next week." I held my breath, expecting revolt.

To my surprise, from all directions I heard shouts of, "I'll stay home next week." And, "I could use a vacation." As it turned out, only thirteen were placed in other departments. No one stayed home who didn't want to. I handed notes to the thirteen, telling them where to report on Monday and making sure they knew where they were going. "Be careful," I said to each one, knowing that learning a new job carries a risk of injury, "We need you back here in a week."

The following Monday all returned. I was surprised at how glad I was to see them all back safely. Several of them came to me in the days that followed with variations of the same story. "Boss, could I do something different next time? Those people put me down in a pit shoveling sludge. The stuff ruined my clothes."

I answered with a promise, "I'll see what I can do." It now made sense why so many had opted to take a week off without pay. That's when the bigger lesson came to me. This automated system for making rocker covers was either "all on" or "all off." There was no way to efficiently run the automation at two-thirds speed. There was also no way to run it with fewer people. It would only run wide open with a person at each station. The path to continuous improvement was blocked.

---

40. Equipment: America began marching lockstep with the American machine tool industry toward a futuristic promise of an affordable "lights-off" factory.

The expanding volume of sales led to cloning factory systems in America. Four and even five assembly plants were being equipped to produce the same model. The American machine tool industry was prospering, building clones. Their pursuit of factories without workers was aligned with ambitions in Detroit's leadership.

The European and Japanese auto plants I reviewed did not lose sight of the importance of hanging on to their own processing knowledge. Their choices in automation were not steps toward lights-off factories. When the era of computerized numerically controlled (CNC) equipment came to fruition in the early eighties, the European and Japanese industrial sectors were able to return to craftsmanship in the production environment that CNC required.

41. Sourcing: The competitive advantage of a surprise in product design was lost when tooling build was out-sourced.

42. Sourcing: The competitive advantage of closely held secrets in processing was abandoned in the surge to out-source.

43. Sourcing: The out-sourcing of die making disconnected vehicle designers from tooling designers and tooling designers from tooling maintenance crews. The natural flow of advancements in American industrial capability feeding up from the front lines stopped.

44. Sourcing: Influenced by automation and out-sourcing, the overhead on the remaining components still built in-house climbed quickly. Any thoughts of calculating the potential value of a reversal and a return to in-sourcing never crossed my desk.

At times in the mid-sixties, industrial engineers were instructed to focus on finding and justifying automated systems. At first we looked for opportunities that would save enough in direct labor expense to recover the cost of the automation; then a savings accumulated over two years was deemed enough; then it became seven years of savings on certain components for power trains and chassis. In the sixties, the cost of doing business in America was becoming secondary to reducing headcount through automation.

45. Sourcing: Out-sourcing without reducing the proportional amount of supporting headcount drove burden rates up. Out-sourcing became a slippery slope. In-sourcing strategies and bringing down the cost of all auto components were key elements of Henry Ford's and William Durant's objectives. But current automotive leaders no longer shared that vision.

In the sixties, decision making was based on a system that spread overhead expenses across all components as a percentage of labor hours and it was dangerously inaccurate. The tail began wagging the dog as burden rates climbed. Even a slight variation in labor requirements between components in the same factory would unfairly allocate overhead and push the more labor-intensive components onto the out-sourcing auction blocks. Out-sourcing is a slippery slope that gets steeper with each transaction. Overhead expenses in manufacturing cannot be reduced at the same rate as the direct labor.

46. Sourcing: Countering union demands for wages and benefits with threats of automation caused burden rates to rise, which in turn helped drive component manufacturing out of operations.

Shareholders chose the adversarial role in dealing with unions and began paying the price for their decision. Union leaders kept demanding wage increases and benefits. Executives continued to carry through with threats of automation and out-sourcing. The manufacturing sites were filling with dedicated automated systems. The floor space vacated by out-sourcing was being refilled with automated equipment that remained idle most of the time. Employment dropped steadily, and burden rates rose. Both union leaders and executives were drilling holes in the bottom of the same boat.

47. Product Design and Development: Annual rearrange work became costly in the late sixties as outside contractors took over.

The era of the skilled gypsy riggers living in local motels had begun. The local maintenance crews were supplemented with fly-in experts during start-up and acceleration and for ongoing maintenance. Response time jumped from minutes to overnight from great distances. Downtime went up, and the cost of doing business in America went up.

The outside contractors also brought longer acceleration periods and smaller uptime percentages as systems grew in size, complexity, and cost. The true cost of automation and out-sourcing installation versus the retooling and rearrangement of universal equipment with local maintenance crews was too complex to evaluate. A strategic decision to counter all union influence was made and then unwaveringly carried out.

48. Product Design and Development: The decision to out-source tooling build would erase an internal balance. Prior to these decades, one side strove to keep the overbuild of tooling (the silver linings) in check, and the other side kept product and tooling designers evolving in their craft experience.

The in-house apprenticeships in die making taught judgment in requirements for durability using ongoing feedback from day-to-day operations. The building of tooling is much more complicated than what can be noted on blueprints or computer-aided design (CAD) screens. When tool build was still in-house, the journeymen coaching apprentices had experience with die maintenance as well

as die build. They balanced die build cost and maintenance cost based on evolving experience. Overbuild in tooling would waste money. Underbuild would lead
to high maintenance cost throughout the model year. Building tooling in-house
kept the knowledge evolving. Sadly, it was an avenue to competitive advantage
that could not be captured on a spreadsheet.

*49. Sales: The legislation pushed through state governments by the NADA
in the fifties all but stopped the direct interface between automobile
manufacturers and their customers.*

*50. Sales: The brief return to ordering options in the fifties and sixties was
a hint that auto buyers in America are being constrained. Entering into an
agreement with the NADA to continue to constrain consumer choice is a
risky position for a high-scale industry.*

*51. Growth: Losing market share (to imports) in North America was
negative growth. So was losing shares of the value added work, as component
manufacturing was out-sourced. Negative growth was also evidenced by
increasing capital expenditures for automation without more than offsetting
reductions in operating cost.*

For the carriage business, growth had come through building and maintaining a reputation for superior workmanship and reliability. Growth for the early
auto companies had been about riding a wave in an exploding market. Growth in
the thirties had been about market share and hanging on with a tighter grip than
the next guy as the economy collapsed. The fifties and sixties were again about a
wave of rapid growth, and the Big Three made decisions to grow only in assembly
and power-train capability. The balance of the automotive component making
was being out-sourced. Sales volume in cars and light trucks grew from 7.7 to
11.3 million. The imports portion of that growth was from near zero to 1.1 million.
Sales by other than the Big Three dropped from 0.8 to 0.5 million. The net effect
was a decline in market share for the Big Three from 89 to 86 percent.

*52. Manufacturing System: The cultural blight of the assembly line that
spread across the Midwest in the teens and twenties was spread across the
rest of the country in the fifties and sixties.*

Resigning yourself of checking your mind at the door in a manufacturing
plant, and knowing that how you make a living would never be a respected career, made it hard for parents to motivate scholastic achievement in their youth.
"Do your homework; you need a good education to get a job" was an especially
shallow admonition in assembly line communities.[1]

---

1 BH p. 10.

53. Manufacturing System: The decisions of the Big Three to move assembly and then component operations out of the hometowns of founders was a decision to walk away from the daily face-to-face interaction with the balance of the business. It was also a decision to walk away from the surrounding community which had nurtured replacement workers.

54. Manufacturing System: The assembly line demanded simple processing to minimize the number of disruptions that would affect the entire line. Keeping things simple handcuffed process development engineers and vehicle designers.

An assembly line is really many processes hooked together in series. A break in any link can shut down a billion-dollar capital investment, idle 1,700 workers, and render $700 million in product development expenses useless. Even momentary interruptions cause a crew of 1,700 to stand idle.

55. Manufacturing System: Equipment investments to install options along an assembly line must run at the pace of the line, not at the rate at which the option is sold.

The result is excessive investments in equipment for installing options.

56. Research and Development: In a world where applications for patents flow freely across borders and protections are limited to countries with legal systems, the law-abiding countries have been resigned to a severe disadvantage.

Henry Ford did not respect George Selden's 1895 patent on the "road engine." Henry was already working on his first prototype when Selden raced to the patent office. Henry drove his first prototype to the banking district the following spring. Henry and others had been working on variations on the horseless version of a carriage for quite some time. Selden filed his notes on mounting a motor and steering system on a carriage to displace the horse. Henry resented Selden's move. Some automakers did pay Selden for each car they made, but not Henry. He would fight Selden in the courts for eight years, finally winning the case in 1911.

57. Research and Development: Carriage makers succeeded by accumulating knowledge and skills in processing. Their success hinged on holding processing secrets close. Achieving a competitive advantage of this kind in the auto business requires a high level of integration; the new generation of automotive leaders was choosing to head in the other direction.

In-sourcing had been one of the earliest objectives on the back of Henry Ford's envelope. This shift to out-sourcing in the fifties and sixties narrowed competitive advantages, especially in leading-edge private-sector research and development.

58. Imports: After the war, the U.S. was producing 52% of global industrial output as the rest of the world's industrial base had been destroyed in the war. Eventually, as a semblance of normality returned, American companies had to face competition from imports.

The agreement at Bretton Woods to peg currency exchange rates encouraged American consumers to buy postwar Japanese, German, and Korean industrial products.[1] At the same time, American companies were lulled into thinking they were the only serious players.

59. Imports: Industry in America is no match for nations where government and industry cooperate.

The Japanese have following MacArthur's instructions since World War II ended. In his send-off, he gave them an explicit objective of cooperation between public and private sectors, one that was intent on achieving a trade surplus in industrial goods and a strong global economic position. China has since set out on a similar course and could well exceed the capability of all nations. Perhaps America needs to follow its own advice.

Recap 1950s and 1960s

As predicted, the postwar years were a time of boom. Annual U.S. auto and light truck sales climbed from 7.7 to 11.3 million in these decades. The objective of driving competitors out of business with a scale race took spending for new models to levels approaching Henry Ford's prolific beginning with models A through T. GM's Chevrolet Division led the way with the most models. Chevrolet had just offered the standard model with different levels of trim in 1950. But by 1969 Chevrolet was offering six and a half models: the standard Chevy, plus the Corvette, Corvair, Nova, Camaro, and the Chevelle with an offshoot called a Monte Carlo. The scale race meant increased spending for annual model changes. The extent to which models were changed each year spirited higher-income consumers into a game of keeping up with the neighbors. Keeping up served to fill the market with a steady supply of good used cars, and used car buyers had a full array to choose from.

The intent of the scale race was to drive competitors out of business, and it worked. Studebaker, Kaiser Motors, Packard, Hudson, and Willys would close their doors forever. Just 4 percent of the market remained in the weakened hands

---

1 Michael B. Lehmann, *Real World Economic Applications: The Wall Street Journal Workbook* (Burr Ridge, Ill.: Irwin, 1994); and *The Dow Jones-Irwin Guide to Using the Wall Street Journal* (Homewood, Ill.: Dow Jones-Irwin, 1990).

of American Motors, International, and Jeep. Perhaps it was the focus on weed-ing out the domestic competition that left the beaches undefended. Imports began arriving in these decades, pursuing their own back-of-the-envelope objec-tives. They proved quite capable of competing in the midst of America's scale race. Import market share climbed to 10 percent. I must clarify here that I have chosen to call all vehicles built in foreign countries, imports, even those built in foreign factories owned by the Big Three, because they do not make a significant contribution to the American economy. Opel is one example.[1]

The fifties and sixties were decades of adjustment in collective bargaining. Threats of reducing numbers of workers, replacing them with automation and out-sourcing were used to curb the enthusiasm of newly elected union lead-ers, but in many instances union representatives would call a bluff, prompting executives to back up their threats. Capital spending for automation climbed and the levels of in-sourcing that had once been so important slipped away. The UAW unified its electorate with a strike every few years, showing that its threats were also real. The payrolls of the auto companies shrank as the number of jobs decreased.

The NADA organizers gained power at a state-government level, and the Big Three countered by offering to fill individual customer orders. The customiza-tions were limited to choices of options, and customers were promised delivery in three weeks or less. The lists of options were so long that it became possible for the Big Three to build ten million vehicles and have no two of them be identi-cal. Putting customers directly in contact with the manufacturer caught on, and by 1969 was exceeding 10 percent of orders. The Big Three were on a path back to where the carriage builders had thrived for centuries in a personalized trans-portation competition. Behind closed doors the NADA began to back off on its demands.

New Technical Center campuses were erected to replace the founding direc-tors of research, including Henry at Ford and Kettering at GM, who had traveled the Midwest carrying briefcases filled with checks in exchange for inventions. New vehicle assembly systems took over vacant war production plants and filled new green-field sites across the country.

---

1 Automotive News (1950–1969).

CHAPTER 6. 1970s AND 1980s: FINANCIAL-CRITERIA-BASED DECISIONS STRIP-MINE THE INDUSTRIAL SECTOR

The seventies and eighties would test the long-term planning capability of a new generation of financial-criteria-based decision makers. Two drumrolls were played by the OPEC nations, and each one attracted another flood of imports.

The National Automobile Dealers Association (NADA) was well organized, and the number of suppliers of automotive components was climbing. The NADA and suppliers were attacking from opposite ends of a narrow canyon. The war chests had been emptied, and billboards were flashing phrases like "rust belt" and variations on "blue collar lazy." The Big Three were struggling. It was time to rethink the back of the envelope.

> *1950s and 1960s—Product Design and Development: Proliferate model offerings to meet the demand for second vehicles in suburban driveways, and begin to proliferate the number of options offered on each model to increase the strategic value of a shift to build-to-order.*

Was totally reversed:

> *1970s and 1980s—Product Design and Development: Collapse the number of option offerings; all but eliminate the annual model change; shift the fundamental design of passenger cars from rear- to front-wheel drive; replace the traditional body-on-frame structure with body-frame-integral structures; expand the platforming concept.*

Alfred Sloan's 1959 prediction of problems with "financial criteria" as the basis for decision making began to unfold. This new objective for product design and development was a harvesting of brand image and product reputation—things that had taken sixty years to construct. It was a textbook decision—a variation of the "sausage game" played for the highest stakes imaginable. It was a move without an exit strategy.

In the sausage game, business school students are required to develop a business plan for quick entry into retail-food chains with a high-quality line of sausage. At first they strive to establish an upscale brand image, by choosing the finest of ingredients: prime cuts of meat and fresh spices. The game's objective then shifts to increasing profitability. Students with a good grasp of "financial criteria" must shift into ruthless decision making. The game steers them into substituting lesser ingredients and stepping up the advertising to improve the bottom line. Winning the game is all about judging when to sell off the company. The students who get the best grades are those who can recognize when sausage sales volume is peaking, when the profits still look good to a prospective buyer of the company, and when the sausage customers are still not sure whether their favorite sausage has been cheapened with a filler. What the game doesn't teach is the importance of getting out of the food industry altogether once the deal is done—before the buyer, the workforce, and a collective of hostile consumers have realized they have been duped.

The equivalent of the sausage game in the auto business is called platforming. Platforming began in earnest at GM soon after the 1959 antitrust ruling pushed the DuPonts out of the Board Room. In 1961 GM would launch the Pontiac Tempest, Oldsmobile F-85, and Buick Special. The unibody under the paint, the carpet, and the trim on all three were identical. Platforming allowed the body shops, paint shops, and equipment to be of common design for all three models, which added to profitability. The sausage game's prediction of higher profits was correct. What distinguished a brand had become little more than a hood ornament and the engine under the hood. This Y-platform was sold for three years, and more platforming followed with longer life spans between design changes. Less and less knowledge in body design and development was handed down, and the knowledge that was passed down shifted into the hands of the machine tool industry. It was a kind of out-sourcing that Henry Ford and William Durant would never have allowed.

Over time, this saving money on product design and development would test the loyalties of many faithful American buyers. As in the sausage game, advertising and salesmanship were seen as the trusted paths to maintaining buyer loyalty. The financial-criteria-based leadership of the Big Three pumped money into balloons and banners and circulated them to showrooms around the country. Brand loyalty was strong in America, and, as the business school lessons promised, only a few customers defected to imports. At first, consumers simply refused to believe that the well-designed and reliable brand their family had chosen for decades would ever stoop to adding filler. I remember heated debates in Florida driveways. The retired new car owners in my grandfather's neighborhood refused to believe that the new Buick LeSabre in one driveway was even the same size as the new Oldsmobile Delta 88 next door or the Pontiac Bonneville down the street. I explained how they were assembled from common bins of components as they passed down a common assembly line. It was beyond their comprehension. Platforms in these decades were on six- to eight-year replacement programs and that was sometimes stretched to ten or twelve during a recession. This avoided expenses for rearrange, design, development, and tooling. Gains on the bottom line assured shareholders that, while market share was dropping and burden rates climbing, capital expenditures were down and profits were still good.

The stage was set for the influx of Asian imports in America in the late sixties. The initial Asian growth objective was to attract used-car buyers away from the Big Three. Prices on imports were set to match a two- to three-year-old used car. Asian imports were advertised as an opportunity to purchase new with a two-year warranty at a used-car price. They established a beachhead in America; their strategies included careful introductions of dealerships and well-developed systems for getting cars to loading docks in Japan, aboard ships, unto unloading docks, and aboard rail transport systems that would carry them into the States from Vancouver and other west coast ports. At first, the Asian product design and development objective was to adapt designs already selling in Asia to meet the evolving safety and emissions regulations in America. The beachhead proved to be a well-timed move when the 1973 oil shock drove American consumers out in search of fuel-efficient vehicles. Careful planning and patience had paid off.

When the second hiccup in oil supplies appeared in 1979, America's Big Three were already on record as having done poorly in their attempts to design and develop small fuel-efficient automobiles. The Ford Falcon and Pinto had not fared well, and the Fiesta was an import. Chevrolet had followed the Nova with the Vega and then the Chevette. Chrysler chose to import the Omni and Horizon as small-car offerings and avoid the development expense. The Asian designers spent the six years between oil shocks working on upscale versions of their original entrants without changing the model names. The second wave of fuel-efficient vehicles from Asia could not have been better timed. Caught once again without an alternative to offer, the Big Three leaned on their foreign operations and imported small cars designed for other lifestyles and very different streets. The Asian designers were one design generation ahead of the Big Three. Sales of imports in 1979 climbed to 2.3 million and 17 percent market share. The German portion remained stable at 0.3 million, while the Japanese imports climbed to 1.6 million.

Platforming caused a condensing and shuffling of engineering teams at a time when frames were being eliminated and new structural requirements had to be engineered into a sheet metal body. The rush to downsize automotive models in the midst of the first oil shock did not go well for the Big Three. The small imports that overtook the market in 1973 may not have been designed for American consumers, but they were well developed. They were designs that had been on the road for years. To top it off, the quick-response skills of the (annual) model-change crews were gone by 1973—wiped out by platforming.

When the second oil shock hit and the Big Three were still not prepared, many American auto buyers turned to what the Asian vehicle designers and developments had put together to meet the needs of American lifestyles. Concerns over lingering currency exchange advantages set by the Bretton Woods Agreement never made it into the media.

America's Big Three responded to the second oil shock with a major shift. For a decade importers had been selling cars without a rigid frame and with small front-wheel-drive power trains. America's Big Three followed suit. Instead of relying on a rigid two-dimensional steel frame to cradle the body and manage the torque of huge engines, designers set out to provide structural support in a three-dimensional body and a stub frame. At great expense, America's Big Three kept their platforming objective and transitioned from body-on-frame (BOF) and rear-wheel drive (RWD) to body-frame-integral (BFI) structures and front-wheel-drive (FWD) power trains. The new approach would be lighter and more fuel efficient. GM started in 1983 with five models made from a single platform: the Citation, Phoenix, Skylark, Omega, and Cimarron. It had been a while since vehicle redesign had required a simultaneous redesign and launch of both a new engine and transmission. It was a shift that increased the complexity of the body design and body-shop automation. Power-train factories had to launch a new transverse-mounted engine and transmission. The transmission had to incorporate the differential.

The mid-sized platform was next in 1985 with the Chevy Monte Carlo, Pontiac Grand Prix, Oldsmobile Supreme, and Buick Skylark. It was a time when all cars looked like jellybeans, but with different hood ornaments. A shift to a different platform was simply a shift to another size of jellybean. The auto shows employed illusionists with "smoke and mirrors" to highlight the variations in the amount of silver in the paint. The Federal Corporate Average Fuel Economy (CAFÉ) standards were unfurled in 1984, a decade after the oil shocks had begun. The Big Three were finally ready to comply.

> *1950s and 1960s—Sales: Continue selling wholesale but accelerate the return on investment from ninety to sixty days; develop counter threats to an emerging national automobile dealers association.*

Was reversed:

> *1970s and 1980s—Sales: Stop the development of counter threats to the NADA; lead customers away from interest in annual model change, custom orders, and choice of options. Get customers back to buying from inventory.*

In the early fifties the decision to counter the ambitions of the NADA with offers to fill orders for any combination of options was given top priority in assembly plant build schedules. Customers gravitated to this semi-custom idea and signed on to wait three weeks for delivery. Semi-custom orders would exceed 11 percent of sales for Blazer, Suburban, and pickup truck models at Flint Truck Assembly in 1971. Countering the NADA with build-to-order was one of the last strategic decisions to receive Alfred Sloan's support. He died in 1967. Behind-the-scenes agreements with the NADA in the late sixties led to a dampening of customer enthusiasm for direct orders. Delays in delivery and lack of dealer interest were enough to shift the emphasis back to buying off the lot.

My grandfather ordered his thirty-ninth new Buick in 1971, and its delivery was three months late. In the back room of a dealership in Florida, I demanded to see the order schedule and found Floyd's order near the bottom of the list. It had been given a priority code that would make it one of the last to be built at year-end. The dealership was having trouble getting enough of the models that local customers wanted, and it happened to be the same model that Floyd had ordered. The dealer knew Floyd's sale was in the bag, and there would be a greater profit in selling from inventory than delivering an executive-discount vehicle. A simple phone call shifted Floyd's order to another dealership and to the top of the list. When I returned to Detroit, I talked at length with the leadership of dealer relations. Floyd had worked for Buick for forty-seven years and was still purchasing a new Buick every year though he had lost his license several years earlier. Taking care of loyal employees was another thing that the financial-criteria-based decision makers were choosing to overlook.

In the seventies an extended warranty strategy was introduced to counter the higher quality of imports from Japan. Twelve months or twelve thousand miles was increased to two years or twenty-four thousand miles. As the warranty offers were extended, efforts were made to improve the feedback from a warranty reporting system. Perhaps it was an idea out of a business school textbook. Dealer service centers were to be compensated based on the invoices they entered into the computerized reporting system. In Detroit a new central warranty group began tallying the input from all dealers and attempted to debit the responsible manufacturing group. The tributaries feeding components to the assembly plants were long and complicated, and warranty subgroups at each manufacturing location began challenging the central financial group. Staffs from all manufacturing locations held hashing sessions to carve and recarve the warranty responsibility. Business school grads went toe to toe each month to hammer out compromises in allocations.

The warranty invoice system increased white-collar headcount but did very little to improve quality. It may have worked in the textbook but not in the real world. Human motivations were misaligned. The mechanics at dealer service centers could not be counted on to report the correct manufacturing diagnosis. They recognized the pieces that were broken, but they did not understand processing well enough to define what caused the problem in processing terms. Only the people on the front lines understood the manufacturing side and whether the material, the component tooling, the subassembly tooling, or some other factor was causing the problem. There were also pressures on the service managers at dealerships to try to find a few more dollars in warranty income to keep the dealership afloat.

To top it off, accurate warranty feedback didn't really matter. For the automotive consumer, the threat of walking home was more significant than the savings in having the repairs paid for under warranty. For manufacturing sites, the struggle to meet build schedules was more important than the slight declines in income levels as debits accrued from warranty charges. The links between the customer and the assembly craftsmen were just too long for any message to make the trip. Improving quality in American autos by using a warranty feedback system simply employed more levels of white-collar jobs. The cost of building automobiles in America was going up.

The real links between customer and component maker disappeared in 1913. Henry Ford's assembly craftsmen in 1912 and prior years had been intimately involved with the assembly of each vehicle and had a grasp of the overall picture. Their networks of runners linked them back to the fully integrated component builders in the same building. Quick diagnosis and alterations had been a matter of pride in these internal networks. Processing was evolving in lock step with product design and with customer feedback to these assembly craftsmen. They could make adjustments quickly that assured the problems would go away. By the 1970s the design staffs were so far removed from daily experience that improvements in design didn't make the trip from customers any more than did the improvements back through the processing networks. The business school game titled "warranty feedback system" with all its little nicks to budgets did not get the job done. Progress on quality improvement was slow for American manufacturers while Japanese manufacturers were advancing a reputation for high quality. They capitalized on Edward Deming's teachings. From 1970 to 1989 the combined market share of the Big Three would drop from 86 to 76 percent.[1] Edward Deming had been right about the importance of continuous improvement in manufacturing; so had Henry Ford in the beginning. Continual tuning along the front lines gave the Japanese an edge.

1950s and 1960s—Imports: Develop countermeasures to the threat of imports.

Was rewritten:

1970s and 1980s—Imports: Develop fuel-efficient and low-priced countermeasures to the

---

1 Automotive News (1970–1989).

threat of imports. Prepare to counter the exchange rate advantages of imports as they move up into higher-priced vehicles. Improve the perception of quality in American vehicles.

Foreign vehicle designs that had been selling for years in Asia and Europe began selling in America when the oil shock awakened consumers. Initially the imports were small, designed to carry a few passengers short distances over narrow roads. They were designed for countries that taxed heavily based on fuel consumption and used engine displacement as a measure of fuel consumption. They were ideal for calming the panic of an American fuel crisis. The seventies still saw lingering effects of the Bretton Woods Agreement. The dollar–yen exchange rate was still around three hundred to one as President Nixon took the U.S. dollar off the gold standard. The exchange advantage let a Toyota Tercel compete with a used Chevrolet, when it should have been priced comparable to a Cadillac. Twenty-five years after the war, the U.S. State Department was still silently swapping pieces of the American industrial sector for world peace.

Imports upset resale values. Consumers that had been programmed to fashionably update the family car each year and counted on high *Blue Book* values to make their annual exchange of vehicles affordable suffered a rude awakening. They were accustomed to passing their used car down through a series of buyers with smaller and smaller budgets. But the market for two-year-old cars began to disappear. America's used-car buyers were looking at the new low-priced imports that came with a new-car warranty. Imports upset the back of the envelope for the Big Three.

The seventies turned the threat of imports into reality for America's Big Three. Many smaller industries had already engaged Asian manufacturers in head-to-head competition and lost. Foreign companies were fast and flexible, while design and development had stagnated in the U.S. with products that were losing their appeal.

In 1977 the import threat reached the heartland of the television manufacturing industry. Rumblings over lost jobs and failing communities grew loud enough to reach the White House, and President Carter stepped in to negotiate Orderly Market Agreements (OMA) regarding the import of televisions to America. Japan complied with President Carter's request and avoided the risk of incurring further protectionist measures by the United States. Import limits on televisions were set to match 1976 import levels of 41 percent. At this point it began to become clear that artificial trade barriers are no match for well-designed products, a serious manufacturing culture, and a positive government–industry relationship.

The OMA on television sets meant Japan's television manufacturers had to try a different tack. Flush with cash, they shifted their strategy. Without fanfare, in the next three years the Japanese television companies would buy out America's struggling television companies at their newly devalued prices. The new wave of business school management in America was trained in the art of merger, acquisition, and in this case divestiture and was focused on immediate income. They welcomed the Japanese buyers. Who could blame them—they had no experience with grabbing and pulling up on one's bootstraps. Faced with rebuilding something they knew little about, they chose instead to convince shareholders to sell out while they still had a buyer on the line. By 1980 four out of five television sets sold in the States were assembled in foreign-owned subsidiaries on U.S. soil. The acquisitions included Matsushita's purchase of Motorola Quasar and Whirlpool's sale of Warwick to Sanyo. Zenith acquired the Heath Company and evolved into the home computer business. Zenith would eventually be acquired by LG Corporation in Korea. America's television manufacturers were strategically acquired under the radar of the OMAs. Their U.S. sites and skilled workforces were put to work assembling increasing numbers of components imported from Asia that also passed under the radar of the OMAs. The subsequent screams of objection in America's electronic components industries were not heard. They had already been to Washington once on this issue. On Wall Street the acquisitions were seen as an infusion of much needed American dollars to spin through the American financial system.

In several papers Michael Lehmann,[1] professor of economics at the University of San Francisco, aptly describes the evolution of the yen–dollar exchange and how the Bretton Woods[2] Agreement was intended to encourage American consumption of German and Japanese industrial exports during the crucial postwar years. Lehmann then describes how the Agreement set in motion the fall of the American industrial sector. It remained in effect for more than twenty-five years, until the war in Vietnam accelerated currency trading with Asian countries and began to seriously damage the world's economic stability. In August 1971 President Nixon took the dollar off the gold standard, effectively dismantling the Bretton Woods system and taking governments out of the role of directly setting exchange rates and currency manipulation.

Lehmann goes on to describe an out-of-the-frying-pan-and-into-the-fire scenario. *It was now the capital markets which took control and in 1971 they began relying on two indirect tools to manage (some would say manipulate) currency exchange: the change in domestic interest rates and the buying and selling of large sums of currency.* Raising interest rates would attract foreign investors. They would return American dollars that kept the American banking system afloat and increase the

---

1 Michael Lehmann, professor of economics at the University of San Francisco, historical overview of the dollar/yen relationship in his presentation. See Rapporteur: Ken Dubin, copyright © 2005-2007 UC Regents. All rights reserved. Site maintained by the Institute of East Asian Studies, a unit of International and Area Studies at the University of California, Berkeley. Page valid: xhtml 1.1 and css.
2 Michael B. Lehmann, *The Dow Jones-Irwin Guide to Using the Wall Street Journal* (Homewood, Ill.: Dow Jones-Irwin, 1990).

strength of the dollar against the yen. The international banking system began buying and selling large blocks of currency. It could be likened to trading large blocks of stock on Wall Street. With Nixon's decision, and without ways to limit imports, the future of America's industrial capability became tied to financial criteria. A devastating series of short-term decisions based on financial criteria began to unfold.

America's playbook, when it came to currency manipulation, is quite remarkable. It started in earnest with Nixon's decision to take the dollar off the gold standard. The exchange rate dropped from 360 to 260 yen to the dollar, providing immediate relief for American industries already struggling with bankruptcy. The high price of oil in the seventies further eroded the international value of the dollar, and currency flowed out of the country at increasing rates to buy oil as well as industrial goods. In 1978, five years after the first oil shock, the U.S. dollar was trading for 185 yen and manufacturing in America was beginning to see a light at the end of the tunnel.

But in October 1979, with oil prices rising again, Paul Volcker, Chairman of the Federal Reserve, a private institution, raised U.S. interest rates in an effort to combat inflation and to attract foreign investments that would return U.S. dollars to the economy. The higher interest rates did attract foreign currency at a furious clip, which pushed the dollar's value back up to more than 250 yen in less than a year. Americans then went on buying sprees. The newly strong dollar made imported goods cheaper, and new bank policies made open-ended borrowing possible. The message was being out that buying on credit was "good."

The Japanese auto companies were prepared and began their next long-term move in the industrial sector. Volcker's move to combat inflation increased the flow of revenue to the Japanese auto industry by 35 percent, without more units being sold or prices being raised. Further, American consumers were back shopping for fuel-efficient imports. Sales of imports rose again, and this time the weakest link cracked. Chrysler was forced to seek federal loan guarantees two years after the second oil shock. Japan's industrial sector and patient economists quietly turned another page.

In the same year that Chrysler sought a loan guarantee, President Reagan stepped in to call for Voluntary Restraint Agreements (VRAs). The agreements spelled out how many cars each Japanese producer could import into the United States in a single year. It was a move similar to the OMAs for televisions. This time the Japanese countered with "transplants"; instead of buying out American companies as they had done in the television industry, Japanese auto companies began shipping automotive components to the States for assembly. In 1982 Honda began assembling the Accord in its new Marysville, Ohio, transplant operation; in 1983 Nissan started an assembly line in Smyrna, Tennessee. America's headlines touted these transplant operations—that they were providing new

American jobs. The politician who had offered the largest local tax concession usually won the favor of the Japanese decision makers. Local American politicians were lauded as heroes and reelected based on their success with landing a transplant. Japan's strategists were playing the American model of capitalism like a violin. By my calculations, the real value added to the U.S. economy by a transplant operation in the mid-eighties was less than 20 percent of gross revenue. Value added in the industrial sector is used to define how much processing or assemble work is done in each factory. For example, if a component is shipped out to be heat treated before it is sent on to a powertrain assembly plant, it might be purchased by the heat treat facility for a $1.00. Then labor, material (natural gas), and overhead are expended to harden the component. It is then sold to the powertrain plant for $1.10. The difference between $1.00 and $1.10 is the value added. The value added by transplant operations assembling components from Japan and relying on design, development and central staff support in Japan was roughly 20 percent. The balance of the gross revenue from selling the car to a dealer was transferred to Japan to pay for components, equipment, tooling, design and development expenses, and of course profits. The profits were huge while the affects of the Bretton Woods Agreement lingered. The suitcases filled with U.S. currency headed for Japan disappeared into the international banking system and were not recorded on the front pages of American media. Again, just as television components slipped under the restrictions of President Carter's OMAs, the imported automotive components and contributions by support staffs in Japan were able to slip under Reagan's VRAs.

Oh, there were some token arrangements with American suppliers for car batteries, tires, and a few other manufactured components. These purchases camouflaged the magnitude of wealth flowing back into Japan's economy. Building transplant assembly plants was a wise strategic move to soothe the unsettled feelings of buyers of Japanese cars. Employing a token number of American workers in the central and southern region was enough to reduce any pangs of guilt for American consumers.

Toyota was three years behind Honda in building its first transplant assembly plant. Toyota was cautious. They first entered into a joint venture with General Motors. The partners agreed on a site in Oakland, California, that had been shut down in 1982, and was far from Detroit. The venture was called NUMMI, an acronym for New United Motors Manufacturing Inc., and included a Detroit-based UAW contingent and included an integral stamping facility, making it somewhat unique in the United States and nearly identical to plants in Japan. Adding integral stamping capability meant simply erecting a plant addition and filling it with stamping presses. The sheet metal used at NUMMI would be fabricated on site. NUMMI began by building the GM Nova in 1985 and two years later the nearly identical Toyota Corolla. Toyota entered America intent on keeping up appearances. JD Powers gave the Corolla/Nova a top rating for quality under $15,000. It was an experiment meant to provide mutual learning to the parallel management teams but with no clear plans beyond the lifespan of a first product line. The site would remain open for twenty-five years and build many different models. The GM managers were there to learn the art of the Toyota production system, and the Toyota managers were there to learn the lessons of managing an American workforce represented by the UAW.

Toyota would learn enough to open its own transplant in Georgetown, Kentucky, in 1988; followed by Princeton, Indiana, in 1998; San Antonio, Texas, in 2003; and engine and transmission manufacturing plants in West Virginia and Alabama. What they learned at NUMMI would enable Toyota to ward off the UAW organizers in years to come. Toyota plants are all nonunion operations.) For the managers at GM, the NUMMI joint venture taught little that they could bring back and apply. The objectives on the back of the envelope were now in the hands of a financial-criteria-based leadership that was more interested in outsourcing than improving operations.

In the spring of 1983, discussions of trade and economics between the United States and Japan finally escalated. It had been thirty-nine years since the meeting at Bretton Woods, where State Department leaders from forty-four Allied nations had agreed to support postwar recovery. The attendees of the original meeting were now dead; the winds of change were blowing. The Japanese government quietly feared the worst.

That spring the Japanese hosted a Japanese Productivity Seminar followed by two weeks of open door tours of Japan's industrial facilities. The invitations came from the Japanese government, not the industrial sector. For two weeks four of us from GM traveled from one automotive complex to the next. Our hosts were reluctant. I viewed it as a poorly thought out attempt to appease concerns over the imbalance of currency and trade. The Japanese government thought they were extending insights into how to rebuild the world's struggling automakers. The seminar bought a little time, but in September 1985 Central Bank and Treasury representatives of the United States, Japan, Germany, Britain, and France met at the Plaza Hotel in New York. They developed a new common policy to strengthen the yen and halt the mushrooming trade deficits. Within five years the yen's value had dropped from roughly 220 to under a 100 yen per dollar. The result made making cars in Japan more than twice as expensive and albeit too late, gave the America industrial sector a fighting chance, that is until China began its own version of industrial development.

The imports objective on the back of the envelope in the seventies and eighties had not produced the desired results. *Quickly develop fuel-efficient as well as low-priced countermeasures to the emerging threat of imports.* The shift to producing fuel-efficient and low-priced vehicles did not go well in America. The Big Three had to abandon their efforts to develop a competitive small engine when they realized their competitors were decades ahead in the development. During these decades the Big Three shifted gears and stepped up efforts to import small vehicles built in factories they partially owned in foreign lands, including Japan, Korea, and Europe. But here again there was a rude awakening. Their cars were not competitive even in their foreign subsidiary country and could not be expected to do better in the American market.

> *1950s and 1960s—Unions: Negotiate labor agreements using threats of automation, out-sourcing, and the shutting down of hometown operations to keep union demands in check. Begin cutting back on apprentice development.*

Was edited to read:

> *1970s and 1980s—Unions: Continue to cut back skilled trades; increase out-sourcing and investments in automation. Introduce a new type of "chips" onto the bargaining tables with the name of a plant site on each one. Turn excess capacity of a plant into a closing-and-reopening threat.*

The seventies brought a struggle for market share with the imports. The Big Three had found a formidable opponent. Disagreements with the UAW over wages and benefits were shifting to a back burner as the transplants proved they could find willing American workers paying equivalent rates of compensation. The new battles at the bargaining tables were over out-sourcing and which plants would close.

> *1950s and 1960s—Equipment: Solicit proposals for automation to displace the universal equipment in production environments.*

Was expanded to read:

> *1970s and 1980s—Equipment: Solicit proposals for automation wherever possible. Avoid using the emerging universal CNC equipment in production environments.*

The seventies and eighties would unfold a reckless shift toward automation. Conscious decisions were made to separate all operators from the pace of the machine and journeymen from roles in setup and maintenance. Machine tool reps would simply hint that workers were the cause of problems, and listening business school grads would add more line items to their appropriations. Getting rid of the last operator was an unwritten goal.

A wave of complex dedicated automation swept through the body and paint shops. The universal gate-line systems with their carefully counterbalanced universal spot-weld guns and the downdraft spray booths with lightweight multicolor spray guns were torn out after decades of service. The universal "body trucks"[1] that followed the chains in the floor were also scrapped. In their place

1 A "body truck" is an old term for a universal steel platform with steel wheels under it. These platforms were connected by a drop pin to a chain running beneath the floor. A car or truck body was placed on top of each body truck. The body trucks served to carry

came complex dedicated systems measured in acres and hundreds of millions in capital. A change in models was no longer accomplished during a summer re-arrange. These new systems demanded the purchase of a new body shop. The systems for machining engine blocks and transmission cases evolved into elabo-rate automated transfer lines. These lines were dedicated to a single engine or transmission design. A redesign meant a new system had to be built from scratch. The systems were so complex and expensive that the machine tool makers added coolant waterfalls and elaborate light panels to amuse their customers.

Capital equipment expenses in vehicle assembly and in power-train manufac-turing rose quickly beyond all justification. Adding robotics to load and unload the transfer lines ensured there would be no worker-related downtime, waiting for workers to return from a break. But the robotics also had breakdown prob-lems that resulted in downtime. The robots were sold under the pretense of their being another step toward lights-off factories and worth the investment. Who needs people when you've got machines?

A selling point in this push toward lights off was the assurance (or hope) of more consistent quality. The automation would repeat the positioning of weld guns and add the correct number of welds every cycle. In the old body shops, the line rate was unrelenting in afternoons when temperatures climbed to over a hundred degrees. Workers wielding the heavy weld guns would begin to miss a few welds. The crew of industrial engineers at Truck Assembly dealt with the missing welds using their handed-down knowledge. One of the solutions was to overstate the number of welds. For example, in their written job descriptions they would specify seventeen spot-welds spaced evenly along a flange when the blueprints called for eleven. The extra welds in the morning didn't add any value, but in the afternoon they assured there were still enough for structural integrity.

The automation investments in these decades were justified with volume pro-jections filled with optimism that consumer interest in the same model could be held for many years. There were also assumptions that a single well-designed platform would draw in a diverse collection of customers. Optimism and as-sumptions inflated the expected volume of lifetime sales. Spreadsheets would then prove with inflated bottom lines that higher expenditures for automation were justified. Reality was that the choices being offered by imports were turn-ing the heads of a fickle market. Customers did not stay with the new platforms long enough for the sales projections to be realized.

The new automation for body shops, paint shops, and machining lines was impossible to update, and replacing it was a long-drawn-out affair taking at least two years and a billion dollars. The new mode of operation was to shut down a plant in one town for two years and restart another. The local factory would go

---

vehicle bodies along the assembly line as it passed through the body shop, paint shop, and trim line.

---

through boom and a long tapering off before closure, the tapering often lasting a decade or more. This new mode displayed a total disregard for the impact of periods of unemployment on the pool of skills in a community. The choices of locations to be shut down and restarted were bargaining table items and served to counter union demands. The American auto industry had found a formula for assuring the culture of craftsmen could not be rekindled. It was on a path toward self-destruction and blaming the union for the losses.

During these decades, the design and build of the new automation was placed entirely in the hands of the machine tool industry. Purchasing Departments were charged with negotiating reasonableness in the investments as cost and size went up year after year. The automation served to keep workers out of areas where weld sparks flew and paint fumes accumulated. Both the financial-criteria-based decision makers and the American machine tool industry hid behind health and safety issues as reasons to invest in these huge automated production systems. At the same time, other countries were finding ways to accomplish health and safety without automation. America's costly strategy was unresponsive to the market and had destroyed the skill base of the culture that could bring competitiveness back to life.

In just twenty years, the words of the process engineer I had worked for in 1965 had spread across the industry. "We are automating these areas to save our children from the temptation of high wages that comes with jobs along an assembly line." The cost of doing business was climbing unchecked by reason and by 1985 was higher than I could have ever imagined.

My visits to plants around Japan in 1983 had revealed they were installing much simpler and more flexible systems in body and paint shops and more universal transfer lines for power trains. Emerging in Japan in 1983 was a trend toward CNC machines in operations. Adding CNC machines meant the Japanese were nurturing craft skills in their workforce. Using CNC machines meant the Japanese automakers expected their workers to develop the skills of a machinist and to learn some simple programming.

When the Japanese transplants opened in mid-America in the late eighties, they were equipped with body and paint systems crated and shipped from Japan. It is not surprising that the American machine tool industry was not invited to participate.

In the early eighties, directives were handed down to search for more robot installation opportunities. As an industrial engineering manager, I was instructed to submit lists of potential sites where a robot might replace an operator regardless of the payoff period. I soon sensed that these were witch hunts; Detroit was seeking more folders to place on the bargaining table.

Research dollars in these decades were spent to push the envelope in lights-off processing. Prototype factories were built that could never be cost justified.

The ones I visited were always limited by the state of the art in some aspect of the technology. Still they served to focus research and provide photographs for bargaining table discussions.

Component processing was being steadily out-sourced during these decades. Floor space opened up in the old plants, making burden rates climb on the remaining components. Once in a while the floor space was refilled with a new generation of processing, but the new generation invariably required fewer operators and more maintenance personnel, which kept burden rates climbing and prompted more out-sourcing.

> *1950s and 1960s—Sourcing: Out-source component manufacturing at the direction of labor negotiating teams and follow up with strategies that will keep prices from rising.*

Became more complex and focused:

> *1970s and 1980s—Sourcing: Prepare proposals that include plans for all components to be out-sourced in the future. Beef up purchasing strategies to control prices.*

Purchasing agents were working to find multiple suppliers that would enable them to play one against the other and keep prices competitive. Sometimes the agents had to develop suppliers large enough to meet the high volume needs of an automaker. Sometimes they even had to furnish leadership groomed by the Big Three. One of them was Dick Dauch, now CEO at American Axle. He had been serving as an assembly line superintendent at Truck Assembly when I arrived.

The decision to begin out-sourcing not only component making but also tooling construction went against the fundamentals of Henry Ford. More than two thousand tool and die shops sprang up around the Midwest during the model proliferation and annual model change era of the fifties and sixties. Most of the tool and die shops were small and kept afloat by as few as four or five contracts per year. The shops clung precariously to their positions on preferred supplier lists. If they made a mistake and shipped a set of dies or tooling that failed and caused an assembly plant to shut down, they could be dropped from the list. Those that survived built exactly to print and erred on the side of overbuild, which drove up the cost of tooling and slowed the quality evolution based on feedback from die maintenance crews.

In the seventies and eighties, Asian auto producers came to America to buy examples from the tool and die shops around the Midwest. They carried home examples of the competitive advantages of seven decades of development in the forming of sheet metal . . . the magic not revealed in notes on blue prints . . . the things handed down by generations of die makers. The solutions to problems not captured on blueprints traveled across the oceans in the form of finished sets of dies. By the time the eighties came to a close, Asian tool making had evolved from stamping out sheet metal boxes to forming curved surfaces. American tool and die shops began subcontracting their work to Asia where wages were lower, which served to accelerate the hand off. The handful of remaining masters of tool making began flying back and forth to Asia where they were paid to coach the Asian tool and die shops. The magic of tool making in America has been handed across the Pacific rather than down to apprentices.

During these decades, GM of Canada experimented with low-cost tooling development. I worked to help them promote their research inside GM explaining how it was ideal for low volume model offerings. In the end, there were no takers. No program manager wanted to be limited in expansion capability by a choice of low volume, low cost tooling. Canada's first customer was Toyota. With one purchase the state of the art in low cost tooling was handed off to the competition. Strategic thinking did not extend to protecting the competitive advantages gained through technical developments in processing.

Some impacts of tooling out-sourcing were subtle. During the seventies and eighties, the mini steel mills were adding new steel chemistries to their catalogs. Their ability to offer higher-quality steel should have led to new characteristics in tooling, but they came too late. The generation of die makers that could have linked the mini-mill operators with tooling designers was already gone.

Changes in the *sourcing* line on the back of the envelope included a new focus on levels of inventory. Japan's just-in-time (JIT) thinking entered into American thinking. The short-term benefits of JIT excited a financial leadership but had subtle drawbacks. Reducing inventory excesses of parts/components provided tangible one-time improvements to income statements and was thought to provide healthy pressures to keep operations running smoothly. But there was no overall accounting of the impact of JIT. America's out-sourcing trend had already filled highways with trucks. JIT just decreased the average number of containers in each truck and conversely increased the number of trucks on the road. The increasing traffic increased the time required to complete each round trip, and in America the distances between factories were far greater than in Japan. Another American drawback involved the narrow roles of workers. Team participation in quick die changes in Japan did not fit with the adversarial union-management relationship in America. Where Japan was busy integrating stamping operations next to the body shops and using universal equipment investments and quick die changes to keep inventories low, America was building networks of outlying factories filled with dedicated automation that sat idle for days until another batch of high-volume production was needed. JIT worked in Japan but not in the States. There was much more to it than simply reducing inventory.

In the late eighties, leadership grew increasingly skeptical of the capability of America's workforce. Ripples of new thinking emerged, "It was far better to be a fast follower than a pioneer. The natives are hardest on the earliest pioneers. Any technical innovation can be copied in two years or less, making investments in innovation pointless." The shift away from competition based on skills in making things was almost complete.

1950s and 1960s—Manufacturing System: Adapt assembly lines to accommodate the build of infinite combinations of options; modify assembly line scheduling systems to ensure an order placed by a customer through a dealer can be produced and shipped in five days or less. Shift high-volume assembly operations away from emerging union strongholds.

Returned to the original build-to-inventory system:

1970s and 1980s—Manufacturing System: Redirect assembly operations back to the efficiency gains of filling wholesale orders received months in advance. Rely on detailed site-comparison systems, and add even more automation to body and paint shops.

The strategy of building new sites away from Michigan continued and was broadened to include a strategy that filled assembly plants with turnkey automation in body and paint shops. New automation had to be purchased each time a platform design was updated; new automation would take two to three years to design, build, and bring up to speed. The cost of automation design and development was increasing steadily in the hands of the machine tool builders.

Equipping multiple assembly plants with exactly the same equipment made comparisons even easier. Roving teams of auditors would strive to fine-tune the roles of all assembly line workers. It was a top-down system of control. The assembly plants in GM evolved to use common methods and lean operating staffs. Comparisons and auditors stopped the flow of continuous improvement suggestions from the front lines.

1950s and 1960s—Organization Development: Continue filling front-line management with professionals; adopt statistical quality control procedures along the front lines; avoid Edward Deming's path toward greater reliance on the workforce; cut back on apprenticeships in anticipation of the shifts to automation and out-sourcing.

Remained relatively unchanged, with one addition:

1970s and 1980s—Organization Development: Add layers of support staff and middle management to deal with more issues as new competitive challenges emerge.

There are inferences in old books describing the earliest automotive business models and how Henry Ford and his designers were unique in their ability to work out problems on the production floor by interacting with assembly craftsmen. They would hash over new ideas and implement changes that would later be captured on a designer's drawings. In the seventies and eighties, large numbers of cohorts would follow around a handful of capable engineers who could grasp the overall consequences of design alterations. Ford's assembly journeymen who also built cars had disappeared seventy years earlier. They had been replaced by a swarm of cohorts handing minutia around in circles. These new engineers were out of touch with daily evolutions in materials, tooling, equipment, and skills, and the silos of production workers were out of touch with the overall design picture. A new engine or transmission developments had become ten-year projects requiring more than a billion dollars.

The seventies brought the launch of the steel industry's nemeses: the mini-mills, which followed Henry Ford's design for an organization. They approached process and product development much as Henry did, from the heart of the operation, and strove to raise their level of integration quickly. The crews on the floor in the mini-mill led the mill in discoveries of a never-ending stream of competitive advantages. The back of the envelope used to set direction for the mini-mill business model did not include a central research facility to match Big Steel's R&D labs or teams of main-office auditors making sure all operations were identical. Innovation and continuous improvement came from the front lines. The value of what has been lost in the auto business cannot be defined by financial criteria. It is a realm of great opportunity for inventors of the "mini auto plants," but again I am getting ahead of myself.

The rules for screening new hires at Flint Truck Assembly in the early seventies were jokingly reduced to one requirement: "A mirror placed under the applicant's nose must show signs of breathing." In what would be the last major round of hiring in Flint, the factories filled with kids who hadn't been lucky enough to escape and find their fame and fortune elsewhere. Ben Hamper was one of them, and he wrote about his experience in *Rivethead*. Youth without plans get caught up in the high-wage trap of factory towns and do not emerge out the other end for thirty years. Along the way, they suffer the cycles of layoffs and rehires based on seniority, not merit. Even the best and brightest come to realize quickly that their income is capped no matter how much effort they put into bettering themselves. The concept of apprenticeship and a long journey of preparation by a master is no longer filling anyone with imagination or keeping them on a track to self-betterment. The need to use intellect and verbally work with others has been designed out of every corner of the industrial sector. Up-from-the-ranks ascension is blocked, and tales of discouragement dash the deep motivations that come with dreams of doing better in life. It seems that if you were not of royal blood (a college grad), you were destined to serve for thirty years in absolute boredom.

Away from the front lines, Personnel Departments were being challenged to attract the top students from surrounding colleges and universities. Dangling promises of promotions and bonuses, recruiters would strap on the uniform of a declining industry and stand beneath unattractive banners trying to entice what a grading system has sorted out as the best students. This approach to selection of employees made my grandfathers' heads droop.

Out-sourcing increased demands on purchasing staffs. Instead of just buying local services, universal equipment, and standard tooling, purchasing agents were beginning to manage tiers of suppliers; in effect they were becoming the new manufacturing managers. Their bonuses would be determined by their ability to keep things running and cut prices. When they demanded price cuts from suppliers, the portion of a supplier's budget that flowed into process and design advancements simply dried up. The race to innovate and make continuous improvements was no longer in the hands of the auto producers.

In 1983 my team of industrial engineers at the Transmission Division was charged with finding the root cause of thirteen model year startup problems pertaining to transmissions. The searches all led to a common ground: somewhere along the path from design idea to the transmission assembly lines someone had tossed some paperwork over the next wall without sensing the ramifications of their contribution. It was as simple: not enough people understood the big picture. During the hunt for root causes, I sat down for a cup of coffee with the manager of transmission research and development. Off the record, he explained something that captured the essence of the problem. He described six of his people who could sit down and design a new transmission on the back of an envelope and he could rest assured that it would work. He then described a sampling of the thousand worker bees who followed the six designers around documenting their every decision. Each of these six was directing the activity of layer after layer of trackers who couldn't help but make mistakes. Since the birth of the assembly line, the evolution in organization development in the auto business has been to build taller and taller silos in ever narrowing fields of expertise. The silos have been erected further and further from daily operations, and the egos inside the silos have swelled to match those of landlords over serfs. This myopic realm has become so complicated that it was difficult even for teams of experienced industrial engineers to track what happened in the thirteen recalls that had cost the division millions to repair and replace, to say nothing of its good name in the marketplace. When the origins were found, it was difficult to hold back the division's leadership, eager to string somebody up by the thumbs. Avoiding recalls in the future was difficult. The thousand cohorts around each of the six engineers needed more experience, and, more important, the six needed to be linked to what was happening on the manufacturing floor. Missing was what the die designers did when they came down to talk to die makers. There is more to getting tooling to produce something than just putting lines on a CAD screen.

By the late eighties American auto companies were nearly free from all responsibility of nurturing craftsmen in operations and were steadily losing market share on their own turf. Japanese transplants were camping in Middle America and refusing to set up bargaining tables in their tents. They were successful in bringing a Deming continuous-improvement approach to the American workforce. America's Big Three were uncompetitive, and the heart of the problem was the organization of the workforce.

1950s and 1960s—Growth: Continue to narrow the competition and strive for increased market share with each exit of a competitor.

Was altered to focus on profitability:

1970s and 1980s—Growth: Focus on holding market share while increasing profits, through a decrease in the number of models and options and with a shift to platforming and packaged options.

The seventies began as a friendly wrestling match over market share between the Big Three. Driveways were already filled with two and three vehicles, and growth was limited to population expansion and conquest over small competitors. Perhaps it was the friendliness of the match that attracted the attention of new opponents. When the oil shocks shifted consumer demand, the Japanese auto producers were ready. They stepped up production of their current offerings and increased the number of ships traveling across the Pacific. The first oil shock gave Japan's sales in the United States a boost. Considering Japan's two decades of grooming an industrial culture with Edward Deming's fourteen points, the Big Three found themselves in a wrestling match with unfamiliar rules. The Big Three countered with extended vehicle warranty programs that were quicker and easier to implement and didn't require a change in direction for the organization. But market share didn't come back for the Big Three. American consumers were demonstrating with their wallets that they preferred not to have problems in the first place, rather than an all-expenses-paid warranty program.

Japanese and Europeans interests were already tuned to smaller, fuel-efficient vehicles. The Japanese industrial sector was already focused on quality improvement and was able to expand quickly in a direction already supported by Allied nations and the Japanese government. The seventies revealed that Japanese auto producers were experts in the art of wrestling for market share. They were quick to gain a better hold with each shift of the American consumer base.

As we've seen, eight of the ten objectives were adjusted again in the seventies and eighties. The Big Three won the scale race but lost ground to imports. The objective adjustments in these decades were made based on financial criteria, that is, seeking improvements in quarterly earnings. They would add thirty-eight more long-term inefficiencies.

LONG-TERM INEFFICIENCIES HIDDEN IN THE OBJECTIVES OF THE 1970S AND 1980S

60. *Product Design and Development: Platforming drove the cost of engineering vehicles through the roof. It crammed many product development engineers together to work on few platforms. The sheer numbers of the engineers slowed the pace of decision making and watered*

down the decisions. The steady annual model change work was displaced by on-again, off-again platforms. Financial-criteria-based decision making was reacting to cycles in sales and the economy. Developments were pushed from drawing boards only to be called back months later to start over.

Too many cooks in Detroit's kitchens in these decades dampened engineering capability. Design meetings would capture fifty engineers in a single room for days. In the end the most adamant would prevail in the midst of an unrelenting hammering for consensus and off line meetings, which favored the most political over the most capable engineers. The postponing of platforms from year to year caused considerable rework to accommodate upgrades in technology, developments in components, and adaptations to ever-changing consumer interest. The small outside engineering houses became recognized for their efficiency and effectiveness. Subsets of product developments began to find their way to the outside. Another of Henry Ford's earliest objectives was being reversed. The basis of competition narrowed once more as the outside engineers harvested innovations from the Big Three and used them to advance their image in the eyes of all companies.

61. Product Design and Development: It is costly to make platforms across several brand names look different enough to fool customers. The nonplatform-based products offered by Asian and European auto companies have an advantage.

Platforming forced customers of the Big Three to choose from a small selection of vehicle sizes and levels of performance. After the second oil shock, imports offered vehicle designs that filled in the gaps. Americans unhappy with limited design choice looked for alternatives in import showrooms.

BUYING CARS BY THE POUND

The sales data of the eighties revealed what must have been on the back of an envelope created by the Japanese Government and carried around by Japan's auto companies. Fill out a simple grid of price versus performance (weight over horsepower) in 20 percent increments. Fill each square with the brand names and volume sold for each model introduced to the American market. A pattern will appear. The first oil shock triggered Japanese product developments that fit over the American market like a quilt. Every square of consumer interest in a combination of price and performance was covered by a single Japanese entry. It was as if some master plan guided the product development teams..

The quilt also reveals the Big Three going head to head. Platforming had steered their engineering teams to a handful of common squares where designers of balloons and banners were going at it hand to hand. The financial-criteria-based marketing was attempting to build brand image and diversify based on price.

Consumers could not see enough difference between a Cadillac Cimarron and a Chevrolet Citation (both members of the X-car platform). The quilt revealed just how many American brands were positioned in the same square. The Japanese invasion had simply blanketed the squares all around the Big Three. Busy with their family feuds. The Big Three did not recognize what was happening.

It is no secret that the imports arriving in response to the second oil shock were not like the ones introduced after the first. It was not a second wave of whatever was driving around the streets of Tokyo. From what I have learned about Henry Ford, I am convinced that he would have sensed what was coming and prepared a surprise. But without Henry, the Japanese industry–government assault simply rolled over one segment of American industry after another.

> 62. *Product Design and Development: American design and development skills fell out of practice.*

The alternative to throwing large numbers of engineers at a problem and hoping for the best was to compartmentalize the overpopulated engineering staffs. But the compartments did not attract young talent. The prospect of spending years focused on o-rings when young engineers had dreams of designing cars made it difficult for recruiters. The talent drained out of the American auto industry.

> 63. *Product Design and Development: The increased organizational complexity in large engineering groups slowed the pace of continuous improvements despite increasing speed in communications. The time for gaining approvals lengthened exponentially to the growing length of signature lists.*

In the eighties in the Transmission Division, a "Request for Change" in design had to pass across many desks. A proposed design change involving several mating components and the function of the hydraulics required signatures from nearly every corner of the business. The paperwork would travel miles to get all the right signatures. Today electronic signatures and CAD screens replace the paperwork but not the length of time that each person signing off must spend verifying that he or she understands the change.

I once commissioned an industrial engineering study of the cost of change on something as simple as assigning a new part for a new model year for a transmission. The study revealed that each Request for Change would cost a minimum of $3,500 in wages and take more than a month to pass through the series of in-boxes. The interoffice mail handling labor was a small part of it and the waiting for the pick-up and drop-off at each desk added a week to the circulation time. The real cost was in the time spent by people pondering the significance of the change and making decisions to verify before they signed. Out-sourcing increased the cost and the circulation delays. The distance between in-boxes albeit electronically is a problem. The value of entering into discussions and solving complex problems with a group of Henry Ford's assembly craftsmen is no longer understood.

64. Imports: Investing in research and filing for patents has become detrimental to both competitiveness and the bottom line for American industry.

Many companies that import to the United States are not voluntarily following U.S. patent law, especially in areas of processing. American companies on the other hand must comply with the patent laws, which put them at a disadvantage in a global competition.

65. Unions: Threatening plant closures and postponing the reopening of plants has served to disrupt the ambitions of the UAW. But it has also brought tremendous burdens to local communities and driven up the cost of doing business.

In the remote green-field sites, there were often no other automotive operations around to absorb the talent being laid off. A workforce attracted to town by high wages in a new auto plant soon discovered their assigned vehicle had tapered off in popularity. The entire community would have to go through the downward spiral. Economists say a dollar trades hands roughly eight times before it leaves the surrounding community. Hiring 3,600 assembly plant workers puts more than 30,000 local people to work. When the popularity of a new car model fades, the plant workforce plus 30,000 other locals struggle to find work. The cycles of models into and out of towns would vary in length from four to twenty years. In every instance, the green-field site has stirred community and statewide excitement only to be followed by devastation. Each time, the local electorate coerced its constituents to offer tax concessions and to pay for new infrastructure through special assessments. The cycle continues today, and even the transplants are playing the game. Perhaps the Big Three have been dreaming that communities would put enough pressure on the union to solve many of the issues on their bargaining tables. I can't help but wonder how America could have forgotten the value of the surrounding community that once helped the automotive entrepreneurs who chose the Midwest.

66. Equipment: In the new era of systems experts being flown in from out of town, no one remembers the value of the silver-haired breakdown crews.

Erecting assembly plants in green-field sites employed some local tradesmen and the local media made headlines out of the increase in construction work. But because of the lack of experience in equipment installation and production launch, both the equipment suppliers and the auto companies poured significant amounts of capital into ensuring that the turnkey automation worked. Without supporting neighborhoods familiar with the auto industry, the acceleration periods were longer. Lags in assembly start-up were the result and sales opportunities were lost during the initial season of advertising hype. There are good reasons why industrial enterprises are still choosing places that value the trades, such as the Czech Republic, to start a factory.

67. Equipment: Automation has become so large that it is impossible to connect all the sections and make a test run before it is shipped.

Today's machine tool suppliers insist that their own crews install their systems, which leaves plant personnel out of the loop until the installers have cycled the system a few times and left the building. Then the struggles to accelerate begin. Many highly automated body shops and transfer lines never reached their promised daily rate in the eighties and nineties. Acceleration periods were career-altering experiences for the young plant managers transferred in to test their mettle. The pace of automation would eventually ease to meet the rate of sales on its way down; the blame for lost sales never seemed to settle on the shoulders of system builders.

I remember standing in the midst of one of these Rube Goldbergs in the Hamtramck plant, talking with a bedraggled superintendent who had been trying to get the system to run at expected speeds for eighteen months. The pressure to fill showrooms with the new Cadillac model had been grueling. The automation stretched in all directions, beyond my field of vision. As I stood there, I remember wondering, *where would I start if suddenly someone tapped me on the shoulder and handed me the reins? Getting the V-8 Rocker Cover Department to run at speed had taken me three months. Automation this large might require a lifetime.*

The system builders would send out their costly fly-in troubleshooters who would get the equipment to cycle a few times and then leave after dropping off another hefty batch of invoices. The system builders blamed the problems on quality of the components they were expected to weld together, the skills of the operators, and the skills of journeymen who tuned the system. The factory management blamed the installers, builders, and system designers. Bottom line, the large automated systems had a higher-than-advertised price tag. The original bid was just the beginning, and the financial-criteria-based decision makers were not grasping the bigger picture.

A LESSON IN MEXICO

One day while I was working in Roger Smith's think tank, I received an anonymous note from upstairs (somewhere above the twelfth floor in the GM building). The note simply asked, "Why are quality audits rating Ramos Arizpe #1?" The Ramos Arizpe plant is in Mexico near Monterrey. It was the home of the fourth A-Body assembly plant. The other three were in the States. I flew to Monterrey and rented a car. I couldn't imagine what I would find that would give Mexico a quality advantage. The three plants assembling A-Body cars in the States were stocked with the latest in body-shop and paint-shop automation. Everything I had heard from visitors returning from Brazil and other overseas operations was that the technical skills and workmanship were not good. Savvy buyers in foreign countries were choosing imports from the States over locally-assembled cars.

When I got to Ramos Arizpe, I saw gate lines[1] in the body shop, something I hadn't encountered since my days at Flint Truck Assembly in the early seventies. Both the pickup truck line and the Blazer/Suburban line had used gate lines. Here was a plant still assembling the new A-Body car using generic gate lines. The local craftsmen had bolted swing fixtures onto the gates and humans were guiding the spot weld guns. All the feeder lines were equipped with flip fixtures enabling them to build a mix of wagons, coupes, and sedans. The equipment, fixtures, and tooling had been torn out of a plant in the States and shipped to Mexico when the plant started building A-cars. The quality auditors must have viewed the plant as far behind the curve in the automation age and they marveled at how the fit and finish flowing out of this body shop were better than the plants in the States. The craft skills, pride, and commitment of the workforce I observed were like what I'd seen in the old days.

My exploration of the surrounding community was a trip back into the fifties. In the evening the streets were lined with cars with hoods up; backyard mechanics were gathered around. This was a culture that still knew how to keep an old car running. Apprenticeships in understanding the automobile were being conducted under hoods in every neighborhood. The supervision in the assembly plant was also different: they were not college grads, and they wore their notches of experience proudly. The small amounts of automation they did use were the kinds of things I had justified with time studies twenty years earlier.

In the evening I visited the neighboring town of Ramos Arizpe and was amazed to see students entering and exiting a well-lit trade school near the center of town. My grandfather Max had attended a night school similar to this in 1909 in Williamsport, Pennsylvania, when he was qualifying himself for a job with the railroad. This was a microcosm of my understanding of the culture of Flint in the twenties and during the Great Depression. The well-lit windows in the trade school were showing off the drafting boards and instruments. On the ground floor was a machine shop with math problems on the chalkboards. While Drucker and Deming were pushing lessons in management and continuous improvement in process, Mexico was busy nurturing a hands-on culture that could build higher quality automobiles. I was in

---

1 The gate-line systems were a solution to the mixing of models in body shops. The systems were interconnected loops of overhead monorail filled with hangers resembling garden gates. Spurs off these rail systems and switches allowed the gates for station wagons and coupes to be mixed in with gates for sedans according to a manifest published by the scheduling department each day. The fixtures on these gates were reworked every model year before it became in vogue to buy all new automation with every model change.

the midst of a culture with a much higher form of control over the process and a much more professional approach to management—things that America has forgotten. It was chance to remember the V-8 Rocker Cover Department as it neared its goal of sixteen thousand per shift, when the hive mind took over. The bottom line in my report: Mexico was building superior quality because it chose to nurture skills and allow workforce pride of accomplishment. I had a feeling that whoever had requested the evaluation appreciated my answer.

68. Equipment: The parade of installers of automation provided by the machine tool industry wiped out the pools of in-house journeymen.

Prior to the seventies, the people who made the annual summer modifications to the gate-line body shops were also the people who kept them running. They were the Clarence Van Wagners of assembly plants. Small in numbers and big in responsibility, they were committed to keeping downtime short as they jumped on breakdown wagons and raced through the assembly plants. The wagon riders would leave the wiring schematics neatly folded in the panel boxes. They were there when the equipment was tuned each summer and handpicked for their mechanical intelligence. Clarence was right, "To fix something you just have to think like the designer."

69. Equipment: For the American machine tool industry, the transition from generic machines and in-house tooling (in the fifties) to turnkey automation for platforms was a boom time. For auto companies, capital expenses began climbing out of control, right under the nose of decision makers using financial criteria.

The machine tool industry was leading the auto industry by the nose toward a common vision of lights-off factories. The smart machine-tool reps were adept at dropping a hint—on a golf course or at the back of a private box at a hockey game—that they had something that might be a solution to another UAW problem. More and more the equipment came specially built for the new component designs. It also became more and more expensive. Capital investments spiraled out of control.

70. Equipment: The auto industry walked away from the generic gate line and body truck[1] assembly system that it had used for decades. A body shop or an engine block line could no longer be reconfigured during two weeks of August to accommodate work on a new model.

When platforming was rolled out in the seventies, all new equipment had to be purchased for each new platform design. The standard reply from machine tool reps for any thoughts of going back toward

---

1 A body truck was a steel platform with four steel wheels and a simple drop-down post on the front that engaged the body truck to a moving chain in the floor. Body trucks snaked through the body shop, the paint shop, and then the trim shop in single file. The body trucks were universal and didn't change from one year to the next.

generic equipment changeovers was always challenging, "Sure you can changeover the equipment you have, but you will need a skilled local workforce in those green-field sites and the body-shop systems—because body-frame-integral systems are more complex." Any suggestion of retooling the existing machining equipment was challenged by sales reps: "You'ill have to invest 80 percent of what it would cost to buy an all new system. You might just as well install new and eliminate all the maintenance headaches." The decision makers chose the all-new equipment each time, and the cost of doing business went up. Once again cost going up had very little to do with wages or benefits.

71. Equipment: Automating body and paint shops was not justified with labor savings.

Roughly 85 percent of the capital spent to equip an assembly plant during the eighties was spent on the body shop and paint shop automation. The average investment was roughly $850 million. At Truck Assembly we stationed 160 workers in the old gate-line system of the body shop and a smaller number in the hand-spray booths. On two shifts fewer than 500 workers were needed to man the body and paint shops. The capital investment in these automated systems was equivalent to the wages of 1,500 workers for ten years. The average life span of a platform was fewer than eight years. The cost of doing business was climbing, and it had nothing to do with wages.

72. Equipment: The "nonperformance" reputation of the automated equipment that evolved in these decades prompted operations managers to insist on extra equipment to ensure they could meet their obligations.

73. Equipment: The real cost of these big automated production systems was not in the initial bid. The eighties was the era of bidding low and making it up in design changes.

The job would go to the low bidder, perhaps prearranged, and once the construction had progressed to the point of no return, an unfailing vehicle design staff would begin pumping out design revisions. The revisions would lead to Requests for Appropriation Change from the supplier, and the profits missing from the initial low bid were refreshed. Once in a while someone would object to the high cost of revisions, which led to compilations of exit costs. The exit numbers were always staggering, and the prospect of program delays was a career-altering risk for any program manager. It was impossible to change horses in midstream, and the machine builder would get to finish the job. Back in the sixties, in-house skilled-trade capability had served as a backup to the mistakes and threats from equipment and tooling providers. They also served as the reality check on pricing. The generic equipment purchased in the sixties was available from several suppliers. The true cost of these large automated systems was unknown.

74. Equipment: New automation was invariably larger and more expensive than the old. Rarely were several smaller versions chosen over the ultimate one-size-fits-all.

This ever-larger investment approach eventually ran into the reality of the limited life cycle of the model platforms. The huge automation would début to meet dramatic sales demand but soon fade to limping along for years. The smaller scaled equipment purchased in multiples up through the fifties had universal capability and allowed the phasing in and out of models with simple tooling and fixture changes. The cost of doing business began to rise exponentially in the sixties.

75. Equipment: Today's assembly and manufacturing systems are too costly to update. Continuous improvements are shelved until a new model is introduced.

76. Equipment: The evolution of dedicated machining automation (transfer lines) preceded the evolution of the body-shop automation. Transfer lines began disappearing in Europe and Japan in the eighties, but not in America.

A machining transfer line is used to turn a block of cast iron into an engine block, or a block of cast aluminum into a transmission case. Like a body shop, an automated machining line is not designed for life beyond the life span of a single product. Basically a transfer line is a cluster of hundreds of expensive precision spindles mounted along a precision transfer mechanism. Many of the spindles cut chips for less than 1 percent of their life spans. During peak sales years, they spin maybe half the time and cut chips maybe 3 percent of the time. As sales drop off, the spindles begin to gather dust more and more days each month because they are mounted to a system that runs only at one speed and makes one product. Like a body shop, a transfer line also has trouble with acceleration and does not live up to the promises of speed made by the manufacturer. The spindles became a poor investment in energy, coolant, and precision bearings back in the eighties. Computerized numerically controlled (CNC) machines began appearing in factories in Europe and Japan. A CNC machine uses one precision spindle. The tooling in the spindle is automatically exchanged with other tools from a magazine. The more useful CNC machines can operate a spindle in five axes of movement and can completely machine a block of metal into a component. Their life spans stretch beyond the life cycle of any vehicle design, which makes purchasing a bank of CNC machines instead of a transfer line an improvement in the bottom line; that is, if you have a workforce capable of programming them and keeping them in good working order. Auto companies in Europe, such as Ferrari, and most of the automakers in Japan have figured this out. America is struggling with the shift because it demands a skilled workforce. America's adoption of an industrial union (CIO) in place of the trade union (AFL) made the shift to a CNC-based operation impossible. GE's main aircraft engine plants were strongholds of the CIO and yet somehow GE executives were able to negotiate an agreement to spin their new remote sites away from the CIO. The remote sites were equipped with CNC equipment and are now building high quality military engines. The American auto industry has not been able to cross this bridge.

77. Equipment: America may be too slow in its adoption of CNC equipment.

In the late eighties, Ferrari chose to equip its new engine plant with banks of CNC equipment built in Italy. The decision would put them on the leading edge in a new generation of competition based on high-paced innovation in low-volume products. Others would soon follow Ferrari down the CNC workforce path, while plants in America still chose turnkey transfer lines.

In 1995 GM made its first major step into the CNC era in Eisenach, a city in eastern Germany. The experiment was positioned in the midst of a culture still valuing traditional industrial trades. For GM it was a decision that admitted the value of the CNC approach over transfer lines. Perhaps it was also an admission that the automotive craftsmen in the Midwest had been purposefully passed over.

78. Equipment: The CNC era came along too late. The American machine tool industry had already "married" the financial-criteria-based leadership of the American auto industry.

For four decades, the smoke and mirrors of the American machine tool industry have served to steer strategic discussions in Detroit by insinuating that the internal culture that once erected, equipped, and maintained the world's largest auto industry had been overrun by the UAW. It may be too late to shift away from the promises of better lights-off solutions.

79. Equipment: The challenge of forcing sheet metal to pass through automated body shops has forced a dumbing down of vehicle styling and a dampening of the creativity that had once flowed from automotive designers.

The robots that position weld guns in body shops mimic the motion patterns of the workers they replaced. If you look up and down one of the robotic lines, it looks as if a volunteer fire chief has thrown together a robotic bucket brigade. Each robot adds a few welds in the same location over and over when a shuttle mechanism presents the next body. The old system had used fixtures they called gates to hold sheet metal components in alignment while they were welded together. Workers tended the spot-weld guns. The gun operators could handle any mix of coupes, sedans, and wagons and conceivably an unlimited number of models. The output of a gate line would include two body side assemblies, a roof assembly, and other major panel assemblies on their way to being joined to a floor pan in the main framing station. In a main framing station, the major panels were aligned and tacked together before loading them on a body truck that would carry them through the finish weld area.

Today's finish weld areas are fundamentally the same, but with robots standing in for operators and expensive stationary automation replacing the flexible and inexpensive body trucks. These are the robots that often appear in television ads. Perhaps they are meant to lull car buyers into believing that precision automation has assembled their purchases. To an industrial engineer, the ads draw attention to how much capital and operating cost is being wasted. There are two huge differences between these robots and the line workers they replaced. (1) When the exciting sparks fly in all directions from a sheet metal miss alignment, the robot on TV isn't smart enough to add an extra weld spot next to the one that burned through or to adjust the positioning of the gun on the next car coming down the line. (2) Workers could be quickly retrained each summer, enabling acceleration to full production in hours instead of months or years. The robots have to be tuned and retuned as the sheet metal zeroes in to the required body shape each time the stamping dies are polished.

There is a big kicker in all of this. The cost of the robots is a drop in the bucket compared to the cost of the shuttle and locating systems that must position the 220 to 300 individual sheet metal components against each other before the robots can begin to weld. The daily challenges of positioning the mating pieces of stamped sheet metal was once handled by a combination of gate-line fixtures, body trucks with flip fixtures, and an experienced workforce. Stamped components vary in shape and size as they flow through the many series of dies in multiple sheet metal plants. The stamping dies are always in varying stages of wear and require periodic repolishing and resharpening. The progression of variation in each stamping was once handled by a skilled group of body-shop workers who understood the mating sheet metal components and when to reject a component or shut the line down. These craftsmen have been replaced with very expensive automation that is rarely tuned to the latest variation in mating sheet metal.

I remember kicking around the idea of using a single weld station to completely assemble the body. The idea was to keep adding components and sending the body truck back into the same weld station. The engineers at Fanuc Robotics agreed it was possible. Human beings would position and clamp each added piece of sheet metal saving more than $500 million in capital investment and enabling the purchase of a single weld station to live beyond the rise and fall of a single model. It was a variation on using a single Pines Bender with an indexing spindle to put all bends in a tailpipe.

80. Sourcing: Purchasing Departments were tasked with spreading acquisitions of equipment and tooling across three or more suppliers in hopes of keeping costs in line as they negotiated prices. At the same time, Detroit's large-machine tool builders were smart enough to track the long-

range model-change plans for every program in the Big Three.

When visiting machine tool builders in the mid-eighties, I was amazed to stumble upon the latest future program plans for GM alongside those of Ford and Chrysler. They were all marked confidential and arranged neatly in a locked cabinet. America's machine tool manufacturers knew more about the flow of their workload than the auto industry's purchasing agents knew about controlling prices.

81. Sourcing: The automotive supply base, which has divided itself into tiers, has its own internal support structure for interfacing with suppliers.

Henry's Ford's fears of buying from outside suppliers and where it would lead are turning to realities. The supply base is sharing all of the process innovations being hammered out by each of the Big Three with other auto producers, both foreign and domestic. The supply base has divided itself into tiers I, II, III, and IV. Each level is taking a slice of profit and compounding prices. The supply base has become global, and suppliers are sharing developments of the Big Three with the other automakers around the world. It is naïve to think that America's supply base will ever again invest in processing research that will provide a competitive advantage for the Big Three.

82. Manufacturing System: Asian auto producers are choosing universal equipment, minimal tooling, and staying close to their home-town original sites, strategies America's auto companies were employing before the UAW began to threaten shareholders.

83. Manufacturing System: Japan's "gift" of a JIT system has clogged the arteries of America's transportation systems with partial loads.

Just-in-time (JIT) systems are simple. An inventory space is allotted for each automotive component and marked on the floor. At regularly timed intervals, a review of inventory is fed back to the supply location, which sends another shipment just large enough to refill the space. This strategy of keeping small inventories has had serious impact on America's transportation system. Passenger trains sit on sidings waiting for freight trains to pass with JIT shipments—often railcars with partial loads. The delays pushed rail passengers into crowded airports. Even worse, our highway infrastructure has become flooded with JIT trucks. JIT was invented to meet the needs of a very different culture with short shipping distances and high property values in the industrial sector. It seems ludicrous that a nation with limited oil supplies would choose a system that drives up foreign oil consumption.

Further, it is mystifying that a nation that uses tax dollars from all citizens to build, expand, and repair its highways and ports is not concerned about the decisions being made by its business sector, especially when the divestiture decisions will cause the expansion of seaports, railways, and highways. America's auto companies in particular with their shifting of operations and suppliers offshore have increased the demand for infrastructure but not jobs that would increase tax revenues to pay for the added infrastructure. The American vision of the proper separation/paring of business and government has developed cataracts.

84. Manufacturing System: Compared to American auto companies in these decades, the Japanese applied fundamentally different thinking about production systems.

America's process engineers were focused on the speed of systems and how long they could run between tool changes, things that financial criteria guiding the decision makers would recognize. The Japanese, on the other hand, were focused on nurturing ingenuity and teamwork to save operating cost while purchasing universal equipment and simpler tooling, things not so easily measured on spread sheets. The Japanese downplay in the importance of sophistication in equipment and tooling was evident in the factories across Japan that I visited in 1983. The five-minute die change gave me a stunning glimpse of the culture they developed. My grandfathers would have described their approach as employing common sense.

85. Manufacturing System: Getting the new automated body shops and transfer lines to accelerate to full speed during these decades took months and was often never fully realized. The losses during assembly line accelerations mounted quickly and often exceeded $100 million for each plant. The collective that now manages auto plants has lost all memory of what my grandfathers' generation passed down regarding acceleration.

An assembly plant employs roughly 3500 workers. During new model accelerations a view from the rafters would reveal only a handful of workers scurrying around trying to get the line going again and again. Many workers standing around is hard to watch if you are familiar with the summer rearrange in the sixties, when the line was up and running in two weeks instead of months.

86. Organization Development: With the secret race to out-source the manufacture of auto components in full swing, superficial goals were introduced in component operations. The authors of bonus checks were definitely not seeking progress in the evolution of workforce skills.

Strong central control led by financial-criteria-based thinking led to poor and narrowly focused measures of performance in operations. Focus would shift every quarter to new measures, such as reducing inventories of auto components, reducing scrap losses, increasing quality audit ratings, improving housekeeping, and of course reducing headcount. The big picture was measured in quarterly earnings watched carefully by a handful of investment group managers who manipulated the majority of the blue chip stocks.

A FEW PLANT MANAGERS DID THE RIGHT THING

A plant manager in Toledo once shared a dilemma. To earn his bonus, he had to shave 150 people off the payroll. The guidelines did not specify whether he should (1) follow the advice of an industrial engineering manager and push for increased effort by his crew of three thousand or (2) send some of the component making to outside contractors. He did the right thing and increased output that quarter because he was a good manager. I soon found out that he had revealed his dilemma with the intent of suggesting that other managers in the division had the same goal and might choose to meet it in different ways. He was also suggesting that I was still näive in my assumptions of the levels of operations understanding in our collective corporate leadership.

At one point in the mid-seventies, maintenance expenses were the targets for quarterly improvement to earn a bonus. I was leading a team that had been asked to compare headcount in Chevrolet's twenty-six manufacturing locations. One plant had an extremely low maintenance headcount. It was a foundry, and its plant manager had decided to go all out for the bonus. He let his foundry fall apart. When I entered the plant for the first time, I was shocked to see the exterior doors had fallen off; there were gaping holes in the roof, and whole sections of the exterior walls had been removed in the summer and never replaced. The openings in the roof allowed the ovens to run without ductwork. The dirt floors had turned to mud in the falling snow. The bottom-line, financially-motivated leaders were not grasping the ramifications of myopic goals.

87. Organization Development: The American auto industry stopped nurturing generalists, people who can tell by walking around if anything is amiss. Specialists took over for generalists, and more of them were needed to keep the business running.

Auditors and financial system trackers eventually identified what was amiss, but not until an error had proven costly to customer satisfaction and the bottom line. The number of people supporting operations was increasing while the breadth of their knowledge and experience was decreasing.

THE VETERAN MAINTENANCE SUPERINTENDENT

The Maintenance Department in the Willow Run Transmission Plant was large. There were 3,500 maintenance employees spread over three shifts servicing the needs of 14,000 employees. All 3,500 reported to one well-seasoned superintendent. Construction, maintenance, tool room, and sanitation all fell under his jurisdiction. The long-tenured superintendent was a master at dodging any hints of streamlining his department. When production schedules dropped, all production managers were expected to reduce headcount, and with some efficiency improvements provided by industrial engineers the laid-off workers did not all return when production went back up. However, cutting back was not a part of this older superintendent's modus operandi. In the meetings where cutting back headcount was discussed, he would begin with his favorite line: "I can cut back, but I'll have to close some of the restrooms." It was all he ever had to say. None of the managers ever wanted to press him for fear of dealing with committeemen when the nearest restroom was closed or not cleaned. A 5 percent reduction in production schedules called for a reduction of 175 people from the maintenance workforce, and the old superintendent's his entire sanitation crew numbered 165. No one ever challenged his bluff, perhaps because there were no generalists left who understood the whole scope of the maintenance staff. Perhaps no one would have been willing to go toe to toe with him.

88. Organization Development: Blocking all up-from-the-ranks promotions was a costly move. Overall performance slipped in both quality and cost improvement.

Some of the college grads placed along the front lines were natural leaders and survived for a year as supervisors before beginning their climb up the ladder. Most however were unfamiliar with their surroundings and dropped like flies. Many caused upward swings of 50 to 60 percent in operating costs. Their formal education was ineffective when it came to judging a fair day's work or sensing the cause of a problem. The front lines were a test by fire that quickly sorted out these college grads, but it proved to be a very costly way to operate the business. The new grads should have been striving for continuous improvements and were instead striving to keep up with the status quo.

89. Organization Development: The American industrial sector lost touch with the importance of completing internships before being licensed to practice.

The days of being recommended into apprenticeships and receiving hands-on learning in side-by-side arrangements disappeared as the UAW emerged. American recruiters began rounding up the top graduates of the top schools, while America's culture became increasingly intent on perfecting how to take the test rather than what could be learned. Between a focus on memorizing the answers to the most likely questions and the unethical pursuit of the answers before the exam, America has gotten off course.

90. Organization Development: A company that does not take the time to apprentice its decision makers is a poor match for companies that do.

Even automotive engineers are no longer required to carry on-the-job knowledge of line worker expertise, skilled-trade capabilities, or knowledge of the challenges in other salaried workforce environments. Engineers strong in theory but boxed in by standardized sizes, cataloged chemistries, and software limits are slowing the evolution of crafts in America.

91. Organization Development: The interviews-and-résumés approach to hiring leadership in America's industrial sector is unable to sort out the educated from those who took shortcuts or those without the intelligences that the industrial sector requires.

FRATERNITY AND INTEGRITY ARE NOT SYNONYMOUS

During the first week of my junior year at GMI, I was cajoled into a life lesson I will never forget. A senior named Arden, whom I knew from Flushing High School, went out of his way several times that week to encourage me to join his fraternity. I knew my grandfather Max had joined a fraternity in Williamsport, Pennsylvania—before fraternities had been banned from recruiting high school students. After several cafeteria discussions, I accepted Arden's offer of a house tour and lunch on Friday.

Arden and the other members convinced me that a fraternity affiliation would increase my network and career opportunities. Looking back, I was an easy mark to join a lifelong brotherhood. I moved into the fraternity on Sunday and started pledging on Monday.

I joined nine freshmen in the first meeting. Our new pledge master began laying down rules. The ten of us would share two study rooms in the basement. My study pattern of staying at the GMI library till 11:00 p.m. had to change. Sleeping arrangements were in the attic with our clothes duffel slid beneath a cot and a few things hung on two hooks along the wall. The attic and the basement had not been part of the lunch tour on Friday.

Only members were allowed in the attractive first- and second-floor quarters. Only members had double-occupancy rooms, and only house officers had single rooms. I listened in amazement as our pledge master filled up every hour of every day with tasks for the next ten weeks. Our schedule would not relax until exam week. Then the following semester would begin with "hell week," famously rumored to be full of unpleasant surprises. Figuring this whole thing was nothing compared to the boot camp my high school friends were going through on their way to Vietnam, I resigned myself to do it.

The ten of us worked together to divide up the chores. Our days began at 4:30 a.m. and ended with lights out at 11:30 p.m. The amount of time I spent studying was reduced to the time between classes, which was just ten hours a week. My midterm grades were terrible. I kept reminding myself of the selling points: that fraternity life was a microcosm of a real life and that the brotherhood we formed would last a lifetime.

The second five weeks of pledging turned out quite different from the first. Two of the nine freshmen were punished several times and then kicked out. One overzealous member doling out pledge punishments was also expelled. The whole thing began to look more and more immature. I was fast losing respect for the leadership of the house, but determined to meet my commitment.

At the end of our tenth week, we were called into the library. Our pledge master said, "Congratulations, you have completed your pledging requirements. Hell week will begin when you return next semester." He walked to the bookcase on the back wall and said, "To help you bring your grades back up this semester, we have a secret that must never leave this room." He slid some books aside and pulled out a wedge. A six-foot section of the bookcase swung forward by itself. Behind it was a long narrow room lined with shelves. "The things on these shelves must never leave this room." he said.

As my turn came to enter the alcove, I could see labels on each shelf. They were the names of GMI faculty members. They appeared to be categorized by grade level, freshmen to senior. Each shelf held copies of midterm, end of semester, and final exams, stacked in order on separate shelves. By the height of some stacks, fraternity members had to have been saving tests for more than a decade. I walked toward the back until I came to first semester sophomore year, Physics II. I found the shelves marked Associate Professor Marsh, my nemesis, and pulled down the stack labeled midterm. There were three exams. At a table I compared them year to year. The multiple choice questions were all the same each year, except for numbers 27, 28, and 29. Marsh had rewritten the same three questions each year. I found his quizzes and final semester tests. They were equally repetitive. My resentment toward him swelled. *What a lazy tyrant.*

I looked at some other final exams. In the heavy freshman and sophomore subjects like chemistry and calculus the questions were repeated year after year. I thought about all the students who had finished exams in half the allotted time while I had struggled to finish before time ran out. Then I remembered an incident in a Metallurgy II midterm. The proctor had gone crazy in the last ten minutes. He had stepped out in the hall and shouted at the backs of students who had finished early and walked out. He called some of them back into the room but did not catch them all. Seven students had not returned despite all his shouting. He then ranted and raved for ten minutes, demanding the return of the copy of the test one of them had taken. At one point he shouted something that didn't make sense at the time. "It was brand new." Now it all made sense. He must have drafted a new test, and it had slipped through his fingers despite a watchful eye. One of the seven who didn't return would surely have made a copy that adorned a shelf in this and the other secret rooms in fraternity libraries.

I sat in the library dumbfounded, growing more and more upset with my naïveté. How could I have entered into so large a competition and not realized that 70 percent of the population (the fraternity members) were taking shortcuts? The 30 percent of us that did not join fraternities, the independents, were jokingly referred to as GDIs (God Damn Independents), and I had assumed it was because we were dodging the payment of membership to a fraternity. I had never stopped to think about why so many independents had dropped out during the freshman competition. Now it made sense. Nurturing a feeling of separation between GDIs and Frat Rats assured that the secrets behind the library walls remained hidden.

While my young pledge compatriots were scrambling to grab notebooks and jotting down answers for the coming exams, I went to the basement. No one noticed me carrying my books out to my car. I went up to the attic and grabbed my duffel and clothes, again without anyone noticing. I sat in the parking lot, thinking about what I was doing and what I should say. I concluded there was no one in the "house" who could agree with my decision without having to be ashamed of his own. I just drove away.

The exam week that followed was a long one. I ignored the frat members in the hallways, and no one approached me about leaving. Over the years I have never volunteered to anyone that I once pledged a fraternity. Instead I just smile when the subject comes up, finding pride in having survived the 33-percent forced attrition in a school where everyone had a full-ride scholarship. I also survived in a competition where 70 percent of the competition had the answers to tests ahead of time. Living in a fraternity did a lot for my self-confidence and self-respect, just not in the way that Arden had described it.

---

92. Organization Development: Auto companies and their suppliers are having to staff up interface teams to run back and forth between decision makers. The value of meetings on the production floor has been forgotten.

Out-sourcing increased the numbers of "keep trackers" who followed the handful of product design engineers. The design engineers did not interface with outside suppliers. Purchasing agents and the keep trackers handled the communications. The numbers of keep trackers increased with the amount of out-sourcing and when tiers were added to the supply base. The pace and frequency of improvements slowed, and the risk of making mistakes climbed.

93. Organization Development: Warranty reporting systems were introduced to try to match the quality and durability of the emerging Japanese imports. The outcome was of little or no value to operations, engineering, or design staffs.

The warranty reporting systems linked dealerships with accounting offices but accomplished very little toward improving quality. The links were refined over the years, but even today provide very little useful information to operations. It is nearly impossible for a service center mechanic to assess what process or assembly system needs a tweak. The expense of fixing a spill of processing errors into vehicles rolling off the line is higher than ever. Until 1912 the customer could link his vehicle back to the assembly craftsmen who put it together. Today the links between customer and assembler must extend across a continent and often an ocean. The cost of fixing even a simple spill can be very expensive.

94. Organization Development: Empire building became a frequent practice in the second half of the twentieth century. Middle managers correlate size of their paycheck to the size of their staff.

In the auto industry, as with other businesses, the second half of the twentieth century was an era of founders stepping down; their replacements seemed unable to judge reasonableness in size of support staff. Empire building became popular. Even the best of CEOs had trouble balancing staffing. It was why the study of indirect labor staffing at twenty-six Chevrolet locations had been such a fertile effort. The business model that evolved after the founders stepped down still struggles with empire building.

95. Growth: America's industrial sector became measured in growth of revenue and size of market share, losing focus on what mattered.

The long-term measures of progress in developing a highly skilled craft culture and a surrounding community to nurture a next wave of apprentices were missing.

96. Organization Development: The shift away from annual model change and into platforming depleted the numbers of experienced tradesmen and engineers. A decade later in the midst of the oil shocks, a decision was made to shift to body-frame-integral (BFI) structures and front-wheel-drive (FWD) power trains. There were not enough experienced tradesmen and engineers to pull it off, and the result was a rapid increase in dependency on the American machine tool industry. This shift proved to be costly.

Long acceleration periods with workers standing idle at their stations became an accepted cost of doing business in the eighties. Plant sites were shut down for more than two years to make the changeovers, and communities were expected to absorb the attendant costs of years of workforce unemployment. The talented workers began to migrate during down periods, and most of them never returned to work in their hometowns. The migrations depleted the pools of talent in the culture surrounding auto plants and blackened the image of the auto industry in terms of cultural involvement. Any community that supported landing some auto industry business was setting itself up to be ravaged.

Platforming enabled a combining of sales projections for several brands. The result was higher volume projections for every platform development. America's machine tool industry stepped up and began offering high priced, high-speed automation. The automation was invariably designed to produce a single model and had to be replaced with each design change. The waste of intellect on getting the automation to run and waste of capital on systems that could not meet the early high demand and then had to limp along for years at low speeds was costly.

97. Organization Development: The decision to dismiss the maintenance crews who once installed new equipment and systems threw away an avenue to firsthand knowledge when breakdowns occur.

Recap 1970s and 1980s

Annual sales volume increased through these decades from 11.4 to 14.1 million. The last of the non-Big Three American auto companies disappeared. American Motors was bought out by Chrysler in 1987. International stopped making light trucks in 1975. Sales for America's Big Three (of vehicles built in the U.S.) increased from 9.7 to 10.7 million, while imports increased from 1.0 to 3.5 million. The net was an increase in volume for the Big Three, but a loss in market share from 85 to 75 percent. Imports of the Volkswagen Beetle and others from Germany grew to 400,000 per year and leveled off, while imports from Japan climbed from 188,000 to 2,275,000. The imports from Korea were just beginning.

In the mid sixties Detroit began its counter to the anticipated arrival of imports from Japan: the Corolla from Toyota, Civic from Honda, and Datsun from Nissan. The Big Three prepared a new generation of small cars: the Pinto, Vega, and AMC Gremlin, and a new wave of light-weight power trains to go with them. All three models, however, would prove to have design flaws, from gas tank ruptures to short life spans on aluminum engines. By the time OPEC's first drum roll reached American filling stations in 1973, the wave of Pinto, Vega, and AMC Gremlin had already made their poor impression. The Corolla, Civic, Datsun, and Subaru were proving to be reliable and fuel efficient. They were also being upgraded.

Imports reached 1.8 million in 1973 in the midst of the panic over oil shortages. The early imports were designed for the heavily taxed fuel and narrow streets of other nations. In America they would suffice for short trips but were not meant for America's life style. Import sales began dropping in 1974. Slipping to 1.4 million and lower as American consumers went back to choosing vehicles designed for their lifestyle.

During the seventies teams of Japanese and Korean designers and development engineers began filling the auto shows with models and options designed for American interests. GM made a third counter move with its Chevette in 1976. Fitted out with a new 1.4 and 1.6-liter engine, it still didn't have much appeal. In 1979, the second oil shock struck and the financial-criteria-based decision leaders were forced to make a major decision. They followed the imports, changing the entire fleet of American automobiles to front-wheel-drive (FWD) and body-frame-integral (BFI) structures. The heavy tubular steel frame was eliminated and the body sheet metal stiffened to give it structural integrity. It wasn't until years later, in 1983, that the first American FWD-BFI developments hit the market. Design and development had been expensive and the production acceleration was slow. For GM and Ford, the shift to platforming was a blow to brand images. GM's first platform was badged as a Chevrolet Citation, Pontiac Phoenix, Buick Skylark, Oldsmobile Omega and Cadillac Cimarron. The models all looked alike and customers noticed.

The Big Three chose to also partner with small foreign companies during this period. They began to import small cars and it was no surprise that this strategy did not go well. The partnerships the Big Three were able to land were with the lesser foreign companies. The companies that had had trouble competing with the giants of their own country had trouble competing with the same giants on American soil.

There were many other things that caused a slump in profits and sales volume. Customers were herded away from ordering their choice of options and pushed into ordering bundles of options. The freedom to custom order, once attractive to carriage customers was taken away again.

The Big Three found the UAW willing and able to sacrifice jobs for wages and benefits. The purchase of automation and the push to out-source increased. Attempts were made to solve problems in operations by hiring more white shirts. The result was an ineffective middle management swelling unchecked. The Big Three were being dealt many blows from many sides.

CHAPTER 7. 1990s AND 2000s: THREE DINOSAURS ARE LURED ACROSS THE PACIFIC

The descriptions of these last two decades, from 1989 to 2009, are not like the others. They do not have the clarity that comes with hindsight. Many of the long-term decisions made in these two decades have not yet played out, making it impossible to back into what was jotted down on the back of the envelope. I can only offer my opinion as to what must be on the back of three envelopes at this time. I offer what I have observed while on special assignments for two Board chairmen in the nineties, both trying to alter the course of General Motors. I add insights gained from serving as chief executive officer of startup, called Hypercar, intent on introducing a hydrogen-powered automobile technology. And I add my observations during an attempt to pull together a collective of American entrepreneurs to introduce a production-ready hydrogen-powered vehicle that would employ a manufacturing system to replace the assembly line and operate under a very different business model.

> 1970s and 1980s—Imports: Continue to develop fuel-efficient and low-priced countermeasures to the threat of imports. Prepare to counter the exchange rate advantages of imports as they move up into higher priced vehicles. Improve the perception of quality in American vehicles.

This objective had to be totally rewritten because it wasn't working:

> 1990s and 2000s—Imports: Go out and meet the competition on their home field. Capture market share as demand for transportation increases in Asian and in South and Central American countries. Use the income from these global operations to offset losses in the American market as it falls prey to government backed imports from around the globe. Trust American consumers to keep America's product development teams on their toes as the Big Three make preparations to manufacture all vehicles in foreign countries and ship them back to sell in Big Three dealerships across America. "If you can't fight 'em, join 'em."

In the nineties and in the first decade of the new millennium, the Big Three and the world's other auto producers stepped up their involvement in expanding ventures in South and Central America; the auto companies of Korea and Japan expanded their exports; China began advertising itself as the new frontier and lured in automakers from around the globe. The wisdom of the Chinese leadership and its long-term planning has already begun to reveal itself as it captures more and more of the world's industrial goods production. The world's auto production seems to be next.

> *1970s and 1980s—Growth: Focus on holding market share while increasing profits, through a decrease in the number of models and options and with a shift to platforming and packaged options.*

This envelope item remained the same for the U.S. market despite the declining market share, but it was expanded to include capturing growth in other countries:

> *1990s and 2000s—Growth: Expand holdings in growth regions of the world including China and India; expand capability in Korea, China, Mexico, and other nations, seemingly with the intent of increasing exports of automobiles back to the United States.*

In 1997 the Big Three began a series of moves to expand their holdings in Asia. China was seen as the world's next emerging region and GM became the first of the Big Three to sign a joint venture agreement with one of China's emerging automakers. China's State Planning Committee traveled to the U.S. from Beijing along with the Mayor of Shanghai for the historic signing of the Joint Venture (JV) agreement. Their trip included a visit to GM's Research Labs and I was asked to be one of three presenters that day. I spoke of the importance of Scenario Planning in steering long term thinking in a large corporation. How ideas can bubble up from a stimulated and interactive gathering of 50 of the company's best long-term thinkers and how documentation of their gatherings can help the leadership in their long-term decision making. Of the three presentations that afternoon mine was the only one to stir a hurried conversation between our guests. Thinking back to their burst of conversation in a dialect that no one understood, I can't help but wonder if they were concerned that we might have already figured out how they were planning to dispose of the world's automakers. Perhaps they thought we had already figured out a counter move.

That week GM became the second major auto company to sign a joint venture (JV) agreement with the Chinese. Volkswagen had signed the first one in the eighties and was already running two successful vehicle assembly plants. Ford quickly followed GM and two of America's Big Three began investing heavily in factories and equipment in China. They also began coercing the American component and tooling supply base to join them in China because the JV agreements insisted that all vehicles assembled and sold in China be assembled from components made in China. Some wise planning in Beijing had already figured out a way to assure there would be no equivalent of Orderly Market Agreements (OMAs) or Voluntary Restraint Agreements (VRAs) to sort out after the JVs began selling cars. They had also figured out a short cut to getting into the auto business. The GM/Shanghai Automotive JV would climb to 1.8 million in sales in 2009 making it the largest foreign automotive JV in China.[1]

Ventures from Europe included Shanghai Volkswagen Automotive Co., Ltd. (SVW) in conjunction with the FAW-VW Automobile Co., Ltd., which together sold 1.4 million vehicles in 2009. Europe's PSA Peugeot Citroen signed up for a JV and so did Fiat. But problems with the Fiat JV would end in Fiat's withdrawal.

Soon after the turn of the century three of Japan's automakers including Toyota, Honda, and Nissan, would sign JV agreements with partners in China. By 2009 they were collectively producing more than 2 million vehicles on Chinese soil. These Japanese companies evolved quickly into exporting at the encouragement of their Chinese partners. Their exports fed into the existing shipping network and vehicles built in China began to arrive unannounced in U.S., Canadian and European seaports.

Korea's Hyundai Kia signed up for a JV agreement and began to also invest in China. In 2009 their volume of sales reached 811,700 outpacing Toyota.[2]

I did not fathom in 1997 that a JV agreement signed with China would evolve in 12 years to surpass U.S. auto production. In 2009 China produced 13.6 million light vehicles surpassing America's 10.4 million. Nor did I fathom that exports from China built in Japanese JV plants would begin offloading at American seaports. GM's production in China reached 1.8 million in 2009 nearing its 2.1 million output on U.S. soil. The signing in 1997 has proven to be far more significant to jobs in America than I had fathomed.[3]

> *1970s and 1980s—Sourcing: Prepare proposals that include plans for all components to be out-sourced in the future. Beef up purchasing strategies to control prices.*

Direction was altered and the emphasis was increased:

> *1990s and 2000s—Sourcing: Harvest price reductions from outside suppliers as they migrate to Asia; focus on developing outside suppliers for all remaining components in Asia as well as the United States, with the exception of the machining of a few components and the assembly of power trains; focus on out-sourcing all vehicle subassembly work and keeping in-house only the body assembly, paint, and the attachments of major subassemblies; step up efforts to build vehicles overseas and import them to the States.*

A century earlier, the strategy for survival as one of the new automakers was to quickly integrate automotive component manufacturing with vehicle assembly; this in-sourcing of manufacturing and assembly processes avoided the con-

---

1 *Global Times*, accessed on March 24, 2010, source Gasgoo (14.44 Jan 19, 2010) http//autos.globaltimes.cn/china/2010-01/499513.html
2 *Automotive News*, Crane Publications, March, 2010
3 Jerry Flint, "Detroit's Long Road," *Forbes Magazine*, April 12, 2010

trolling carriage-component supply network that was spreading the secrets of processing to all automakers and erasing a basis of competition. For half a century, Ford Motor Company's evolution in technology had relied on the ingenuity of its internal manufacturing workforce. But beginning in the fifties, their in-sourcing focus was displaced by out-sourcing. Purchasing agents were charged with keeping prices in line, the supply of components flowing, and technical advances from being shared with competitors. But the expectations did not produce the desired result. For example, in '92, General Motors enticed J. Ignacio Lopez de Arriortua to Detroit from Europe with an offer of a position of vice president in charge of purchasing. Lopez appointed disciples who were instructed to send ripples through the component, tooling, equipment, and raw materials supply base across America. Lopez would auction off GM's internal contracts to the lowest bidders. He broke good-faith relations and trust with many long-standing suppliers. Some were cut off because they had been lent development funding to get started but had never delivered or repaid their loans. Until Lopez came along, many outside component suppliers had been shut out of doing business because in-house component divisions at GM had a lock on dealing with operations and design. Lopez offered all suppliers a chance to bid directly against the in-house providers. Lopez vowed, "There will be no politics, no protection, for GM parts divisions." He even invited unsolicited bids for contracts already signed for future models.[1]

In nine months Lopez would bring all GM purchasing activities worldwide under a single roof. In-house component and system builders were forced to compete for work. Lopez employed a bullying routine on price reductions and used the withholding of a share of volume if the supplier did not comply. Suppliers were placed on preferred lists. Ranking on the list determined the amount of volume being allocated. The media around Detroit was filled with hype from the disgruntled suppliers. Ford and Chrysler were affected. The in-house component system providers at GM and Ford began to struggle. Seven years later, on May 28, 1999, GM cut loose its DELPHI organization. The goal of out-sourcing all automotive component making at GM was complete. Ford Motor Company followed suit, on June 28, 2000, spinning off its Visteon Division. These two divisions would have to seek contracts with the other auto companies to survive. The transplant operations in middle America provided some contract opportunities, but Asian auto companies would never really subscribe to the Lopez approach to sourcing.

Fifty years of stacking out-sourcing threats on bargaining tables at Ford and GM culminated in the out-sourcing of all automotive components. What started

---

1   Michael G. Sheldrick, "A Sea of Change in GM's Purchasing—General Motors Corp. Vice President of Worldwide Purchasing J. Ignacio Lopez de Arriortua," *Automotive Electronics, Electronic News* (June 22, 1992).

as threats to keep UAW demands for wages and benefits in check evolved into what Henry Ford and William Durant would proclaim as an untenable position.

There was something else that came with Lopez. He brought his vision for Volkswagen with him. At Volkswagen and other auto companies in Europe suppliers were expected to provide a great deal more than components including: engineering support, and even basic technological advances. In America only the internal supply base had been allowed "inside" until Lopez came along. Lopez opened the doors and allowed the supply base inside. They began working elbow to elbow with design and development teams inside GM. By the time DELPHI and Visteon were spun off six years later, members of the American supply base were on the inside looking out. These same suppliers were also agreeing to begin joint ventures in China to help the Big Three comply with the Chinese requirement that all cars built in China be assembled from components made in China. It is not a stretch to imagine a supply base linked into the Big Three in the States sharing as they learn with their new Chinese partners. But it is a stretch to imagine Henry Ford willing to make the Lopez decision.

> *1970s and 1980s—Product Design and Development: Collapse the number of option offerings; all but eliminate the annual model change; shift the fundamental design of passenger cars from rear- to front-wheel drive; replace the traditional body-on-frame structure with body-frame-integral structures; expand the platforming concept.*

Was somewhat reversed:

> *1990s and 2000s—Product Design and Development: Increase the apparent differences between models from the same platform. Cultivate interest in custom pickup truck designs and SUVs to harvest sunk cost in large rear-wheel-drive power-train developments. Begin to publicize new alternative fuel developments to shore up stock-market value and make preparations to follow if other pioneers succeed in setting direction on the issues of global warming and peak oil.*

The body-on-frame–front-wheel-drive (BFI-FWD) objectives for cars in the eighties continued to evolve, saving money and reducing weight. The nineties brought new emphasis on visible differentiation in the designs of models from a common platform. Engineering expertise in BOF-RWD design and development was transferred to upscale pickup trucks and SUVs. The light-truck designers targeted consumer interest in: a means to commune with nature if busy schedules ever allow an escape; a better-than-average means to escape insecure urban environments; a better-than-average means to escape from a disaster; an ability to survive in increasingly frequent inclement weather. Developments in new alternative fuels were tracked to hold the interest of more shareholders.

> *1970s and 1980s—Organization Development: Continue filling front-line management with professionals; adopt statistical quality control procedures along the front lines; avoid Edward Deming's path toward greater reliance on the workforce; cut back on apprenticeships in anticipation of the shifts to automation and out-sourcing. Add layers of support staff and*

middle management to deal with more issues as new competitive challenges emerge.

1990s and 2000s—Organization Development: This envelope item remained unchanged, making America more vulnerable every year.

1990s and 2000s—Unions: Continue cutting back skilled trades, increase out-sourcing and investments in automation. Introduce a new type of chip onto the bargaining tables with the name of a plant site on each one. Turn excess capacity into closing and reopening threats as part of the bargaining process.

Was rewritten entirely and requires some explanation. By 1990 the battles between union and management were all but over. The objectives of bargainers on both sides had been met. Both sides were proud that they had won their battle not realizing they had lost the war. The new charter for union and management at the Saturn Corporation had been overthrown by a joint effort in Detroit. Roger Smith had been ushered out and the Saturn experiment was shut down. Its dealerships and brand name were folded into the mainstream.

The post-war effort to tie Japan to the West had been successful. The yen was allowed to float in the global currency exchanges.

As more U.S. manufacturing plants were closed, the UAW was left without a workforce to represent. The objective for dealing with unions was re-written.

1990s and 2000s—Unions: Shift all financial responsibility for benefits for UAW-represented workers onto the shoulders of the UAW organization.

The spinning off of Visteon by Ford and DELPHI by GM were the final all-in plays, with each side of the bargaining table gaining something, while the last of America's automotive craftsmen were cast to the four winds to the great delight of the Asian competition. In Detroit there was no more need to stack out-sourcing threats or automation plans on bargaining tables. Most of the high-roller chips, marked car assembly or power-train manufacturing plant, were disappearing fast. The game of collective bargaining was over. It had employed many negotiators for half a century.

1990s and 2000s—Sales: Stop the development of counter threats to the NADA; lean customers away from interest in annual model change, custom orders, and choice of options. Get customers back to buying from inventory.

It was time to get back to a traditional business school objective:

1990s and 2000s—Sales: Increase effectiveness in advertising and salesmanship.

The number of import dealerships and the competition among dealerships increased, and the behind-the-scenes battles for a balance of rights between dealer and manufacturer resurfaced. Behind closed doors, the dealers negotiated the right to offer products from multiple manufacturers in their showrooms and in their new dealer malls. It was a shift in power in favor of dealers. It gave customers a better opportunity for side-by-side comparison of brands and manufacturers. It is logical that showing multiple manufacturers would allow dealers to pressure manufacturers to stop forcing excess inventory onto their lots during sales slumps. Dealers could also focus their advertising and salesmanship on products for which manufacturers were offering the highest margins.

In the 1990s and 2000s, the cost of delivering an automobile was rising. Fewer sales per dealership for the Big Three meant dealer expenses had to be spread over fewer sales. At the same time, import sales were rising which meant foreign dealerships were operating at lower margins. Sales for the Big Three were dropping, and they had too many dealerships. This problem was solved when bankruptcy court protections in 2009 allowed the Big Three to trim out their least effective dealerships.

> *1990s and 2000s—Equipment: Solicit proposals for automation wherever possible. Avoid using the emerging universal CNC equipment in production environments.*

Was expanded in the 1990s and 2000s to read:

> *1990s and 2000s—Equipment: Expect machine tool companies to take full responsibility for the design, build, and launch of automated systems in the United States and abroad, including the acceleration of production. Continue to steer clear of CNC machining in American operations but not in regions like the Czech Republic.*

By the early 1990s, the evolution in machining equipment had gone full circle. The auto business had begun with standard mills and lathes and with standard cutting tools used by highly skilled apprentices. It had evolved to use special equipment with preset stops and tooling that could be operated by quickly trained line workers and tuned by highly skilled setup men. Then came the shift to transfer lines dedicated to a single component design and producing one finished part with each cycle. These transfer lines were attended by skilled setup men and by full-time tool changers. The next step was to automate these transfer lines, adding the robots to load and unload and well-lit control panels and lighted waterfalls of coolant. At this point, only the fly-in experts could get the machines to run, and they never ran at published speeds for more than a few minutes.

The 1980s brought the introduction of more durable computerized controls into the production environment in Europe and Japan. CNC production was part of the early planning for the 1989 opening of Saturn's Springhill operation. These CNC machines were really the machines of Henry Ford's early days but with computers taking over for the attentive hands of the craftsmen who operated them. Applying Kentucky windage (getting the basic machine to produce more accurately than what a machine builder could promise) became the responsibility of the computer. The CNC machines could be programmed to adjust for deflection in the part and temperature and tooling wear. Unlike the blind automation that had become so popular, the new CNC machines could be programmed to make adjustments on the fly and reprogrammed to make other components instead of purchasing new equipment.

But for production operations to shift back to using Kentucky windage—to take advantage of the capability of CNC machines—the knowledge and skills of the attending workforce would have to increase. The skills gained through apprenticeship would have to return. Machining equipment had made its full circle from high skills requirements to low and back again. It had circled from standard machines and standard tooling to turnkey automation and back again. America's assembly line workforce and its management, locked in labor disputes, could not adapt. As a result, CNC was avoided rather than welcomed by the Big Three.

In 1995 the General Motors management in Europe approved the building of a CNC-equipped engine plant in Eisenach, Germany. The shift away from transfer lines that Saturn had planned four years earlier but was unable to execute was approved for this site, which was surrounded by an industrial culture. GM in Eastern Germany was stepping up to match the technological skills that Ferrari had been using for more than a decade. The trouble is there are only a few places left in the world like eastern Germany and the Czech Republic where the culture still nurtures industrial craft aspirations. It made sense to choose Eisenach for the introduction of a CNC-based engine plant.

LONG-TERM INEFFICIENCIES IN THE OBJECTIVES OF THE 1990s AND 2000s

98. Organization Development: The shift toward CNC machines introduced many new classifications into the American workforce when it should have simply been a new tool for existing journeymen and line workers.

99. Growth: There is little evidence that the decision makers of this nation are planning for growth through higher levels of domestic industrial investment and domestic sourcing; there seems to be no effort to counter the dependence on sourcing from foreign manufacturers.

100. Sourcing: A squeeze on prices slows supplier investments in research.

101. Sourcing: There is an intangible value in the secrets of getting machines, tools, and fixtures to mass produce components. Out-sourcing and letting the Masters of component making leave without training a new round of apprentices meant the retirees would take their handed-down secrets of processing components with them as the headed home for the last time. There was no going back.

102. Sourcing: Considering its experience base, America's industrial-sector leadership is no longer capable of planning or implementing sweeping

reconsiderations of its out-sourcing strategy.

To reestablish the involvement of front-line craftsmen would require a reevaluation of staffing across the entire industry.

103. Sourcing: Important intangibles have been erased from America's memory: those gained from linking assembly operations to component operations and those gained from engaging the hands-on intellect and creative energy of the entire workforce.

104. Sourcing: As the supply base moved overseas, the direct links between vehicle developers and component makers became a struggle. The high speed visual links attempt to duplicate hands on decision making but are not as effective.

Day-to-day face-to-face communication between the hands-on tooling maintenance crews and the engineers assigned to oversee product development became increasingly impossible as industry walked away from Henry Ford's approach to organizing a workforce. Increasing distance and adding translation problems to component manufacturing evolved to make the Big Three less and less competitive. At the same time it has been getting easier for Asian automakers backed by their governments to achieve long-term industrial objectives.

105. Sourcing: Initiating continuous improvements is almost impossible for an outside supplier.

Changes in current automotive component designs to accommodate a supplier's innovations rarely get approved. They introduce risks to the flow of operations in the midst of struggles to keep up with demand. Similarly, it is difficult for a component supplier to get an innovation into a new car program. Each new component adds another risk to the success of the launch.

106. Product Design and Development: With platforming as a strategy innovations in design are especially difficult for the Big Three. The competition is not using platforming.

Designers must strive for a perfect balance of style, performance, handling, and now energy efficiency. They must then meld their creation into a common platform when it is often uniqueness that sells.

107. Organization Development: American industry once thrived on its hive-mind capability. But decision making during the last two decades has shifted to a focus on equipment and not the workforce producing industrial goods. The auto industry in particular may have forgotten how to rekindle a hive-mind environment.

108. Organization Development: America has filled its management ranks with the in-experienced. Auto manufacturers in Japan, Mexico, China, and the Czech Republic are using up-from-the-ranks management in operations.

The decision to fill the leadership along the front lines with college graduates has proven to be a poor tactic, negatively influencing our ability to remain competitive.

109. Organization Development: It is a mistake to assume American competitiveness has ever been firmly rooted in patents or on drawing boards. The real roots are in the evolving knowledge base of the workforce, and in this regard American industry has lost touch.

The real foundation of competition has been systematically handed over to turnkey automation providers. The interfaces between automation builders and either the customer or operations have become so convoluted with levels of management that nothing gets through.

110. Organization Development: In the few locations in America where CNC equipment has been introduced, it has been difficult to manage a CNC workforce in the midst of the larger workforce tied to the mindless tasks of bucket brigades. Even when both workforces are compensated equally, there is a division in commitment to the job that breeds ill will.

Expectations that well-suited workers will flow toward the right jobs does not work in a free-choice environment where there are a limited number of jobs. In actuality, workers with the most seniority migrate to jobs that look easier. In industry all workers cannot do all jobs though they do not realize it. The right of higher seniority is a significant cultural issue in need of reform.

111. Unions: Thinking that the battle for profitability can be won by holding wages and benefits in check may serve to shore up share price, but it doesn't begin to address the problem of losing market share.

112. Unions: Threats of out-sourcing, automation, and plant closings were played like chips in a game of cards till the bluffs were called too many times, resulting in trends. The union threats of strikes led to higher wages and benefits but only for those still around to elect another round of union leaders. The bargaining tables were serving up short-term wins on both sides. The real loser was America and its economy.

The union's rank and file must trust their elected representatives. The major shareholders must trust the company's appointees. Neither side wants to allow cameras behind its closed doors. Cameras would reveal UAW representatives choosing to sacrifice one plant site over another and answer why they chose to give away jobs for one group and not the others. The company appointees would have to reveal to shareholders the amounts of wealth in their tradeoffs and why they chose one over the other. Both are complex subjects too complex for cameras to pick up.

The bottom line after five decades of collective bargaining has been a steady decline of America's industrial base. Wages and benefits rose to make America fourth[1] on the scale of highest-paying industrial nations but smaller in terms of industrial exports. The automobile exports of other nations have become more popular. The real losers in all of this have been the American economy and America's standard of living. National security will be next as the industrial base collapses.

113. Sales: The competition for automotive customers requires more than good arrangements of balloons and banners or price incentives.

Henry Ford knew it was about having a superior product, which demanded the nurturing of continuous improvement skills in his workforce. He established a system of manufacture and level of integration where a hive mind could thrive. Component suppliers today are spreading themselves around the globe in search of lower wages. The required complex innovations involving combinations of mating components have begun to bog down without daily personal interactions between knowledgeable parties. This is something that cannot be accomplished online in the middle of the night by parties only concerned about profitability.

114. Sales: There have been many costly business practices rolled into the price of an automobile at dealerships in America.

Local media in the thirties was sometimes paid to print notices that the local dealer was going to cut their margin on Saturday. Henry Ford was often the culprit, paying for notices that proclaimed the local dealer was going cut his operating margin from 14 percent to 12 percent. In the fifties the NADA made this practice illegal. Today manufacturers can no longer quote selling prices if they also sell the model through a dealership in the same state. Dealer margins today are closer to 25 percent. They vary from year to year and dealer to dealer depending on how many cars are sold. Current bankruptcy proposals include provisions for GM and Chrysler to close dealerships, which will enable the remaining dealers to lower prices and hopefully increase their sales—this at a time when the dealer approach to retailing cars is becoming obsolete. Selling wholesale was chosen by Henry Ford and others a time when all buyers needed lessons in how to start the engine and operate the features of their first automobile including; the shifting of gears, controlling the throttle, applying the brakes, and advancing or retarding the spark. They also needed a complex set of lubrication instructions. Selling

---

1 Kevin Phillips, *American Theocracy: The Perils and Politics of Radical Religion, Oil, and Borrowed Money in the 21st Century* (New York: Viking, Penguin Books, 2006).

through dealers was also a vital means by which manufacturers could quickly recover their investments in materials and labor.

American dealers today participate in a "dealer trade" system that appears to be a free service for consumers, but in fact adds roughly $100 to the cost of delivery of all new cars. It gives consumers more vehicles to choose from as dealers swap vehicles to make a sale. There are already companies selling used cars on line and delivering direct to your door. It is only a matter of time until foreign manufacturer will make a move and by-pass the investment in a chain of dealerships. A head of research at one the leading information companies told me in 1997 that it would be possible to make money, operating at a 9 percent margin, connecting retail customers to cars sitting on the docks at American seaports.

Automobiles assembled in America today are assessed a $300 to $600 delivery charge. The charge has been rising with fuel prices and traffic congestion. Imports are assessed another $300 to $600 for shipment across the ocean. Localizing the manufacture of automobiles and selling them direct to local consumers would increase profit margins. And while there are state laws against manufacturers selling vehicles directly to retail customers, the banning of manufacturers from selling cars is only applicable if the vehicle is that is only if the vehicle is not also sold through dealerships in the same state.

One of the hidden costs for dealers is the financing of the inventory of cars on the lot. This expense has been part of the automotive dealership business model since Henry Ford began. The norm for inventory is now one hundred days. The number is a rule of thumb for providing consumers with enough choices of optional features and color and serves as a buffer between dealer and manufacturer. Doing the math—a hundred days of inventory across America at an annual sales volume of 12 million means there are 3.28 million vehicles on dealer lots. If the average dealer cost per vehicle is $10,000, the investment in dealer inventory is $32.8 billion. The interest payment on $32.8 billion at 5 percent for one hundred days is $449 million. The inventory holding cost tacked on to each selling price at 5 percent for one hundred days would be $137.

Without knowing it, car buyers are being assessed:

$137 to keep inventory selection on the lot;

$100 for access to a dealer trade system;

$400 for delivery from the manufacturer; and

$450 more if it has to be shipped across an ocean.

These are all ballpark figures and meant to simply suggest that there could be advantages to building cars in local factories.

115. Manufacturing System: The emerging era of multiple choices in energy and propulsion systems is pointing toward increased proliferation in vehicle structure and styling, all of which is pointing toward further incompatibility of the assembly line decision.

High-scale producers spinning out platforms and trying to limit consumer choice cannot expect to continue to control the market.

Recap 1990s and 2000s

The growth in volume of new automobile sales leveled off in these decades. The 100,000-mile warranty programs had lengthened product life cycles to the point where they reduced the requirements for new vehicles. The desire to have more vehicles in the driveway also waned, perhaps because the reality of only being able to drive one at a time was settling in. There were 16.0 million new cars and light trucks sold in 1989 and 16.3 million in 2007.[1] The volume of production by the Big Three in American factories dropped from 12.0 to 7.1 million, while import volume rose from 3.5 to 7.0 million with a small portion of them being produced in foreign plants partially owned by the Big Three. The transplant production that began on American soil in the eighties reached 2.2 million in 2007. The misconception that transplants employed Americans was well advertised. In reality a transplant operation employs only 20 percent of the people that would be required if the vehicle and all of its components were designed and built on American soil. Transplants are good for the Asian economy and largely for appearances in America.

The bottom line of these most recent decades is simply that less than half of all auto industry jobs are still performed on American soil. Over half of the revenue spent on new automobiles is now flowing to other nations. The impact on the American economy is much larger than people realize. Every autoworker job that is lost must be multiplied by eight to arrive at an approximation of how many other American jobs go with them. A dollar earned by selling an automobile changes hands roughly eight times before it leaves town. The impact of wiping out America's industrial sector is huge.

All of the adjustments to the back of the envelope in these decades have so far resulted in negative growth for America's auto industry. The Big Three have struggled to find balance in the midst of their downward spiral, cutting back in one facet and then the next. The shifting of blame led to more slashing of headcount, which led to more imbalance and so on. The Big Three became the Big Two for a while when Daimler Benz purchased Chrysler in 1998. Hopes were high that adding lower-priced entries to the Mercedes lineup would somehow add profits on both sides of the Atlantic. Nine years later it is was clear that the joint venture was not going to work. Daimler sold 80 percent of its interest to Cerberus Capital Management for $7.4 billion. Financial officers were back in charge of making the long-term decisions at Chrysler.

---

1 Automotive News Data Books (1989–2007).

The nineties were ushered in with the launch of Saturn Corporation by GM. It was a prototype of a new back of the envelope for the rest of the corporation. It had been a decade in the making and was Roger Smith's move to introduce sweeping change to the Detroit business model. Its hive-mind characteristics would have impressed Henry Ford, but the rest of the corporation pushed back, proving that even a Board chairman could not alter where the union/management battles were taking America's industrial base. Saturn's approach to resolving a half century of conflict between union and management was rebuked by both sides at Detroit's bargaining tables. Roger Smith failed to anticipate just how great a threat Saturn's partnership with the UAW would become. It threatened the livelihood of both union and management leaders in Detroit whose kingdoms were erected on a foundation of conflict. What happened in the hallways outside the collective bargaining rooms is not documented and not yet revealed in memoirs.

Michael Moore's *Roger and Me* hit the movie theaters in 1989 just before Saturn's new line of vehicles began rolling out of Springhill, Tennessee. The movie publicly saddled Roger Smith with the desertion of towns across America, when desertion was the doing of Roger's predecessors. It made Smith appear a fool at a time when he was launching a sweeping change in business model that would drive imports back to their ships. More important Smith's new business model would stabilize communities, just the opposite of what was being portrayed in the movie. Saturn's Springhill site actually rivaled Henry Ford's Rouge complex both in level of in-sourcing and in its potential for longevity in the community. Moore's movie made no mention of the return to cultural stability inherent in Saturn's new operation.

The Saturn engineering center was disbanded soon after the movie hit the theaters. The highly skilled hands on the team that had built its own prototypes were told, "Spread what you have learned to the other engineering centers across the company." It was the beginning of the end. No more Saturn models would be developed. The team at Springhill faced the daunting task of the launch of a new body shop and paint shop and the simultaneous launch of a new engine and new transmission. To everyone's surprise the plant accelerated quickly. Within three years agreements of production launch agreements across the bargaining tables in Detroit began forcing the Springhill site to hire disgruntled UAW leaders from other plants. The harmony of the hive-mind workforce in Springhill ran into disruptive union leaders from other sites. The wheels were being yanked off the pilot of GM's new business model. By the time John Smale took over as chairman it was clear that the hopes of Saturn were dismissed forever. Smale attempted to make a more palatable course correction and was placated with agreements to spin off EDS, Hughes Defense Systems, and GM's military vehicles division. But the course of the giant dirigible was not altered.

Perhaps when organizations become too large, their fiefdoms become too numerous and resilient for any leader other than the founder to steer. Today the leadership of North America's automotive segment is counting on financial gains through bankruptcy protections to bring the balance sheets around for the next few quarters and bring the stock price back above the horizon line. Hopes are high in Detroit that enough fabric can be pulled together for another round of golden parachutes. Things like: wage reductions, shifting pension burdens onto the shoulders of the Pension Benefit Guaranty Corporation (the government), and cutting back on the number of dealerships, are supposed to make the Big Three competitive. But thoughts of coming to agreement on new objectives for the back of the envelope are not emerging from the smoke and mirrors of bankruptcy proceedings. The North American portion of the leadership of the Big Three does not seem to realize that their seat belts will not release before their empty fuselage hits the ground. Reshaping America's Big Three does not seem to be a priority.

CHAPTER 8. ASSESSMENT OF CHINA'S INDUSTRIAL SECTOR

It all began with a phone call in December 2003 from someone in Beijing who the previous summer had politely listened to my harangue of Detroit's poor decision making. We had spent five hours together, on an eighteen-hole golf course. I will name him Chris, and his wife Joelle. They were both Americans back home for a visit after living in Beijing for six years. Chris was the chief operating officer and Joelle the personnel director for a successful joint venture that imported and distributed American baby care products. On the phone Chris explained that he had related my thoughts on auto making to a member of a private equity firm in China named Eric. This Eric wanted to hear more, and Chris suggested I meet him in San Francisco the following week.

In doing some homework for the meeting, I discovered that Eric was one of three members of an investment group with roughly $75 million in assets. They were doing business out of an office in Shanghai and a small office in San Francisco. Chris had explained that they were looking for their next business opportunity and might be supportive of a venture that could evolve into an automotive company.

Eric and I met in his office in San Francisco on December 24 for lunch. We reached an understanding of where our interests were common and agreed that I should travel to China to see some things for myself. We would meet again in Shanghai at the end my travels. I would contribute my assessments of the possibilities for the business model, and Eric would bring his findings on the interest levels of other Shanghai investors.

Chris and Joelle made the arrangements for as many meetings as possible before the Chinese New Year began. With a visitor's visa in hand, I landed in Beijing on January 13. Joelle served as my interpreter and proved to be highly skilled. We jumped from meeting to meeting until the weekend when we shifted to cultural exposure. Nine days and seventeen meetings later Chris, Joelle, and I flew to Shanghai to meet with Eric.

My reasons for wanting to consider doing business in China had been three: (1) the twenty-two provinces of China had all been encouraged by Chairman Mao to start a car company. The scaled-down approach to auto production I was carrying would make it possible for each province to have an automotive manufacturing site. For all the small plants to be competitive, they would need to have close ties to a central research, development, and training center. It was a business model that suited the interests of China's State Planning Committee. (2) I carried a proposal for a hydrogen-powered vehicle that was supported by researchers back in the States who were eager to get their concepts out from under the thumbs of the Big Three. The proposal included a shift to lightweight all-composite bodies, to electronics in place of hydraulic and mechanical controls, and to hydrogen fuel cells in place of combustion engines. It was an offer of a path that skipped over many of the traditional and costly processes for making automobiles. I believed that a government that had already skipped over the setting of telephone poles and stringing wires would be interested in another leapfrog opportunity. (3) The high-scale operations in the present approach to making and selling automobiles are vulnerable to the low-scale-factory assault I was proposing. America's dinosaurs were busy showing China how to build and operate huge assembly plants; I was going to offer a highly efficient low-scale development opportunity. China's Provinces could be the first to implement and set an example for other nations to follow. I thought it was bold move and it had certainly attracted Eric's interest.

With the help of Chris and Joelle, I talked to people in the U.S. Embassy and met American joint-venture attorneys and business managers. I talked with practitioners of imports and exports and met entrepreneurs. I attended a party at the American Club and listened intently to the Americans' tales of life in China, all of which made me feel like I was in an old black and white movie in the British sector of Shanghai. My conversations in the embassy and in legal offices were laced with subtle warnings. The civil courts handling international disputes always favor the Chinese partner. If you get into a dispute with your joint-venture partner, expect that your idea of a fifty-fifty settlement will resolve at eighty-twenty with you on the short end and expect that reparation payments will take decades. Despite all the cautions, there were enough plusses to make China the location for the launch of a new business model without assembly lines, without dealerships, and with a very different level of responsibility for a collective of workers.

On my seventh day, arrangements were made for me to be picked up at 7:00 a.m. A black sedan pulled up in front of the condo and a driver held a piece of paper with my last name on it. Giving him a simple nod, I slid into the backseat. We rode in silence for ninety minutes, heading southeast toward Tianjin. The empty winter fields and leafless trees along the fencerows reminded me of farms in the Saginaw

Valley in late November. All that was missing were the high-ceilinged two-story houses with Centennial Farm markers in the yard.

We pulled up in front of an unmarked building, and I let myself into a tiny unattended lobby at the foot of a stairway. After a moment or two, I climbed to the mezzanine. Paul, a lanky Canadian entrepreneur, greeted me in an open office environment where only Asian employees attended the drawing boards and desks. He introduced me to those who spoke English, and I nodded politely to the rest.

The mezzanine windows across the back provided an unobstructed view over the eighty-thousand-square-feet of factory floor. Paul pointed to a nearly completed bulk material conveyor six feet wide and so long that it was being assembled on a diagonal in three sections spanning the entire building. The conveyor was intended for a seaport where it would load and unload grain, ore, and other bulk goods. The place reminded me of the construction shop in Plant 7 where mill-wrights would rework hundreds of conveyors to meet the specifications for the approaching annual rearrange. While conversing we walked out onto a balcony and down a stairway to the floor. Paul was a proud and engaging fellow, charged with energy. "I understand you are here looking into starting your own business?" he asked.

"Just looking," I replied, "I'm trying to get a feel for what it will be like to do business in China."

With that, Paul began his tale of one of life's lessons. "I came to China in 1996," he began. "Shipping docks were expanding in every port, and they needed conveyors. I sold my Canadian partner on the idea of setting up a satellite in this new frontier. It was a place for us to expand." He paused and then added, "But I was wrong."

I returned a puzzled look and we walked on.

"This one here," he said, tapping the freshly painted steel, "is destined for western Canada."

Now I was really puzzled.

"Back in '96 the Chinese government would not allow a private company to do business in bulk-material handling systems. They appointed a fifty-fifty joint-venture partner, and I signed an agreement." Paul looked at me and added, "Business laws here have changed since then, and a partner is no longer required. I'm not sure about automobiles."

"An auto industry venture still requires a joint-venture partner," I replied.

"China is like the wild west," he said. "My assigned JV partner was located in Harbin, six hundred miles northeast of Beijing.

"My partner in Canada purchased and shipped what we needed to get started. I stayed on-site for three years, overseeing the construction of the factory and the equipment installations. Much longer than I had planned. I dealt with the design, import, export, and training issues, and my JV partner was supposed to be lining up the Chinese customers." Paul frowned. "My JV partner did not live up to their end of the bargain. Oh, some customers did come calling, but I had to jump through one hoop after another. We demonstrated capability after capability, but still there were no orders. It was very frustrating."

As we kept walking, I listened intently but couldn't help myself: I slipped into industrial engineering mode and began to visually assess the skills in the workforce. There were machinists and millwrights here with limited skills and many seemed to be trainees. When we approached the assembled sections of the conveyor running down the center, Paul described a telling mistake in one of the early units they had built. "It was ready to ship," he said, "and I was giving it a last once over when I noticed one of the shafts extending from a pillow block was slightly askew. I grabbed it, and it snapped off in my hand."

"What?" I exclaimed.

"One of my newly trained machinists had made a mistake," he explained, "and rather than expose his error by scrapping a six-foot piece of axle rod that he had cut two inches short, he covered the mistake by making a short piece that extended the right distance out from the pillow block." Paul paused and gave me a warning glance, "You will have to check the workmanship closely. Workers here do not understand the rigors that their workmanship must withstand. Most of these people have never seen a seaport. They mean well but lack understanding of functionality and sometimes common sense."

"I have been to Silk Alley," I said. "I understand what you mean about emphasis on appearances." Joelle and Chris had taken me to Silk Alley on the weekend. It had reminded me of the Ann Arbor Art Fair with its hundreds of white canvas walled booths. But instead of original art work, Silk Alley was stocked with garment knock offs that even included fake tags strung around the buttons for each brand name and store. China's industrial sector was good at copying anything and everything. But just how shrink-resistant, washable, and color-fast the fabrics were could be determined only after a few washings or cleanings.

Heading back toward the mezzanine, Paul continued his tale. "One day in 1999, I was riding back from the airport after another frustrating trip to Shanghai when my loyal driver spoke out. He told me that I should not put so much trust in Chan. Chan was my number-one guy, who covered in my absence. When I asked what he meant, he turned off the highway and drove twenty miles out of our way. He turned into a parking lot and pulled up to the front door of a strangely familiar factory. It was identical to the one we had just built. As I got out, Chan came out to greet me. He was smiling and invited me in for a tour.

"The factory was identical in every detail," Paul said. "The equipment, the building, everything."

"Wow," I exclaimed, wondering what I would do in his shoes.

"I had trusted this guy with the keys," Paul said sadly. "I fired Chan on the spot, and he had the audacity to put forth a sad smile and say that he hoped we could still be friends. On the bright side," Paul added, "all of the frustrations of being unable to make a sale went away."

We stared at each other as his lesson sank in.

"Doing business in China is unlike anywhere else," Paul said quietly.

Back on the mezzanine we were served a cup of tea. Paul continued, "I confronted the leaders of the JV partnership and told them our agreement was dissolved. I told them I was shutting down the operation and taking my share of the investment back to Canada. They also had the audacity to offer hopes that we might still be friends."

I couldn't help but smile.

"I hired an attorney to define my share," Paul continued, "only to discover in the fine print that I was entitled to the building but not the equipment that my partner had shipped over from Canada."

"This is unbelievable," I whispered.

Paul grew cool as he continued. "I called my Canadian partner, and he told me to give it all up and come home. But I couldn't. They were thieves, and I just wasn't going to walk away and let them have it all. I asked my partner to wire some money and hired a construction crew and forty flat beds. The crew disassembled the building and loaded it onto the flat beds." Paul smiled a little. "The fine print proclaimed that I also owned the concrete slab, but not the land. I ordered a crew with jackhammers and backhoes. They had jacked me around for three years, and I was going to do a little jacking of my own. I was determined they weren't going to keep a dime of what I had invested." Paul continued, "No sooner had the jackhammers begun to deaden eardrums than a black sedan rolled up. The leadership of my JV partnership stepped out and offered to buy the slab on the spot. We negotiated a cash settlement, and I drove away, leading my caravan south for six hundred miles. We parked the trailers in a field outside Beijing, and I dismissed the drivers. I checked into a Holiday Inn and opened a bottle of Canadian Club. I called my Canadian partner again and recounted what had happened. Again he urged me to sell everything and come home."

Paul sipped his tea with a glint in his eye and continued, "By the afternoon of the fourth day, my hangover was wearing off. A knock at my door revealed four of my devoted employees from Harbin. They had driven the six hundred miles to convince me of their loyalty and willingness to help me rebuild it all again. We talked through the night discussing a plan for how to start over. The laws banning private ownership of bulk loading systems had changed in the four years, and we would be able to start again without a JV partner. We were up and running in eighteen months under the same roof but in a new location and with all new equipment."

We talked for a while about hydrogen-powered vehicles and the proposal I had pulled together. He jokingly warned, "Be sure to read the fine print."

As Paul's driver pulled away and we headed back toward Beijing, I thought about just how long it would take the culture of China to begin spinning out well-grounded automotive apprenticeships. Nurturing a craftsman's culture could not happen in a single generation. What I had in mind for changing the scale of the world's auto industry would require skilled apprentices born into a nurturing culture and led by skilled craftsmen in the workplace. There didn't seem to be anyone in China who knew something about building carriages or fixing automobiles. There weren't people under the hoods of cars along the road, as I had seen in Mexico. On my silent ride back to Beijing, I recounted the little things I observed here that gave me pause. Some of the exterior tile work on the new condos was popping off several stories above ground. Probably moisture was getting behind the tile, now freezing and thawing in the winter. It was probably just a simple error made by a newly trained mason. Or perhaps it was a materials problem. The culture here is racing headlong into a global competition. What I was proposing would require a much higher level of skills than laying tile or making garments.

I considered the probable back-of-the-envelope objectives guiding China's automotive sector. The world's major auto companies were here by invitation. Each one teaching its version of automotive design and organization in exchange for a piece of the world's next expanding market. All of them were using some version of Henry Ford's assembly line. Learning to run a business without an assembly line at the core might be difficult to sell, but then again there were many advantages that might be viewed as ideal.

Was China's government out to carve out a position in the world's automotive sector? They might be interested in a direction not being taught by the world's dinosaurs. It was a direction that could evolve into the production of special models for each provincial climate and terrain and for each specified energy source. It could evolve into setting up many small plants in many countries on many continents. Their present course seems to be heavily vested in the old business model and outdated processing. Then again, why did China's visionaries decide to invite all of the world's dinosaurs to join a venture partner of their choosing? I had to wonder what was really on the back of their envelope.

As the miles clicked away, I realized how different this experience was from my trip to Japan in 1983. China is still in the conceptual stages of an entry into the automobile business. There isn't a General Douglas MacArthur at the helm here pulling in the next Edward Deming to teach classes on continuous improvement. China's government was definitely sifting through the manufacturing conventions of America, Europe, and Japan, but its path to superior automobiles was not clear. A century ago America was fortunate to have had a carriage culture from which to draw its earliest autoworkers. The skill base of the carriage culture had already been focused on extremes in lightweight and durable personal transportation. Carriage-making skills were vital to the success of the early underpowered automobiles. The culture of America's carriage craftsmen had been accustomed to sharing challenges and lessons learned about wood, wrought iron, cast iron, and even the characteristics of teams of horses. China didn't seem to have an equivalent base of handed-down skills. In Ramos Arizpe, Mexico, I drove through neighborhoods with cars in driveways, hoods up, and sitting on cement blocks. In the evening the night school in Ramos had been filled with young adults who already knew things about keeping the family car running. The young night school students of Ramos were learning the language of blueprints and the logic behind the steps in machining. China didn't have Mexico's path to assure that common sense prevailed in its factories. There were things that would be difficult to kindle in China.

All of the global auto companies were interfacing with China's auto industry. They were all building vehicles designed and developed for customers in this country and others. How were the Chinese going to fill in the gap of design and development and begin to build something more suited to their culture, climate, and terrain? I wondered if they wanted to enter into production of lightweight alternate-fuel vehicles. If China could offer a leg up and launch an alternate-fuel vehicle, I could help them erect a network of factories and a business model that would compete with any of the companies they had invited to set up shop.

That evening I walked through the neighborhood around Chris and Joelle's apartment. The vehicles parked along the streets were not old cars and yet many of them had had their interiors altered from what flowed off assembly lines. Beijing's car owners were expressing themselves with customized interiors. Perhaps the aspiration to own a custom carriage was here in China as well as in the States. I walked down a dead-end street. Near the end, on the left, I saw a cluster of high-performance two-seaters produced in Europe and Japan. They were all nosed up to an open door under a small neon sign. The smoke, loud voices, and music spilling out suggested the neon was blinking "Crazy Horse Saloon." The noses of two-seaters pointing toward the door could just as well have belonged to a collection of fine-spirited horses. Paul was right when he said, "If you scratch the surface, you will find this place is like the Wild West."

On Sunday Chris and Joelle joined me for a 1,600-mile round trip to Shanghai. It was time to review my findings with Eric and discuss whether there was any reason to continue the discussion of the formulation of a venture. I expected the meeting to pick up where we had left off in San Francisco. I would discuss my nine days of experiences, and Eric would bring the essence of what his circle of Shanghai investors thought about the idea. Truthfully, I was still vacillating on whether a start-up here would be a good idea.

We left Beijing at 7:30 a.m. on a new Airbus 330 and were in Shanghai in plenty of time for the 1:00 p.m. meeting. The roads leading to both airports could have been mistaken for limited access highways in any city. The light Sunday traffic consisted of the same late model automobiles you might see in any American city. The only thing that gave away the location was the writing on the billboards.

Eric directed us to a large conference room on the twentieth floor of an office building. The panoramic wall of glass facing west unveiled the cranes that mark high-rise construction stretching out toward the horizon. The conversation began with an informal discussion of holiday travel plans. Chris was surprisingly subservient around Eric, and the conversation dragged on for fifteen minutes until I interrupted, "I wonder if we could pick up where we left off in San Francisco?"

Eric looked at his watch and smiled. "Let's wait a few minutes. I've asked someone to join us." He and Chris returned to memorable vacations.

My mind raced. Maybe Eric had found someone interested in a JV? Maybe he wanted one of his two partners to be present? The buzzer in the office lobby sounded and Eric stepped away. I looked at Chris and Joelle for some sign of what came next, and they both shrugged.

Eric reentered, followed by a well-dressed person in his early seventies. After Eric's introductions, we all sat down. I knew the guest was a primary figure in one of the auto companies already doing business in China. Eric's demeanor in front of his guest was too respectful and too distant for it to be a friendly relationship. Perhaps someone interested in our proposal had wanted to test its soundness.

"So, Tom," the guest asked when the formalities were covered, "What is it that you are proposing? Eric told me it had something to do with automobiles."

I spoke quickly. "I've put together a team back in the States capable of designing, equipping, and launching a factory to produce a lightweight full-sized vehicle that can achieve the BTU equivalent of one hundred miles per gallon of gasoline and run on hydrogen. The vehicles can carry enough energy in the form of compressed hydrogen to offer a three-hundred-mile range. Their lightweight fuel cells convert the energy stored in the hydrogen to electricity. Either a battery pack or a much lighter bank of capacitors can serve to store the excess energy generation for acceleration. The vehicle is lighter than electric and hybrid-electric vehicle designs and can be refueled faster than even a gasoline-powered automobile. For China, it would mean access to evolving technologies in processing and an accompanying business model that would enable a competitive advantage over assembly-line-based auto companies." I paused to see if there was any interest.

Met with silence, I continued more slowly. "I've come to China to propose the launch of a new joint venture under the umbrella of the Chinese government. What I have to offer will be a serious threat to all current auto companies steeped in the traditional assembly line business model. Ken Iverson once launched his Nucor Steel business model under the umbrella of Cargill, a privately held grain conglomerate. I'm hoping to find a similar protective shield here in China." Again I stopped and waited.

Eric's guest showed hints of surprise and anger and then spoke. "Auto companies here already have this market covered." The visitor had an air of confidence. "We expect sales in 2004 to far exceed previous years. There are already plans to introduce more models here in China. This market is saturated." Then, with a slightly threatening tone, "It would be unwise to try and launch a new auto company here."

Glancing at Eric for a signal of what comes next, I saw he had turned to stone. I began again, unwavering. "China is just the right place for such a launch. China has a real need to move beyond dependence on oil and natural gas. In Beijing, there are leaders keenly interested in alternative energy and in technology sharing. I find long-term vision discussions around energy play better here than they do in Washington, perhaps because the Chinese government has a much greater ability to make sweeping change. A shift to hydrogen-based mobility could be done much more quickly here than in the U.S."

Again I stopped. Again the visitor remained silent. "There are actually many reasons for coming to China to launch this effort," I began again. "We can bring an evolutionary path in technology that has been avoided in the U.S., Europe, and Japan. The technologies required to do this have been sitting on shelves for years. Some are product innovations—like a shift from steel to composites and a shift from combustion engines to fuel cells. But more important is the shift in business model. The assembly line is being pushed down China's throat. It is obsolete. Avoiding further introductions of the assembly line will save China from a terrible drain on its cultural development. There is a more efficient alternative to the assembly line, but it requires intellect in a workforce to keep it running. The things I am offering to bring to China could accelerate the advancement of capability as a global auto producer." The visitor was becoming tense.

I kept going. "A century of building barriers to entry in the high-scale auto industry around the world has also built barriers to change. China is being led down a path to an entrenched position. My partners and I see China as an ideal place to shelter a fledgling venture that can escape the gravity of the current business model." The visitor was now visibly tight.

"The Chinese are being hoodwinked into partnerships with the current auto producers," I added. "These partnerships are introducing old technology and a hundred-year-old system for doing business. China skipped the landline approach to phone networks when it chose cell towers. We can bring China a chance to make another leap. It is quite possible to scale down the auto business in China to a point where every one of the twenty-two provinces could have a competitive auto factory. A network of small, highly integrated factories could allow provinces to improve on the designs of foreign producers for their climate, road conditions, and way of life. From a portfolio of new provincial designs could come some uniquely 'Chinese' products for export into developing regions."

I stopped and stared back in silence. If I was right, Eric's investment partners had arranged for this surprise visitor. They were expecting more than a simple dismissal, and I had to hope that I had struck a nerve.

The ten seconds of silence ended with a burst, "We already offer the things that make sense for this market. We are soon going to be building four different models in the same factory. You need to take your crazy ideas back to California or wherever you came from." The visitor stood, proclaiming, "I have another appointment," and walked out, with Eric scrambling after and disappearing down the hall.

I turned to Chris and Joelle and asked, "What do you think Eric will say when he returns?"

Chris replied, "I'm not sure." Joelle gave me a warning glance.

"Do you think he's still interested?" I asked.

Chris would not commit, and Joelle again said nothing. She had already privately shared with me that I should not trust Eric.

Eric returned and spoke quickly. "Could you put what you just said in writing? Just a two- or three-page overview, and I will take care of getting it translated. I want to run your ideas past several people here in Shanghai." I smiled to myself, deciding the encounter had been convincing. I agreed to send an overview via e-mail when I returned to the States.

Early the next morning, back in Beijing with my suitcases packed, I waited in silence on an empty street for a prearranged driver to take me to the Beijing Capital International Airport. My twenty-five-hour journey back to Washington had begun. A dusting of snow was gently floating down in the little circle of light around the entrance to the apartment. There were little flecks of coal dust mixed into the snowflakes like pepper. As my eyes began to adjust to the darkness, I could see a white carpet of snow leading in all directions to an undisturbed scene in infinite shades of gray. A black sedan pulled up with headlights off, making the first tracks in the new snow. The trunk opened automatically and a second circle of light appeared on the snow. The driver took my suitcase, and I slid into the backseat.

I looked to my right as we pulled away. Down the alley was the base of one of the many smokestacks that stretched out in a grid pattern to the horizon in all directions. From my sixth-floor window, I had marveled at the mix of old and new, the old smokestacks and the new condos. My one evening walk around the neighborhood had taken me to the base of the closest smokestack at the end of the adjacent alley. A small, darkened guard shack with windows on three sides had challenged my approach when I walked up. Behind the glass I could hear the deep rumble of a coal-fired boiler. Tracks in the snow indicated that a truck had just delivered a load of coal. As I approached the shack, I noticed a few small lights on a console inside. I stepped near the glass and shaded my eyes to peer inside. I was startled by the figure of a man with arms folded standing inside in the dark and staring back at me. His uniform had a short upright collar. His presence epitomized what I had felt since arriving in China. An element of this culture was operating just behind the scenes. As my driver pulled away, I peered down that same alley and sensed someone vigilant was still standing there in the dark.

I settled back for the forty-five-minute ride in silence. We wound through the deserted streets and merged onto the new toll road headed northeast. As the city faded behind us, I took stock of all that had happened.

The factories around Beijing were pages out of the sixties. Wooden block floors served as nonskid surfaces, and the equipment was the kind that my grandfathers would have chosen. The sites reminded me of my days in the apprentice shop and in Mexico with roving masters coaching the workforce. China is working on a "leading industrial nation" status at its grass roots and getting some help. They are also learning some bad habits from the world's auto producers. As suspected, China might be a very good place to launch a new business model in the auto industry.

As we neared the airport, I flashed my ticket jacket, and the driver stopped at the specified departure gate. The meter showed sixty-four yuan, roughly $8. I handed him a twenty and motioned for him to keep the change. It was less than half what it was going to cost me to get home from Washington Dulles. The driver smiled graciously and jumped out. He ran inside and returned with a luggage pushcart. He unloaded the trunk and ushered me through a doorway. He pointed toward the airport exit tax window. I returned his bow as we departed.

As I stood in the lines, I was reminded of an Englishman at the American Club party who told a story of an obnoxious fellow who came to China many times in the early nineties. He had been peddling technology to the defense industries conglomerate, and after a number of visits, the man was invited to his last dinner. When the grand meal was over, he was driven to the airport, where his passport was ceremoniously stamped "Not to Return." The point of his story had been that there is much more interconnectivity between business and government than you might think in this fast-evolving landscape. The person looking at my passport was probably viewing my itinerary on a screen. He finally passed it under the scanner and handed it back without a stamp. I smiled thinking to myself, *I can come back. Perhaps I still hold something of interest despite my unwelcoming reception in Shanghai.*

Somewhere over Canada I concluded that the Big Three might think China's automakers are following the path they have chosen for them. America's automakers might think they have started them down a path toward an excessive hierarchy of management and high numbers of supporting white-collar jobs. They might think China's auto companies are started down an irreversible path toward mind-numbing assembly lines and imported automation and that labor unrest will follow as aggressive union leaders take over. In my ten days I reached a very different conclusion. China's leadership is smarter than the companies they are luring ashore. The concept of striving for a flow of innovation from the bottom up might very well suit China. A minimalist approach to capital spending, that is, striving to make long-life investments in equipment and buildings, was something that would suit this culture. But the idea of sharing profits and losses would probably not. It was a communist country after all. China was in for some rough days ahead as the dinosaurs they have attracted come to realize they are little more than shells of political correctness.

A few days after my return to the States, I sent Eric the three-page summary. He did not acknowledge its receipt. In fact, I never heard from him again. Catching up on the news after ten days out of the country, I came across an article, "States Are Wooing Foreign Car Makers"; Michigan's Governor Jennifer Granholm was urging state lawmakers to bypass the usual bidding process and authorize the sale of a parcel of state land to Toyota to build an engineering center.[1] To her it was a chance to keep jobs in Michigan. To me it was another long-term bold move by the world's number-one auto company. Toyota was tapping another segment of the American workforce in a move presented as caring about employment in southern Michigan. I knew the landscape architect who had created the curb appeal of Toyota's small engineering center on the east side of Ann Arbor. It has been operating for decades. This new land grab would position a much larger engineering center close enough to Detroit to pick up the talent spinning out as the Big Three down shifted their engineering activities. With America openly walking away from making automobiles, the Asian automakers are wisely picking through what might still be of value. It is amazing how Asian strategists are able to find ways to line the pockets of New York brokers and legislators while always appearing socially correct. America is asleep.

I came across an article in the *Shanghai Star* that confirmed the fears I had formulated while in Beijing. It was dated July 7, 2003:

> Near-Identical Car Sparks New Chinese Piracy Fears, Automakers in the country's booming vehicle sector, frustrated with what they deem intellectual property theft, suddenly face a new threat: the copying of cars, which take anywhere from US $500 million to US $2 billion to design from scratch.

The Silk Alley approach to doing business was beginning its takeover of the world's auto business.

A similar announcement appeared in the *Shanghai Star* four years later. "Plucking Chevy's Chery [Cherry]",[2] a story China's Chery Automotive copying GM's Chevrolet's design for a Chinese car. The same lawlessness of China's Wild West that had robbed a Canadian conveyor company was training its sights on the more lucrative auto industry."

The long-term thinking in Beijing is to do what will benefit the nation, not a handful of corporations. And their approach was picking apart capitalism all around the world. Five years, later George Soros would concur in his October 2009 lectures at Central European University in Budapest, Hungary.

China has discovered a remarkably effective method of unleashing the creative, acquisitive, entrepreneurial energies of the people. They are allowed to pursue their self-interest while the state skims off a significant portion of the surplus value of their labor by maintaining an undervalued currency and accumulating a

---

1 Norihiko Shirouzu, "States Are Wooing Foreign Car Makers," *Wall Street Journal*, December 14, 2004, p.a A-3.

2 Plucking Chevy's Chery [Cherry]— "The plucky little automobile company, Pride Autos, based in the city of Binzhou in Shandong Province, has pulled a fast one over on Chery [Cherry]. We're not sure if Pride paid Chery [Cherry] for the technology behind their Saloon which looks a lot like the Chery [Cherry] Eastar. Prides 'traveling wagon' also seems to resemble an extended station wagon version of the Chery [Cherry] Windcloud, which was based off an older generation Seat Toledo [The Toledo is model offered by the Spanish auto maker Seat]. *Shanghai Star*—February 8th, 2007."

trade surplus.[1] Soros has supported this conclusion with investments in Chery Automotive and their plans to export cars from China to the United States.

China's central authorities have insisted on joint ventures with a fifty–fifty Chinese partner, which has been a good move—for them. Their insistence that all automobiles that are assembled on Chinese soil be composed entirely of components manufactured in China was also a good move—for them. Wise but simple strategic moves are maximizing the rate at which industrial capability is transferred into China from around the world.

These strategic moves are moving China ahead rapidly while accelerating America's slide into rentier collapse. Why America and other nations cannot alter their course is hard to fathom.

With the world's leading auto producers setting up assembly plants in China and their entire supply base forced to follow suit, six more long-term problems emerged. These six are too complex to be solved by a shift in business model. They will also require legislative change.

ASIA IS COMPOUNDING THE PROBLEMS OF AMERICA'S INDUSTRIAL SECTOR

116. Imports: The Big Three have been choosing to invest in China rather than American communities. The financial return to investors compared to the loss of jobs in America is causing economic imbalance.

117. Imports: Automotive component companies have been required to follow the Big Three. They have made similar investments in China, also hoping for a financial return. But the magnitude of the job and craft skills migration for the components segment is five times greater than for the assembly plants.

118. Imports: The key to survival in an industry with a complex product line is more about knowledge of craft than business acumen. An experience base is needed to keep a line of automotive products advancing in market acceptance. Moving the role of nurturing knowledge of a craft outside the borders of the United States has created a precarious position.

119. Imports: Since US corporations stepped up their outsourcing of a wide array of jobs, both China and India have become significant players in whole segments of the US economy under the banner that reads, "Go Global."

---

1 George Soros, *The Soros Lectures*, (New York, NY: Public Affairs, Perseus Books, 2010) p. 110

The Big Three spent a half century striving to bring component manufacturing in-house and away from the carriage makers' supply base. Both Henry Ford and William Durant knew that exposure to an uncontrolled supply base was dangerous. It is ironic that in the second half of the 20th century, in hopes of escaping the grip of the UAW, the Big Three laid out capital to set up multiple suppliers for all of their components, including overseas. I can't imagine either Henry Ford or Billy Durant settling easy in their graves knowing their companies have reversed an objective they felt was so vitally important.

120. Imports: Asian transplants on US soil do not compensate for the net outflow of good jobs.

The transplants have settled in places in America's South where they received the greatest tax incentives and assurances of protection from Northern union organizers. They have filled the media with the misconception that they are building cars in America when in fact they adding just 20 to 25 percent of the wholesale value. Sales of automobiles assembled in a transplant operation generate a flow of 75 to 80 percent of revenue back to the home country, increasing the imbalance of trade. Unlike China, the US does not insist that cars built in transplant operations be comprised entirely of components made in America.

121. Imports: The push for a "global economy" may stoke the bank accounts of a handful of big financiers, and it may fill Wal-Mart stores with cheap goods for a few years, but it is steadily eroding the foundation of the American economy.

America's Big Three jumped on what they saw as a heaven-sent opportunity and invested heavily in China for the past decade, proclaiming it as the last frontier for growth in auto sales. China itself has long since planned its next strategic move. In 2009, auto exports from China began appearing in American showrooms. They are joint-venture-built automobiles with familiar hood ornaments, and US consumers cannot tell where they are made.

CHAPTER 9. SOCIAL AND LEGISLATIVE HURDLES

At a time when the leaders of America's auto industry are retreating to foreign lands in search of the few remaining pockets of low-paid craftsmen, I am convinced that it is possible to turn the US industrial sector around. The turnaround of just the auto industry could reemploy more than a million US workers and pull the nation back from the brink of a rentier collapse. I am also convinced that the United States is capable of developing personal transportation for individuals that is not dependent on foreign oil. That said, I do not believe it can happen without supportive social and legislative change.

Adopting a new version of an old business model with craftsmen at its core is at the heart of the change. But new players cannot enter the field the old-fashioned way, with a simple frontal assault by an entrepreneur with a great new prototype. The world's dinosaurs know how to crush this type of entry. A new business model is needed, along with a collection of automotive craftsmen from a new generation, in it for the long haul.

A few years back, a speaker at the Hotel Jerome in Aspen triggered my realization of how much potential remains from inventions in processing. A single spider can produce six distinctly different strands, one of which has better strength-to-weight ratios than steel or carbon fiber. The strands have different degrees of elasticity and adhesiveness. The spider produces these varieties in continuous strands in a portable factory set up at each job site. The factory is so small it can fit on the head of a pin and uses a single raw ingredient, bug juice, at room temperature. I walked out that evening with confidence that many inventions in processing await discovery and that a shift away from the inefficiency of high-scale thinking is the first step toward enabling an evolution in industry.

That Aspen lesson spurred thinking into other dimensions. Along with being a factory that produces continuous strands, a single spider is also the architect, engineer, builder, and web operator at each job site. In the United States we have forgotten the term generalist and the value that a broadly skilled craftsman once brought to any barn raising. America needs to get back to nurturing generalists.

To bring the auto industry back, the assembly line must be recognized as a bad decision. It tried to force skilled craftsmen into stanchions, and they walked away. It has been my family's experience that checking one's mind at the door day after day leads to social unrest and social decline. It will be difficult to change the foundation, but I believe it is necessary.

There have been times when a shift down in scale of processing, rather than up, has provided the impetus to bring an uncompetitive business back to life. Look at the eyeglass industry. In rural America it was once common to run around with your old glasses taped together until the lens grinders in a major city could mail you new ones. What emerged in the eyeglass business was a semi-custom franchise business model that handles the complexity of lens grinding on scaled-down equipment and offers the fashion-conscious frame manufacturers more lucrative marketing opportunities. Eyeglasses became "eyewear" processed in small shops in the midst of an era of mass producers pumping out brightly-colored sunglasses to fill revolving racks near check-out lines. Demand grew for a scaled-down lens grinding process that could match the shapes of new fashion-industry driven designer frames. Lens grinding equipment and craftsmen began filling the back rooms of upscale eye-ware showrooms. I believe there is a willingness to pay higher prices for custom craftsmanship in personal mobility. A century ago carriage makers thrived on the profit margins of custom made. Making choices in personal mobility can again accompany making choices in clothing, housing, furniture, interior decorating and food.

The steel industry's mini-mill story remains the most comparable example of what scaling down and reintroducing craft skills can do for American industry. The mini-mills increased their levels of integration, proliferated their offerings, and began selling direct; these are all things that could be formidable elements of a business model in the hands of a new wave of entrepreneurial automotive craftsmen. Steel's mini-mills began with reinforcing rod, a simple chemistry, sold in small lots to construction crews who wanted it preformed, bundled, and delivered each day to their ever-changing construction sites. These mini-mills began in a segment of the steel market that Big Mill owners didn't care about.

A similar opening in the auto industry might be in the special-use families of vehicles—a line of ambulances tailored to the needs of each community, a line of custom fire trucks, or special-purpose designs for taxis or some other service industry vehicle. The opening could also be a line of vehicles for government fleets meant to lead the evolution in alternative energy or serve some purpose that cannot be met without aftermarket alterations of what the Big Three can offer. A vehicle that requires periodic upgrades could be ideal.

For more than a century, attempts by new entries into the automobile business have always come up short when the large dinosaurs begin to focus. The parade of entrepreneurs has included the familiar Cord, Tucker, Pagani Zonda, Panoz, Corbin, and DeLorean. These were the "namesake" attempts to offer a better "shiny red two-seater." More recent attempts to strap on waders and wade into this revenue stream have included the alternative technology players, Think, Aptera, IT, Solectria, Hypercar, and others. Current moves to accommodate alternative fuels have included Tesla, Fisker Automotive, Gordon Murray Design, Think Global, Loremo, Mindset, Tata's Nano, and others. Each of these attempts is making preparations to enter the stream with its own version of the back of an envelope. The resemblance to what happened to 142 companies that preceded Henry Ford in 1903 is uncanny. The few entrepreneurs who get it right this time will again have to avoid the financial-criteria-based leadership that will push their company into an initial public offering (IPO) or into the hands of foreign investors. Both Ford and Durant were successful because they set out to build a corporation and not simply peddle their holdings to an investment group. Brokers are as eager today as they were a century ago to sacrifice a company for the chance to haul away a slice of the deal in wheelbarrows. Only vigilant communities nurturing craftsmen, and that are in it for the long haul, will survive in the 21st century.

There are perhaps more hurdles to clear today than a century ago. But the glitter of the gold in the manufacturing revenue stream is still alluring to the entrepreneur. And there are still financial-criteria-based thinkers lying in wait, counting on the inventor growing tired of the challenges.

Today there are arrogant beliefs that America's financial prowess and that America's circle of FIRE will somehow remain attractive to foreign investors into the future. Kevin Phillips shows America's manufacturing sector as having dropped from 29.3 to 10.9 percent of the gross domestic product (GDP), and that it will not have to drop to zero before the economy collapses. Bringing the auto business back to life could begin a return of widespread employment and economic stability. For automobiles, the return begins with retracing steps all the way back to 1903 and starting down a path that avoids all markers that say: "This Way to the Culture of Assembly Lines and Transfer Lines."

The reemergence of America's industrial sector will also require some rethinking of legislation involving;

- currency exchange rate adjustments,
- antitrust legislation affecting boardrooms,
- inheritance legislation for industrial enterprises,
- craft education curriculum and the focus of its funding,
- proficiency testing that needs to be broadened,
- patent law restrictions in a global economy,
- and some new guards against rentier collapse—before it is too late.

Poring over shelves in libraries helped me to understand the magnitude of change that I had sought when I naïvely joined GM's corporate think tank in 1988. At the same time studying the evolution of the back of the envelopes of the Big Three solidified my convictions that it is possible to rebuild America's industrial sector. It is difficult to predict whether automobiles will continue to be produced by the Big Three or a new wave of entrepreneurs will take over. But what is very clear is the need for adjustments in long range thinking (the back of the envelope). It is conceivable that pension fund managers and others, looking for dividends and long term growth, will begin checking to see what is on the back of the envelope before they invest. My hope is that they recognize that more can be accomplished by a "hive mind" than by a small group of clairvoyant authoritarians.

EPILOGUE: COUNTERING THE PESSIMISTS IN FUNERAL HOMES

Getting a culture to change begins with unsettling the things believed to be true. Delving into history uncovered the sources of the funeral home "myths." Tracking Henry Ford, his company and the auto industry over the course of a century revealed many brilliant and some very risky shifts in objectives. Henry didn't make the shifts abruptly and never before they were absolutely necessary. The brilliance of Henry Ford became clear when I realized each of his shifts addressed several and not just one emerging threat. It was amazing how he was able to re-knit the strands on the back of his envelope each time. Henry Ford was patient.

RESPONSES TO THE MYTHS

1. **"Of course the auto industry needs to be located in Detroit."** — That was true when cars were made of hickory. It was also true before decisions began to eradicate the role of craftsmen and devastate the communities that nurtured them.

2. **"Of course the role of unions should be to fight for all they can get from management."** — Saturn disproved this adage with its corporate structure that called for elected union positions throughout its organization. The role of the union was to represent the opinions of the workforce in every discussion of financial interests. America's population chooses to live in a republic, and it only makes sense that its workforce would prefer to work in one.

3. **"Of course an assembly line is the most efficient way to build cars."** — The assembly line is less than 50 percent efficient. It severely limits ability to meet consumer needs and adapts poorly to swings in customer preference. The ideal increments of capacity for assembly lines affect every other segment of the

business and the increments are now too large to suit the fragmenting market as Americans unknowingly strive to return to custom made.

4. "Of course American autoworkers are paid too much." — Wages in industry in America are not as high as they are in Switzerland, Japan, and Germany, and these are all countries with higher rates of industrial exports. Out-sourcing and automation are driving up the cost of building cars in America. The tiers of suppliers and the machine tool industry have too much influence and are too absorbed in their own interests.

5. "Of course it takes years and billions of dollars to design and develop a new vehicle. — The first decade of Ford Motor Company and his assembly journeymen was a time when the adoption of new models and continuous improvement were part of the daily regimen. Designers were on the floor each day to banter around new ideas to put down on paper. There was no equipment expense for new model introduction, only a resetting of tooling as if the factory were a basement workshop. Design and development has since evolved to become too far removed from day-to-day operations. It has also evolved to cater too much to the capability of automation builders and not enough to customer needs.

6. "Of course there are unbeatable advantages to high-scale operations. — The mini steel mills proved this adage to be false. The scale race, to outpace the competition, took the big steel makers too far, and it has done the same to the auto industry.

7. "Of course outside sources can make parts for less than the auto companies." — There are technologies today that have the flexibility to fabricate components as needed inside scaled-down vehicle assembly operations. A shift back to high levels of integration will eliminate the profit taking of each tier. It will also eliminate transportation between tiers of the supply base, taking trucks off the highways.

8. "Of course transfer lines and automated body shops are the only avenue to quality." — In the 1980s General Electric chose CNC equipment to machine new jet engines and Borg Warner chose CNC to machine a new 4x4 transfer case. For them it was a move to keep ahead of European and Asian competition. Today there are CNC alternates for all types of machining, welding, bending of pipes, and even automotive body assembly. The ability to adapt to rapid changes in design, the inherent low cost tooling and fixtures, together with the long life span make CNC equipment superior to transfer lines and automated body shops.

9. "Of course lights-off factories are the future." — New technologies that link the machine to the operator's intelligence rather than just his brawn, coupled with a fragmenting car market are pointing toward a return to custom build; they're telling manufacturers that robots are not industry's saviors.

10. "Of course cars have to be sold and serviced through dealerships." — Today used cars are being sold by linking individual cars to individual customers via the Internet. Delivery is to the customer's door, where the ritual of kicking tires still takes place before payment is authorized. It would be even easier to do this with new cars. Steel's mini-mill entrepreneurs strategically positioned their startups near large numbers of customers and began offering full service; from melt, to mix, to pour, to roll, to cut, to form, to package and even delivery, which took out all of the middle men. New cars could be built and sold in the same way. Factories will have to be equipped with very different technologies and staffed with a highly skilled workforce. Selling out of the factory and not through dealerships is legal in all states if the model sold in the factory is not also sold through dealers in the same state.

11. "Of course research has to be done by scientists and protected by patents." — The number of innovations conjured up on drawing boards to meet customer expectations is small compared to the number dreamt up by craftsmen innovating process solutions for making something new. Some of the ideas end up as patents, but many do not because there is a greater chance of competitive advantage if the processing is not revealed thought the circulation of a new patent application. This has become alarmingly true as Asian automotive capability comes on line beyond the reach of patent enforcement.

12. "Of course imports will always be cheaper than American-made cars." — The rising cost of transport, reversals in protections of currency exchange rates, and longer distances between consumer and manufacturer are already making it difficult for imports to compete. Adding the element of skilled workforce requirements will make it more and more difficult for foreign transplant operations to compete.

APPENDIX 1. TABLE OF THE EVOLUTION OF INEFFICIENCIES IN THE CURRENT AMERICAN AUTOMOTIVE BUSINESS MODEL CAUSED BY ADJUSTMENTS TO OBJECTIVES DURING THE 20TH CENTURY

THE EVOLUTION OF INEFFICIENCIES IN

PRODUCT DESIGN AND DEVELOPMENT OBJECTIVES

THE EVOLUTION OF INEFFICIENCIES IN
GROWTH OBJECTIVES

THE EVOLUTION OF INEFFICIENCIES IN
ORGANIZATIONAL DEVELOPMENT OBJECTIVES

15. The supporting white-collar organization became top-heavy with far too many levels of hierarchy. 60

24. The well-compensated executives who appeared soon after the union won the right to represent the workforce may be the price that had to be paid to ensure that the interests of the represented workforce remained under control while the shareholders harvested profits. But high-paid executives are not the right choice for building a competitive industrial sector. 74

25. The 1941 decision to manage the front lines with professional managers (business school grads) would steer America's Big Three into a vulnerable position. Decreasing quality levels accelerated the decline in sales. Japan's auto makers gradually increased their U.S. market share. 74

26. With the UAW came enforced delineation of journeymen trades. Maintenance and construction projects suddenly required full complements of trades on standby. 77

27. Further separation of blue and white collars in 1941 drove up the cost of both. (A carriage company that valued its intellect and brawn equally could avoid the inefficiencies of class structure.) The UAW was broadening the cultural gap between office and floor workers and between skilled trades and both floor workers and contractors. 78

30. When the 1959 antitrust ruling dismissed the DuPonts from GM's Board Room, it allowed financial officers to take control of long-term decision making. Moving component manufacturing to the outside where wage rates were lower (on paper) became a short term avenue to increased quarterly earnings. How to compete using a common supply base became a concern for the new Board. 106

31. The value of a supporting community was erased when culturally led aspirations around Detroit shifted from recognition in craft to recognition of ability to rise through the ranks. 106

32. When the front-line managers with hands-on experience began to disappear in the fifties, the informative link between line workers and maintenance crews began to break down. 106

33. The shift to quality control procedures during these decades wiped out a parenting culture—inspectors—that kept a workforce on its toes in mind and spirit. 107

34. America has lost market share for many reasons; one of them is the slowing rate of continuous improvement. 107

35. Organization Development: Frederick Taylor's 1911 goal of taking the intellectual and skill contributions of craftsmen out of the workplace was expanded in the fifties and sixties to begin taking away control of the pace on all operations. 107

36. Organization Development: "If you give anything back, you might not get as much the next time": such statements in budget discussions indicated that America's business model and staff goals were not aligned. 111

37. The shifts toward automation began eliminating journeymen from the rank and file. The machine tool industry began taking over, wiping out the remaining pockets of supporting skills that had once built the world's finest carriages.   111

86. With the secret race to out-source the manufacture of auto components in full swing, superficial goals were introduced in component operations. The authors of bonus checks were definitely not seeking progress in the evolution of workforce skills.   154

87. The American auto industry stopped nurturing generalists, people who can tell by walking around if anything is amiss. Specialists took over for generalists, and more of them were needed to keep the business running.   155

88. Blocking all up-from-the-ranks promotions was a costly move. Overall performance slipped in both quality and cost improvement.   156

89. The American industrial sector lost touch with the importance of completing internships before being licensed to practice.   156

90. A company that does not take the time to apprentice its decision makers is a poor match for companies in nations that do.   160

91. The interviews-and-résumés approach to hiring leadership in America's industrial sector is unable to sort out the educated from those who took shortcuts or those without the intelligences that the industrial sector requires.   157

92. Auto companies and their suppliers are having to staff up interface teams to run back and forth between decision makers. The value of meetings on the production floor has been forgotten.   159

93. Warranty reporting systems were introduced to try to match the quality and durability of the emerging Japanese imports. The outcome was of little or no value to operations, engineering, or design staffs.   159

94. Empire building became a frequent practice in the second half of the twentieth century. Middle managers correlate size of their paycheck to the size of their staff.   160

96. The shift away from annual model change and into platforming depleted the numbers of experienced tradesmen and engineers. A decade later in the midst of the oil shocks, a decision was made to shift to body-frame-integral (BFI) structures and front-wheel-drive (FWD) power trains. There were not enough experienced tradesmen and engineers to pull it off, and the result was a rapid increase in dependency on the American machine tool industry. This shift proved to be costly.   162

97. The decision to dismiss the maintenance crews who once installed new equipment and systems threw away an avenue to firsthand knowledge when breakdowns occur.   163

98. The shift toward CNC machines introduced many new classifications into the American workforce when it should have simply been a new tool for existing journeymen and line workers.   172

107. American industry once thrived on its hive-mind capability. But decision making during the last two decades has shifted to a focus on equipment and not the workforce producing industrial goods. The auto industry in particular may have forgotten how to rekindle a hive-mind environment.   173

108. America has filled its management ranks with the in-experienced. Auto man-ufacturers in Japan, Mexico, China, and the Czech Republic are using up-from-the-ranks management in operations.   174

109. It is a mistake to assume American competitiveness has ever been firmly root-ed in patents or on drawing boards. The real roots are in the evolving knowledge base of the workforce, and in this regard American industry has lost touch.   174

110. In the few locations in America where CNC equipment has been introduced, it has been difficult to manage a CNC workforce in the midst of the larger workforce tied to the mindless tasks of bucket brigades. Even when both workforces are com-pensated equally, there is a division in commitment to the job that breeds ill will.   174

THE EVOLUTION OF INEFFICIENCIES IN
SOURCING OBJECTIVES

23. The purchasing objectives would prove to be no match for the financial ambi-tions of the suppliers.   73

41. The competitive advantage of a surprise in product design was lost when tool-ing build was out-sourced.   117

42. The competitive advantage of closely held secrets in processing was aban-doned in the surge to out-source.   117

43. The out-sourcing of die making disconnected vehicle designers from tooling designers and tooling designers from tooling maintenance crews. The natural flow of advancements in American industrial capability feeding up from the front lines stopped.   117

44. Influenced by automation and out-sourcing, the overhead on the remaining components still built in-house climbed quickly. Any thoughts of calculating the potential value of a reversal and a return to in-sourcing never crossed my desk.   117

45. Out-sourcing without reducing the proportional amount of supporting head-count drove burden rates up. Out-sourcing became a slippery slope. In-sourcing strategies and bringing down the cost of all auto components were key elements of Henry Ford's and William Durant's objectives. But current automotive leaders no longer shared that vision.   117

THE EVOLUTION OF INEFFICIENCIES IN
EQUIPMENT OBJECTIVES

THE EVOLUTION OF INEFFICIENCIES IN

SALES OBJECTIVES

THE EVOLUTION OF INEFFICIENCIES IN

RESEARCH AND DEVELOPMENT OBJECTIVES

THE EVOLUTION OF INEFFICIENCIES IN
MANUFACTURING SYSTEM OBJECTIVES

THE EVOLUTION OF INEFFICIENCIES IN
UNION OBJECTIVES

22. The political maneuvering in local union elections is not much different from that in any election. The local plant management sometimes gets involved.   71

28. With the rise in numbers of outspoken union loyalists came a rise in the numbers of workers holding back in quiet eddies. A silent majority emerged that never bothered to vote in union elections. The union did not represent their interests beyond fighting for wages and benefits. Management was struggling to counter the union leaders and failed to engage this silent majority.   93

29. Many of the out-sourcing decisions were made at a time when true cost was not as important as putting threats on Detroit's bargaining tables.   106

65. Threatening plant closures and postponing the reopening of plants has served to disrupt the ambitions of the UAW. But it has also brought tremendous burdens to local communities and driven up the cost of doing business.   145

111. Thinking that the battle for profitability can be won by holding wages and benefits in check may serve to shore up share price, but it doesn't begin to address the problem of losing market share.   172

112. Threats of out-sourcing, automation, and plant closings were played like chips in a game of cards till the bluffs were called too many times, resulting in trends. The union threats of strikes led to higher wages and benefits but only for those still around to elect another round of union leaders. The bargaining tables were serving up short-term wins on both sides. The real loser was America and its economy.   172

THE EVOLUTION OF INEFFICIENCIES IN
IMPORT OBJECTIVES

58. Imports: After the war, the U.S. was producing 52% of global industrial output as the rest of the world's industrial base had been destroyed in the war. Eventually, as a semblance of normality returned, American companies had to face competition from imports.   121

59. Industry in America is no match for other well-organized nations.   121

64. Investing in research and filing for patents has become detrimental to both competitiveness and the bottom line for American industry.   145

116. The Big Three have been choosing to invest in China rather than American communities. The financial return to investors compared to the loss of jobs in America is causing economic imbalance.   191

117. Automotive component companies have been required to follow the Big Three. They have made similar investments in China, also hoping for a financial return. But the magnitude of the job and craft skills migration for the components segment is five times greater than for the assembly plants.   191

APPENDIX 2. BRINGING AMERICA'S AUTO INDUSTRY BACK TO LIFE

Suppose that Henry Ford reappeared. The preceding chapters provide a sense of what he would remember and the conclusions he would reach as he set out to trace what happened to his life's work in the second half of the twentieth century. It was Henry who launched the fundamentals of the current business model, and he would undoubtedly comprehend how it changed over time. He would think about sweeping course corrections and the things thrown off the wagon. His early experience, attracting a workforce away from the carriage industry and working side by side with them in the early years, would give him a strong sense of what Americans are capable of building. There is a good chance that Henry could pull together a back of the envelope that would bring America's industrial sector back from the brink of extinction.

It wouldn't take Henry long to conclude that America is being dragged toward the world's greatest rentier collapse and that Asia is holding the leash. He would sense that a new set of interlocking objectives was needed, and he would set to work, trying to define it. Finding a new course that would evade the industrial ambitions of Asia would have to be every bit as creative as his earliest envelope—when he set out to take the auto industry away from the carriage makers. This time, however, the future of America's entire industrial sector would be hanging in the balance. The envelope would have to map a route to a business model the low-wage regions could not follow.

Henry's study of what has happened would uncover three areas where his early decisions had evolved to make America uncompetitive: (1) choosing the easy path of selling to wholesalers, (2) narrowing the scope of training and development of apprentices, and (3) choosing the simplicity of a bucket brigade system for manufacture and assembly. Henry's study would reveal how communication, training, and manufacturing systems technologies have evolved, and he would envision envelope adjustments.

First, it is now technically feasible to custom-build and sell direct to customers across the country. Customers in 1903 had been accustomed to waiting ten months from the time they mailed in full payment till the day their customized carriage was delivered. Today it is technically feasible to deliver a build-to-order vehicle in two days. Henry would remember the days of customer pride in customized carriages, and he would discover the margins of upwards of 25 percent at current dealerships. Dealing directly with the customer had been lucrative and can be again. Offering direct ordering from the factory and establishing factory outlets for delivery could lure Americans away from buying imports. The new back of the envelope must enable ways to walk away from sales through dealerships.

Second, Henry would remember how he had chosen shortcuts in training his automotive component makers and assembly craftsmen. Hindsight would tell him that he made the decisions without a sense of the outcome. As he sorted out what happened in the second half of the century, he would see how the union used his narrow definitions of trades to increase the numbers of tradesmen on the payroll. He would discover the technology used by the military to educate on the job and remember what was expected of the old master craftsmen. By setting new objectives, he might be able to rekindle lifetime aspirations for higher levels of combinations of learning, experience, and skill. Henry would know how far American business has wandered from what Americans did so well when they built carriages and put together the first automobiles. Increasing the contributions of the workforce would have to be a consideration in every item on the back of the new envelope.

Third, Henry would remember his reluctance to turn to the assembly line. He would realize that he'd been right in being cautious. His assembly line decision devastated the American culture. Spending their days doing mindless tasks along an assembly line destroyed the surrounding carriage builders' culture and disenchanted the line's entire second generation. He would remember the carriage builders' system of assembly that he pushed to reach 750 per day. He would study later experiments with alternatives to his bucket brigade: the Saturn skillets, the teams at Volvo and Saab, the engine assemblers at Ferrari, Volkswagen's new Phaeton plant, and others. Henry would realize that reversing his assembly line decision could affect every item on the back of the envelope. Conjuring a manufacturing system that would enable rather than constrict, as has the assembly line, would be important especially as it supported the other objectives.

Henry would study the history of other traditional industries and how they fared. He would come across an upstart like himself named Ken Iverson, who picked apart the business model of Big Steel in the seventies. It was a move that would impress the wise Henry Ford, having picked apart the carriage maker's industry seventy years earlier. Like Henry, Iverson insisted on in-sourcing everything to protect his fledgling company. Iverson chose to build a network of mini-mills near major market hubs. America's steel-making capability came back to life as result of Iverson's back-of-the-envelope choices.

It is conceivable that Henry would decide to make his own mini-assault. A chain of mini auto factories might be able to push imports and transplants back into the sea. An entrepreneur or stand-alone division of the Big Three, with the right back-of-the-envelope objectives, might just succeed. The lobbies of these mini auto plants would become factory outlet showrooms that would offer custom-design services; here customers could kick around ideas with the people who would build their cars. It could be a return to wide-ranging personalization, including special interior features and electronics. A chain of mini-plants serving local interests could flood the market with models tuned to match local terrain and weather as well as fashion. The era of financial-criteria-based decision making would be over. Getting back to craftsmen making things that people want could lead American culture back to health.

Along with Ken Iverson at Nucor, there have been two other major successes involving a shift in business model: Sam Walton with Wal-Mart and Fred Smith with Federal Express. Like Iverson, they were both familiar with the traditional business model. They knew its weak points and forged ahead with new back-of-the-envelope objectives that exploited those weaknesses.

HENRY FORD'S BACK OF THE ENVELOPE FOR THE TWENTY-FIRST CENTURY

The ten areas of objectives on the back of the envelope would be the same but the wording would change. The strategic moves deployed under each objective would need to be interrelated and well timed.

Manufacturing System: *Build plants around the country scaled not to exceed a maximum of five hundred employees. (The two-shift daily build volume would not exceed two hundred vehicles.) The manufacturing system would accommodate the build of up to twenty different models at the same time. It would accept a steady stream of new model introductions, accommodate the gradual phase-out of old models, and welcome a continuous stream of design improvements without ever shutting down. The system of manufacture would use moving rooms[1] and reject all considerations of an assembly line.*

1 A moving room is a large self-propelled body truck. It operates in a system that replaces the assembly line. It keeps the vehicle, workforce, and components moving into successive areas of stationary tooling and equipment.

Strategic moves enabled by this new Manufacturing System objective:

- Introduce custom-built unique designs into a high-scale market.
- Offer many propulsion alternatives in a coming age of energy uncertainty.
- Take over for the up-fitters.
- Harvest the losses inherent in assembly line systems.
- Eliminate the penalties of unbalanced workloads between multiple models and the inefficiencies of seasonality.
- Reduce losses due to breakdowns by more than 90 percent.
- Reduce assembly operating cost by more than 50 percent.
- Reduce component cost by more than 60 percent.
- Accelerate new model introductions to a matter of weeks instead of years and catch the peaks in market demand.

Organization Development: *Bootstrap the development of twenty-first-century assembly craftsmen. Nurture a hive-mind capability in teams that can accelerate the rate of innovation in both processing and product design. Return to an up-from-the-ranks leadership selection. Use a central development and training center to keep assembly craftsmen at remote plants on a common track. Keep a central staff in tune with operations-led innovation and regional adaptations of customer feedback.*

Strategic moves enabled by this new Organization Development objective:

- Empower lifelong improvements in craftsman performance.
- Increase output and quality with a system that accommodates variations in human capability, both physical and mental, and that adapts to variations in daily levels of energy and ability to focus.
- Harvest the value of lifetime contributions of employees; lay out lifetime career paths that recognize progress throughout a career.
- Reduce maintenance and repair expenses by returning to in-house craftsmen assuming roles of installation and debugging.
- Reduce operating expenses by softening the lines between trades and shifting focus toward nurturing generalists.
- Provide opportunities for ongoing hands-on experience for product and process engineers and for all supporting segments of the organization.
- Expect the numbers in support staffs to drop to one-tenth of current levels, as direct links develop between assembly craftsmen and product designers.
- Provide opportunities to share bootstrapped learning across the organization, with a focus on increasing levels of integration.
- Improve the motivation and contributions of individuals with a return to up-from-the-ranks management selection.
- Improve performance and quality with direct links between assembly craftsmen and customers.

- Improve vehicle performance and quality by links along the assembly crew—using "runners" who relay information to upstream component operations.
- Reduce component cost through direct involvement of CNC operators in both programming and fixture design.
- Refocus measures of worker performance toward skills in craft development.
- Stop the practice of spending all allotted capital funding.
- Attract community participation in the grooming of new generations of craftsmen.
- Localize career opportunities.
- Empower a natural hands-on apprenticeship screening process that avoids the mistakes inherent in professional résumés, test scores, and well-rehearsed interviews.
- Restore the links between the front lines and the office, leading to significant advantages in a global competitiveness.

Unions: *Embrace America's cultural insistence on living and working in a republic. Let elected union officials represent the needs of the workforce at every level of decision making. Disburse gains and losses in operating profit based on input from elected representatives.*

Strategic moves enabled by this change new Unions objective:
- Reduce the losses caused by narrowly focused local union objectives.
- Replace union ambitions to hang on and protect the number of jobs with ambitions to improve the quality of lifetime achievement and the income of communities through mutual interest in profits and growth along with wages and benefits.
- Replace bargaining tables with business decision tables. Let elected union representatives assume responsibility for the republic they represent.
- Kindle more community involvement in future workforce development through union leadership.
- Gain lifetime commitments from communities.

Sourcing: *In-source all automotive component manufacturing that is even close to being cost effective. Establish a level of integration that exposes no weakness to competitors trying to corner the supply base.*

Strategic moves enabled by this new Sourcing objective:
- Restore the advantages of high levels of integration/in-sourcing that founders once used to accelerate their takeover of the industry.
- Stop the losses due to suppliers' sharing of competitors' innovations.

- Return the value of innovation to the pockets of its implementers and step up the pace of approval and implementation.
- Rekindle the value of the handed-down knowledge that never makes it onto blueprints, AutoCAD screens, or the forms circulated by the ISO system of sharing job secrets.
- Take sourcing beyond the financial-criteria-based decision making and out of the hands of purchasing agents; take it back to being a strategic business issue.
- Reduce material handling expenses, taking shipping containers off the highways and out of railcars.
- Reduce in-process inventory and erase the unnatural forces of just-in-time systems that put partial truckloads on American highways and consume increasing amounts of a declining supply of petroleum.
- Eliminate the profits paid to each tier throughout the supply chain.
- Reconnect tooling design and product design on a daily basis.
- Reconnect the two-way streets between tooling maintenance, tooling build, tooling design, and product design.

Equipment: *Take back full responsibility for the design, build, and launch of systems of manufacture; return the decisions on equipment purchase to the hands-on craftsmen; stress the importance of generic (CNC) capability, of lifetime equipment purchase, of the ease of repair and rebuild, and of low-cost tooling; discontinue efforts toward lights-off factory development; tie capital expenditures to overall profitability for each site.*

Strategic moves enabled by this new Equipment objective:
- Bring equipment-design decisions back in-house to stop equipment builders from using an escalating capital investment cycle.
- Eliminate the practice of buying transfer lines that cut air instead of chips.
- Stop the habit of buying equipment that is more costly to retool than it is worth.
- Stop the flow of capital into the costly cycles of "Request for Appropriation Change."
- Stop the buying of capacity in large increments and its resultant life cycle losses.
- Enable a near ideal harvest of the value of CNC equipment.
- Enable a harvest of the true value of robots by separating them from sequential lines.
- Stop the American practice of unjustified capital expenditures on slow-to-accelerate automation.
- Expect reductions in annual capital investments for new equipment and facilities by more than 90 percent.

- Expect reductions in start-up expenses of more than 90 percent.
- Expect reduced investments in equipment for options by a factor of four.
- Eliminate the inherent losses on model-specific investments, which occur as popularity falls off and the investments become poorly used.
- Increase the usage of capital equipment and buildings.
- Expect improvements in the effectiveness of maintenance and construction services.
- Focus on equipment choices that are controlled by the operator rather than operators controlled by the equipment, and minimize the number of workstations.
- Enable the rapid learning of CNC programming skills in both prototyping and production operations.
- Focus on eliminating the devastating impact of dedicated automation on communities across America.

Research and Development: *Rely on a central factory and training facility to ensure that all technical advancements are gathered and disseminated. Insist on weekly links between research and development and the network of operations. The central facility is to include: market definition coordination, styling coordination, product design and development coordination, process design and development coordination, and upgrades. Seek competitive advantages in superior processing by choosing the optimal scale of operations and engaging a new type of workforce.*

Strategic moves enabled by this new Research and Development objective:
- Strive for a high-paced evolution in process and system design.
- Conjure products for smaller market segments—products that competitors would not be able to deliver.
- Develop uses for regional materials, energy storage, propulsion devices.
- Develop vehicle features well suited to climate, terrain, and social demands.
- Coordinate the local site development of hands-on advancements in processing and continuous improvements.

Product Design and Development: *Walk away from platform thinking. Design new vehicles that will stretch the limits of a new generation of universal equipment and the minds of craftsmen who use it. Design products to meet both the short and long life span segments of customers. Capitalize on regional interests and worker capability. Develop prototypes in-house under lock and key, and use production equipment and tools to build all prototypes. Great innovations are often born of necessity in hive-mind environments. America's industrial sector has forgotten the value of this capability.*

Strategic moves enabled by this new Product Design and Development objective:

- Link the hive mind of the collective of assembly craftsmen and their daily encounters to product designers.
- Enable links between consumer interest and the core of assembly craftsmen.
- Increase the frequency and extent of change in design.
- Design features that capitalize on the evolving skills of assembly craftsmen.
- Enable a continuous flow of design improvement from the hands-on assembly craftsmen.
- Play to local consumer interests in their version of "custom made."
- Enable custom upgrades, downgrades, and refurbishing, including upgrades to propulsion and energy storage devices.
- Allow a fragmenting of the market that high-scale designers cannot follow.
- Encourage a design shift from steel to composites for structure as well as outer skin.
- Encourage increases in the rate of continuous improvement in durability, reliability, and cost to produce.
- Encourage a design shift from hydraulic and mechanical systems to all electronic systems that will enable refinements in customization.
- Reduce investments in new model developments by a factor of ten.
- Shorten the lead-time for new model introductions to less than a year.

Growth: *Turn away from scale advantages and focus on workforce advantages. Increase market share through greater concern for regional interest. Return to using high levels of integration as a growth opportunity. Focus on leading the evolution to vehicles that do not run on petroleum. Find a balance between the interests of shareholders and those of the workforce.*

Strategic moves enabled by this new Growth objective:
- Slow the rate at which innovation is leaking to competitors through shared suppliers.
- Introduce ongoing vehicle modifications for changes in lifestyle and upgrades to enhanced performance, handling, fuel alternatives, and electronics.
- Enable gains in revenue through accelerated rates of innovation.
- Access the high-profit segments of the customer base that high-scale producers cannot reach.
- Grow through secured debt, using generic equipment as collateral.

Imports: *Switch to playing offense and bettering the competition on the "away field." Nurture American interest in a position from which to weather all swings in currency exchange. Pressure the U.S. government and the Federal Reserve to view a strong industrial sector as a* *cornerstone in our national security and not to give it away while courting future allies or short-term benefits.*

Strategic moves enabled by this new Imports objective:

- Strive to cater to local needs and shift model designs quickly.
- Expose the true factory outlet advantages of direct customer ordering and ongoing product feedback.
- Encourage the support of state, county, and city government with offers of stable employment rather than the whipsawing of new model introductions.
- Counter imports with a manufacturing system that harnesses the value of handed-down knowledge.

Sales: *Sell factory direct. Offer individual options instead of packages of options. Offer custom colors and fabrics and even custom designs. Fill custom orders within two days. Offer them factory service and damage repair. Offer them refurbishing and updating as well as trade-in and resale opportunities.*

Strategic moves enabled by this new Sales objective:

- Evade the controls that dealerships place on manufacturers and pocket the dealerships' operating margin.
- Provide immediate and accurate feedback to the assembly craftsmen through direct contact with the consumer during the sale, service, resale, and refurbishment of personal vehicles.
- Enable consumers to "kick the tires" of all vehicle designs and options at the factory.
- Eliminate the dealer exchange program and the carrying cost on a hundred days of inventory.
- Rekindle the inherent customer interest in a custom-built product.

Each of the above ten areas of objectives must be carefully interwoven into a business plan. Combinations of choices of strategic moves must be carefully interlinked and altered as the business climate and development of the workforce evolves. The current 121 long-term problems in America's auto industry have solutions and they provide opportunities to become more and more competitive with imports.

To think that the path to recovery is as simple as changing the wording of ten items on the back of an envelope seems naïve when considering the magnitude of the auto industry. And thinking that the auto industry could lead America's industrial sector back to life makes the magnitude of proposing a solution seem unfathomable. But if you start with an understanding of the evolution in decision making that has brought America's industrial sector to its knees, you can begin to get comfortable at the helm of something large. The course ahead now calls for matching wits with some significant Asian competitors. The standard of living for grandchildren in America will begin to improve if each industry chooses the right course. It will help if you expand your knowledge of the strengths your competitors.

INDEX

A

A-Body radiator support, 97, 99-100, 102, 105

A-cars, 147

Acceleration
    of production, 169
    periods, 118, 146, 160

Accepted cost, 160

Accounting offices, 159

Adaptable workforce, 115

Advantages of imports, 129, 163

AFL's trade unions, 80

Aggressive union leaders, 82, 189

Air-cooled vehicle, 92

Air conditioning

Airbus, 185

Alabama, 27, 133

Allis Chalmers, 57

Alternate-fuel vehicle, 185

Alternative
    energy, 187, 195
    fuels, 167, 195
    technology players, 195

Aluminum engines, 161

AMC Gremlin, 161

America's
    costly strategy, 136
    culture, 156, 161, 184, 217
    population, 197

    problems, 52

American
    automotive business model, 201
    Axle, 137
    banking system, 130
    economy, 66, 122, 173, 175, 192, 211
    Federation of Labor (AFL), 65
    financial system, 130
    Motors, 85, 92-93, 122, 161
    suppliers, 132
    Theocracy, 1, 173
    workers/ workforce, 27, 132-134, 141, 170, 190, 205

Andrews, Jim, 53

Annual
    funding, 68, 85
    model, 7, 39, 69, 85, 89, 92, 121, 123, 126, 137, 143, 160, 167-168, 201, 204
    sales, 92, 161, 174
    summer modifications, 148

Antitrust legislators, 11

Apperson, Pete, 41

Apprentice
    development, 81, 134
    programs, 26, 82, 202
    selection, 20
    shops, 56

Apprenticeship, 9, 20, 53, 56, 82, 118, 139-140, 147, 156, 167, 170, 183, 217

Architects, 91

Arden, 157, 159

Area foreman, 105

Arlington, 114

H

I

members, 109
of engineers, 48
participation, 138
Teams of workers, 33, 51
Television manufacturers, 129-130
Tiers of suppliers, 140, 198
Time
card, 71
clock, 96, 105
Time-study man, 42-43, 75
Tokyo, 144
Toledo (OH), 155, 190
Toyota
Corolla, 93, 132
Crown, 92
managers, 133
plants, 133
Tercel, 129
Transport systems, 125
Transportation system (US), 153
Transverse-mounted engine, 126
Treasury, 133
Truck assembly line, 47-48

U

Uddevalla (Volvo plant in Sweden), 51
Underbuild, 119
Underpowered automobiles, 184
Undervalued currency, 190
Unibody, 124
Unions
abatement, 106
ambitions, 217
elections, 71, 93
electorate, 70
leadership, 81, 217
and Management, Adversarial role, 70, 118
organizers, 66
positions, 197
United Auto Workers (UAW), 5-6, 8, 46-47, 65-68, 74, 77-82, 84, 88, 90, 94, 122, 132-134, 145, 148, 151, 153, 156, 162, 167-168, 172, 176, 192, 203, 209-210
United Rubber Workers (URW), 66
United Steel Workers (USW), 66
United States
Embassy, 180
Government, 220

Universal
gate-line systems, 134
steel platform, 134
transfer lines, 136
Used-car buyers, 125, 129

V

Van Wagners, Clarence, 148
Vancouver (Canada), 125
Verbal Orders, 75, 100
Vietnam, 130, 157
Viking, 173
Vinyl, 63
Visteon Division, 166
Volcker, Paul, 131
Volkswagen Beetle, 92, 161
Volume
allocations, 86, 90, 114
model offerings, 138
of production, 24, 27, 33, 175
of sales, 36, 58, 69, 91, 117, 165, 174
projections, 135, 160
rose, 175
Voluntary Restraint Agreements (VRAs), 131-132, 165
Volvo, 51, 214

W

Wages, 34, 36, 44, 56-57, 65, 67, 70, 73, 76, 82, 86, 90, 94, 106, 118, 134, 136-137, 144-145, 149, 162, 167, 172-173, 177, 198, 202-203, 206, 210, 217
Wal-Mart, 192, 211, 215
Wall Street, 19, 30, 77, 121, 130-131, 190
Walton, Sam, 215
War-time production, 81
Warranty
feedback, 128
offers, 127
responsibility, 127
subgroups, 127
Warren Tech Center, 110
Wealth, 3, 6, 29, 56, 66-68, 80, 83-84, 132, 173
Weld nuts, 102-103
Welder repair, 100, 102